Inquiries in Psychoanalysis

The papers of Edna O'Shaughnessy are among the finest to be found in psychoanalytic writing. Her work is unified not so much by its subject matter, which is diverse, but by her underlying preoccupations, including the nature of psychic reality and subjectivity, and the psychic limits of endurance and reparation.

Here a selection of her work, edited and with an introduction by Richard Rusbridger, is brought together in a collection which demonstrates the contribution that O'Shaughnessy has made to many areas of psychoanalysis, from personality organisations, the superego, psychic refuges and the Oedipus complex to the subject of whether a liar can be psychoanalysed. *Inquiries in Psychoanalysis* is a record of clinical work and thinking over 60 years of psychoanalytic practice with children and adults.

This wide-ranging selection of work will be essential reading for psychoanalysts, psychotherapists and students.

Edna O'Shaughnessy is a Distinguished Fellow of the British Psychoanalytical Society and a training and supervising analyst for adults and children. She is also a supervisor in the Adult Department of the Tavistock Clinic as well as in the Child and Family Department.

Richard Rusbridger is a training and supervising analyst of the British Psychoanalytical Society and an Honorary Reader at University College, London.

THE NEW LIBRARY OF PSYCHOANALYSIS
General Editor: Alessandra Lemma

The New Library of Psychoanalysis was launched in 1987 in association with the Institute of Psychoanalysis, London. It took over from the International Psychoanalytical Library, which published many of the early translations of the works of Freud and the writings of most of the leading British and continental psychoanalysts.

The purpose of the New Library of Psychoanalysis is to facilitate a greater and more widespread appreciation of psychoanalysis and to provide a forum for increasing mutual understanding between psychoanalysts and those working in other disciplines such as the social sciences, medicine, philosophy, history, linguistics, literature and the arts. It aims to represent different trends both in British psychoanalysis and in psychoanalysis generally. The New Library of Psychoanalysis is well placed to make available to the English-speaking world psychoanalytic writings from other European countries and to increase the interchange of ideas between British and American psychoanalysts. Through the *Teaching Series*, the New Library of Psychoanalysis now also publishes books that provide comprehensive, yet accessible, overviews of selected subject areas aimed at those studying psychoanalysis and related fields such as the social sciences, philosophy, literature and the arts.

The Institute, together with the British Psychoanalytical Society, runs a low-fee psychoanalytic clinic, organises lectures and scientific events concerned with psychoanalysis and publishes the *International Journal of Psychoanalysis*. It runs a training course in psychoanalysis which leads to membership of the International Psychoanalytical Association – the body which preserves internationally agreed standards of training, of professional entry, and of professional ethics and practice for psychoanalysis as initiated and developed by Sigmund Freud. Distinguished members of the Institute have included Michael Balint, Wilfred Bion, Ronald Fairbairn, Anna Freud, Ernest Jones, Melanie Klein, John Rickman and Donald Winnicott.

Previous general editors have included David Tuckett, who played a very active role in the establishment of the New Library. He was followed as general editor by Elizabeth Bott Spillius, who was in turn followed by Susan Budd and then by Dana Birksted-Breen.

TITLES IN THIS SERIES

TITLES IN THE NEW LIBRARY OF PSYCHOANALYSIS TEACHING SERIES

THE NEW LIBRARY OF PSYCHOANALYSIS

General Editor: Alessandra Lemma

Inquiries in Psychoanalysis

Collected papers of Edna O'Shaughnessy

Edna O'Shaughnessy

Edited by Richard Rusbridger

LONDON AND NEW YORK

First published 2015
by Routledge
27 Church Road, Hove, East Sussex, BN3 2FA

and by Routledge
711 Third Avenue, New York, NY 10017

Routledge is an imprint of the Taylor & Francis Group, an informa business

British Library Cataloguing in Publication Data
A catalogue record for this book is available from the British Library

Library of Congress Cataloging in Publication Data
O'Shaughnessy, Edna.
[Works. Selections]
Inquiries in psychoanalysis: collected papers of Edna O'Shaughnessy/Edna O'Shaughnessy;
edited by Richard Rusbridger.
Pages cm. — (The new library of psychoanalysis)
1. O'Shaughnessy, Edna. 2. Psychoanalysts—Great Britain. 3. Psychoanalysis. 4. Child
psychology. 5. Psychology. I. Rusbridger, Richard. II. Title.
BF109.O84A3 2014
150.19′5–dc23
2014017582

ISBN: 978–1–138–79644–7 (hbk)
ISBN: 978–1–138–79645–4 (pbk)
ISBN: 978–1–315–75446–8 (ebk)

Typeset in Bembo
by Swales & Willis Ltd, Exeter, Devon, UK

For Brian with love

Contents

Preface

It has been my good fortune to have worked in psychoanalysis from the 1950s until the present day. During this time Freud's late great legacies to psychoanalysis – his map of the psyche in terms of ego, super-ego and id, anxiety posited as elemental, and his final view of human instincts as the conflict, in all their many aspects, of Eros and Thanatos – were explored and developed by Klein (among others) in analytic work with children and adults. And in their turn, Melanie Klein's new findings and theories offered to those who worked with them a rich field for further psychoanalytic inquiry.

In the 1950s I trained as a Child Psychotherapist at the Tavistock Clinic. Dr Bowlby was Clinic Director, while Esther Bick and Mattie Harris lead the Child training in an atmosphere of all of us being at the forefront of research from different perspectives. In the 1960s I trained at the British Psychoanalytical Society where I met for the first time the full blast of group hostilities, in themselves disturbing and unproductive, yet even so new ideas flourished. Over the years a spirit of inquiry has prevailed and group hostilities have mostly given way to an acceptance of our excess of diversity and the concomitant pursuit of varied psychoanalytic paths.

Now, in my old age I still recall my training supervisors: Esther Bick, Betty Joseph and Hanna Segal for my young Tavistock patients, and for my adult training cases Herbert Rosenfeld and Hanna Segal. To these foundational influences I add the writings of Wilfred Bion. How different they all are! How different too was the way of inquiry of each into the analytic process. In another, more interior, mode my own analysis endures. A first analysis of 2 years with Dr Charles

Anderson was cut short by his sudden early death. A little later I went to Mr Roger Money-Kyrle and I owe him much.

I am proud to belong to the British Psychoanalytical Society and glad of the long years of work with colleagues there and at the Tavistock Clinic. I am grateful to the Melanie Klein Trust for financial support in the production of this book. And to the Editor of this book, Mr Richard Rusbridger, I offer my warmest thanks.

Edna O'Shaughnessy

Acknowledgements
and permissions

'The absent object', 'Bion's theory of thinking', 'Seeing with meaning and emotion' and the review of Herbert Rosenfeld are reprinted from *Journal of Child Psychotherapy*, 1964, 1: 39–43.

A commemorative essay on W. R. Bion's theory of thinking. First published in *Journal of Child Psychotherapy*, 1981, 7: 181–192.

The Invisible Oedipus Complex. First published in E. B. Spillius (ed.), *Melanie Klein Today*, Vol. 2, London: Routledge, 1988, 001: 191–205. Reprinted in J. Steiner (ed.), *The Oedipus Complex Today*, London: Karnac Books, 1989: 129–150.

Seeing with meaning and emotion. First published in *Journal of Child Psychotherapy*, 1989, 15: 27–31, as one of a number of papers reflecting on Lynn Barnett's film Sunday's Child. Reprinted in Lynn Barnett, *Sunday's Child: the Development of Individuality from Birth to Two Years of Age*, Parts I–VIII. Part IX: 2 to 3 years, 1988. Part X: 3 to 6 years, 1989. Concorde Films, 201 Felixstowe Road, Ipswich, Suffolk IP3 9BJ.

Psychosis: not thinking in a bizarre world. First published in R. Anderson (ed.), *Clinical Lectures on Klein and Bion*, 1992, London: Tavistock/Routledge, pp. 89–101.

A projective identification with Frankenstein: some questions about psychic limits. First published in E. Hargreaves and A. Varchecker (eds.), *In Pursuit of Psychic Change: the Betty Joseph Workshop*, London: Routledge, pp. 168–180.

Intrusions. First published in J. Steiner (ed.), *Rosenfeld in Retrospect*, London: Karnac Books, 2008, pp. 3–14.

Review of Herbert Rosenfeld, *Impasse and Interpretation*, London: Tavistock Press, 1987. Published in *Journal of Child Psychotherapy*, 1988, 14: 99–101.

All of the above reprinted with kind permission of Taylor and Francis.

'Interminably a patient'. First published in *International Journal of Psychoanalytic Psychotherapy*, 1980–1, 8: 573–576. Kindly reprinted with permission of Jason Aronson, New York.

A clinical study of a defensive organisation. First published in *International Journal of Psychoanalysis*, 1981, 62: 359–428.

Words and Working Through. An enlarged version of the paper read at the London Weekend Conference of English-Speaking Psychoanalytical Societies on 3 October 1982. First published in *International Journal of Psychoanalysis*, 1983, 64: 281–289. Reprinted in E. B. Spillius (ed.), *Melanie Klein Today*, Vol. 2, London: Routledge, 1988, pp. 138–151.

A 3½ year old boy's melancholic identification with an original object. First published in *International Journal of Psychoanalysis*, 1986, 67: 173–179.

Can a liar be psychoanalysed? First published in *International Journal of Psychoanalysis*, 1990, 71: 187–195.

Enclaves and excursions. First published in *International Journal of Psychoanalysis*, 1992, 73: 603–614.

What is clinical fact? This paper was presented at the IJPA 75th Anniversary Celebration Conference, London, 14–16 October 1994. First published in the *International Journal of Psychoanalysis*, 1994, 75: 939–947.

Relating to the superego. First published in *International Journal of Psychoanalysis*, 1999, 80(5): 861–870.

Whose Bion? First published in *International Journal of Psychoanalysis*, 2005, 86: 1523–1528.

Review of *Wilfred Bion: his Life and Work, 1897–1979* by Gérard Bléandonu, translated by Claire Pajaczkowska, with a foreword by R. D. Hinshelwood. New York: Guildford Press, 1994.

Review of *The Dead Mother: The Work of André Green*, edited by Gregario Kohon, London: Routledge, 1999. Published in *International Journal of Psychoanalysis*, 1999, 82: 619–621.

All the above kindly reprinted with permission from the *International Journal of Psychoanalysis*.

On gratitude. First published in P. Roth and A. Lemma (eds.), *Envy and Gratitude Revisited*, London: IPA, reprinted London: Karnac Books, 2008, pp. 79–91. Kindly reprinted with permission form Karnac Books.

Melanie Klein: her world and her work. First published in *International Review of Psychoanalysis*, 1987, 14: 132–136. Kindly reprinted with permission from the *International Review of Psychoanalysis*.

All reasonable efforts have been made to contact copyright holders, but in some cases this was not possible. Any omissions brought to the attention of Routledge will be remedied in future editions.

INTRODUCTION

The papers of Edna O'Shaughnessy are amongst the finest psychoanalytic writing. Her papers have a rare combination of an incisive clarity, imaginativeness and a great sensitivity to her patient, including his or her deepest and most psychotic anxieties. She has made important contributions to many of the areas of most current interest in psychoanalysis – personality organisations, the superego, (both abnormal and normal), the Oedipus complex, psychic refuges, and technique; as well as writing with originality about topics not touched on by other writers, such as whether a liar can be analysed. Her work is unified not so much by its subject matter, which is very diverse, but by her underlying preoccupations. These include psychic limits, of both patient and analyst; and the nature of psychic reality and of subjectivity. She is interested in how these can be apprehended with the help of the particular situation of an analysis. She often starts by trying to puzzle out why an impasse has developed in an analysis – and this frequently provokes a new and original line of thought. In this way, theoretical and clinical issues are inseparable in her writing, even more so than in most writing by Kleinian analysts, which is usually very focused on clinical material. Her use of language is precise, free of cliché, and has, as she says of Bion's writing (1981: 1), a 'high yield of exact meaning'. At the same time, she writes with great emotional resonance, evoking poetically her patients and the clinical situations in which she encounters them. This is the corollary of her finely attuned and imaginative sense of the patient's unconscious.

Background

Edna O'Shaughnessy was born in South Africa in 1924. She read Philosophy at the University of Witwatersrand, before going to

1

Oxford to do a B.Phil., where she pursued her interest in the work of Wittgenstein. She then held the Susan Stebbing Fellowship at Bedford College, London University. She was one of the first to train at the Tavistock Clinic as a child psychotherapist. She then worked as a child psychotherapist, and lectured for 13 years in the Department of Child Development at the Institute of Education, London University. During this time she trained as a psychoanalyst at the Institute of Psychoanalysis, London. Her first analyst was Dr Charles Anderson, and her training analyst was Roger Money-Kyrle. She is a child analyst and a training and supervising analyst of the British Psychoanalytic Society.

The Kleinian tradition

O'Shaughnessy works in the Kleinian tradition, although her work shows a sympathetic engagement with other ways of thinking, and has in turn been valued by many analysts working in different traditions.

Melanie Klein worked first with children, and her firsthand contact with their violently loving and hating phantasies underpins all her work. O'Shaughnessy, too, feels that her initial training with children has influenced her in being able to see the child, and the baby, inside the adult patient. As Spillius (1988: 3) describes, Klein emphasised the psychic reality of unconscious phantasy, and the conflict between love and hate in the Unconscious; and she saw babies as being object-related from birth. Klein thought that feelings represented the basic data, some of the fundamental givens, of our existence. She thought that feelings were the manifestation of the drives, and, as with Freud's view of the drives, that they lay on the boundary between the mental and physical (in this sense her theory is both an instinct theory and an object-relations theory). She saw love as a manifestation of the life instinct, while hate/destructiveness was a manifestation of the death instinct. She followed Freud in his thinking about this basic dichotomy between life and death instincts, and her view was that anxiety, the main problem confronting the ego, arose from the conflict between the two. She says in 1948:

> I would also think that if we assume the existence of a death instinct, we must also assume that in the deepest layers of the mind there is a response to this instinct in the form of fear of annihilation

of life. Thus in my view the danger arising from the inner working
of the death instinct is the first cause of anxiety. Since the struggle
between the life and death instincts persists throughout life, this
source of anxiety is never eliminated and enters as a perpetual
factor into all anxiety situations.

(Klein 1948: 29)

She thought that how the mind deals with this conflict has
a structuring effect on the mind, and determines character and
personality. For example in 1937 she writes:

the child's development depends on, and to a large extent is formed
by, his capacity to find the way to bear inevitable and necessary
frustrations [of life] and conflicts of love and hate which are in part
caused by them: that is, to find a way between his hate, which
is increased by frustrations, and his love and wish for reparation,
which brings in their train the sufferings of remorse. The way
the child adapts himself to these problems in his mind forms the
foundation for all his later social relationships, his adult capacity for
love and cultural development.

(Klein 1937: 316)

Klein thought that the death instinct, as manifested in hatred and
destructiveness, was dealt with immediately at birth by projection,
which led to the baby at first feeling that he inhabited a world of
dangerous objects. She thought that the baby deals with this situation
by means of splitting its picture of the world between ideally good and
terrifyingly bad part-objects: objectively part of the same mother, but
subjectively wholly separate. At this stage, which in 1946 she called the
paranoid–schizoid position, the leading anxieties are persecutory and
to do with the survival of the self. Given what she called mitigation by
love, and (Bion added later) containment by an understanding object,
the baby is enabled to take into himself not only milk but also an
experience of understanding and of being loved, which enables him
to establish inside himself a good internal object, the foundation of
his ego. If, because of constitutional elements, or because of a failure
of containment or of being loved, this stage miscarries, the baby's
picture of the world is of an extremely dangerous and terrifying place.
She came to think that envy, which she thought of as largely innate
and an expression of the death instinct, made establishing a good

internal object particularly difficult, as it both constituted and fostered a destructive attack on the good object for being good, not on the bad object, and thus endangered normal splitting. More drastic defences of extreme splitting or psychotic fragmentation may ensue.

With maturation as well as emotional containment, the earlier split world is superseded as the infant comes to understand that the wonderfully good and the terrifying mothers or breasts are in fact the same. This ushers in the depressive position, characterised by anxieties about loss of and damage to this more whole object. The characteristic anxieties – the emotions – of the depressive position are guilt, grieving and loving concern. A particularly important emotion in the depressive position is mourning – over the loss of the perfect object that was previously possessed in phantasy and is now recognised as imperfect and above all separate. Facing these feelings is so difficult that we all regress to paranoid-schizoid position functioning at times in the face of them; and therefore these fundamental positions alternate throughout life.

Influences

As a philosopher O'Shaughnessy published two papers: one, 'The picture theory of meaning' (Daitz 1953), about Wittgenstein's *Tractatus*; and a paper on the enigma of the assertion 'I can if I choose' (O'Shaughnessy 1952). Of these she says:

> These papers were of course philosophical analyses: later it turned out that these topics held also a psychoanalytic interest for me: meaning as given in internal pictures by certain images and dreams in the mind, and the claim to inner freedom – which may be true or may be false – made by saying 'I can if I choose'.
> (O'Shaughnessy and Arundale, 2004: 528)

Her philosophical background is particularly explicit in a number of her papers. See, for example, her discussion in 'What is a clinical fact' (1994) about the possibility of accessing the emotional reality of the relationship between patient and analyst, and of what it means to make a claim about the truth of this reality; or her discussion of the role of words in enabling us to link the past with the present, the transference and the patient's life. Her paper on whether a liar can be analysed discusses the philosophical background to the question. And in her paper 'Mental connectedness' (2007), writing about a paper by the philosopher Richard Wollheim, she discusses the relationship between philosophy and psychoanalysis. She says that analysts need philosophers 'to clarify for us and our critics – in relation to our clinical method of enquiry – the perplexities of how there can be objectivity where there is also subjectivity; the nature of clinical facts; and the problems of evidence and verification'. However, the influence of her philosophical training can be felt much more widely in her papers, in the precision and clarity of her thinking.

O'Shaughnessy's work is part of the rich flowering of psychoanalytic thinking that has developed from the work of Klein and Bion. She feels particularly influenced by Roger Money-Kyrle; by her supervision by Esther Bick, Hanna Segal, Herbert Rosenfeld and Betty Joseph; and by the writings of Wilfred Bion and the work of many contemporary colleagues. She was part of the group that edited Klein's collected writings (Klein 1975, 1980), and wrote the helpful explanatory notes in that edition. She bases her work, she says, on Klein's hypothesis that unconscious object relations and identifications will be found to underlie all mental and somatic phenomena – and on Klein's general theory, dating from 1940 onwards, that in the mind are continual unconscious phantasies of an inner world of objects which, by identification, projection and introjection, are continually interacting with outer reality ('Clinical facts', 1994: 945). Just one example in her work will stand for many. In her paper on 'Seeing with meaning and emotion' (1989), she gives her response to a film made by Lynn Barnett of the evolving relationship between a mother and baby in the first weeks of the baby's life. The mother was depressed and only to a limited extent able to receive the baby both emotionally and physically. O'Shaughnessy describes the evolution of one particular internal object in the baby. His mother's cold, hostile depression meant that she shut him out when he is not perfect, and this had, O'Shaughnessy suggests, led to a hole in the baby's experience. At one point in the film he is seen noticing a cheese grater. He saw it, was transfixed by the sight of it, reached for it and got it. He played with it, intensely investigating its properties, as his mother watched him. O'Shaughnessy suggests that this object, cold, hard, cutting, and with holes, represents the external correlate of one of his internal representations of his mother. O'Shaughnessy comments: 'we see here a beautiful example of how mankind gives meaning to his world, how from his internal elemental objects he proceeds outwards and invests objects in the world with significance' (1989: 31).

Of Bion's writings, O'Shaughnessy is particularly appreciative of and influenced by his earlier papers, thinking that his later work became less disciplined and more diffuse (see 'Whose Bion?', 2005). Two areas in particular have influenced her: his understanding of thinking; and of its vicissitudes, notably in psychosis. Central is Bion's extension of Klein's idea of projective identification to embrace normal communication and to explain the very origins of thought. Bion held that thinking developed from the emotional experience of a baby having his or her projected feelings known and contained by the mother. Bion describes this link with the mother as a K link, a getting-to-know. K, this trying to know the mind of the object, is Bion's development of Freud's idea of an epistemophilic instinct, and Bion adds it to Freud's duo of L, love, and H, hate, as the three central governors of psychic life. Over time, in favourable circumstances, what O'Shaughnessy calls this 'momentous process' of emotional containment gradually establishes a reality ego, a normal mind, where there was before only a pleasure ego evacuating unpleasure. However, if there is a failure of containment, or excessive envy on the part of the child of the mother's capacity, attacks on the K link can bring about psychosis (no K). The replacement of learning from experience by omnipotence and further attacks can lead to K being replaced by minus K (−K), a cruel and empty link, when the infant is filled with nameless dread. In her paper on Bion's theory of thinking (1981), O'Shaughnessy brings beautifully clear vignettes from work with children operating in each of these different realms. She thinks that Bion's 'emphasis on the vicissitudes of K and −K, how contact between analyst and patient is won and lost in the course of a session, changed the way we work' (O'Shaughnessy and Arundale 2004: 532). This conception of mental development arising through the containment by another's mind of otherwise unbearable experiences is also the foundation of her clinical approach, as I describe more fully below. In the same paper she outlines how Bion's ideas enable us to understand in greater depth Freud's idea that analysis consists in extending the patient's knowledge about himself. She says that the patient's insight 'rests on primitive introjections which are emotional experiences of psychic reality linked to his analyst'. Correspondingly, 'the analyst's understanding rests on emotional experiences of knowing his patient in the original and deepest mode, i.e., through reception, containment and thought about his patient's projective identification'.

If projection is used by the infant, not to communicate his distress, but to fragment and expel the means by which the ego knows reality, the outcome is abnormal development and psychosis. This can be either because of adverse endowment, with a predominance of destructiveness and envy; or because of an adverse environment, with an unreceptive caregiver; or both. O'Shaughnessy writes about her work with psychotic patients, especially with psychotic children, in several of her papers. In 'The invisible Oedipus complex' (1988) she illustrates how, at moments of psychotic anxiety, her 11-year-old patient fragmented his perception of her, and of his sexual parents, into dots and patterns, all that remained of two terrifying internal objects, a vagina and a penis. In 'Psychosis: not thinking in a bizarre world' (1992b), she shows a similar massive fragmentation of thinking in a 5-year-old boy and an adult woman patient. She emphasises Bion's view that, as well as having a psychotic personality, the psychotic patient also has a non-psychotic personality, potentially able to respond to understanding of his projections. In 'A projective identification with Frankenstein: some questions about psychic limits' (2004), she writes about a psychotic boy of 12 who 'seemed to exist in a world of terrifying small particles'. During the analysis, which the boy and his parents broke off after 3 years, he evolved an identification with Frankenstein, a monstrous second skin formation that nevertheless integrated his fragmented mind into a coherent identity. She thought that his realisation that his predicament was, as he put it, 'too big' had led him to join with the hard impervious figure of Frankenstein.

The subtitle of the Frankenstein paper is 'Some questions about psychic limits', and one could describe all O'Shaughnessy's work as having that focus. She is interested in contact with psychic truth, and with what limits the patient, and analyst, or both, in making this contact. There are two overarching manifestations in her work of this interest: her interest in impasse; and her approach to psychoanalytic technique.

Impasse

As already noted, the clinical and the theoretical are always intertwined in O'Shaughnessy's work; and a clinical impasse is very frequently the starting point of an enquiry that leads to new theoretical thinking. Patients come to analysis because of reaching a block in their development; and this block is frequently reproduced in the course of the analysis in the form of an impasse. As with Freud, who took the remarkable step of taking the Rat Man's obsessional thinking seriously, and as with Klein, who did the same with the play of children, O'Shaughnessy takes an interest in the stuckness of a patient or an analysis, and this interest generates new thoughts. For example, in 'A clinical study of a defensive organisation' (1981), her patient arrived in an almost broken down state of mind, and then instated what she calls a defensive organisation: an 'interlocking use of several defences, omnipotent control, denial and the several forms of splitting and projective identification described by Melanie Klein'. He became cold and distant, projecting his disturbance into his analyst so that she felt helpless and tortured. This strategy had a markedly anal quality to it, immobilising the analyst and the analysis. Rather than giving up at that point, or during the subsequent phase, where the patient started to exploit his inaccessibility for perverse ends and became high and triumphant over the immobilised analyst, O'Shaughnessy took an interest in the process, and in the patient. This containment of his disturbance led to a further phase, during which the patient could be aware of the different sides of himself, and of a view of the analyst as potentially friendly and interested, rather than as, at first, terrifying, and, later, as both terrifying and useless.

Similarly, she notices two contrasting states of impasse in her paper 'Enclaves and excursions' (1992a), describing them as two variants of psychic refuge. The first is the setting-up – by patient and analyst together – of an 'enclave' – an area of restricted object-relatedness which is meant to be comfortable. The second, the 'excursion', is in contrast a total avoidance of emotional contact because of a terror of knowing, particularly of knowing about an underlying psychotic state.

In her paper on the superego ('Relating to the superego', 1999), O'Shaughnessy describes a similar impasse in the analysis. This reflected a developmental impasse, in which her patient Mr B tries to escape into erotised drowsiness from the worrying situation between him and his analyst. She understands this retreat as both a defence against, and an expression of, an abnormal superego in him that aimed to pull him away from links with his object. His terrifying, non-containing superego is the reverse of an internal object that modifies anxiety: it magnifies anxiety and is a culture of the death instinct rather than an expression of K. She points out that Freud, Abraham and Bion had recognised the existence of an abnormal superego: in her paper she brings clarification and clinical instantiation of this notion, and shows in fine detail a patient's movement away from its 'protection' (actually its dangerous seductiveness and destructiveness) towards relating to the analyst as a normal superego.

The analysis of the patient described in 'Dreaming and not dreaming' (2004) had become such an enclave, a 'not get-attable structure'. Through the understanding and interpretation of a dream that the patient both reported and enacted in a session – that is, by trying to K her patient, to know him in the deepest sense – O'Shaughnessy takes an interest in this blocked state of affairs. This interest uncovered, but in turn also provoked, the hatred of Oedipal reality that underlay the patient's deadening of contact with her analyst and with herself. Other papers where she describes an impasse include 'Intrusions' (2008a) where the impasse takes the form of an intrusive erotised attack on the work of the analyst; and 'Where is here? When is now?' (2008c), where she describes her patient's gradual emergence from an enclave in which he presented himself as little and impotent, which she understood as a complex combination of communication and of attack through erotisation and regression.

Clinical approach

As can be seen from these examples of situations of impasse and their resolution, O'Shaughnessy pays close attention to the vicissitudes of K and −K as they are lived out in the analytic session. She believes that 'the place with the more determining role in the patient's illness [is] not external reality but psychic reality with its unconscious phantasies' ('Where is here?', 2008: 1). She writes: 'The analyst's evenly suspended attention, as I understand it, hovers over, and has a focus on illuminating the psychic reality, while material reality is kept in relative darkness (not darkness, mark you) but relative darkness.' Her focus is on this psychic reality as it is materialised in the relationship between the patient and the analyst. She says: 'interpretations should be about the interaction of patient and analyst, rather than on the patient's intrapsychic dynamics' ('Words and working through', 1983). This leads her to be interested as much by the pressure, unspoken or spoken, exerted by the patient on the analyst to respond in a particular way as by his actual words. For example, in 'Intrusions' (2008), she focuses not on the details of the patient's gender problems but on the functions, both defensive and attacking, of the way in which he spoke about them. In this way, processes such as denudation of meaning 'can be caught in the immediacy of it happening' ('Bion's theory of thinking', 1981: 182). The analyst needs to contain the patient's projections with 'strong plain words' (as she describes Rosenfeld as doing ('Intrusions', 2008: 2).

This interest in psychic immediacy and acting in is similar to, and was influenced by, the work of Betty Joseph (Joseph 1989). Both were influenced by Klein's description of projective identification, and its extension and broadening by Bion. O'Shaughnessy describes projective identification as an object relations perspective on the discharge of unpleasurable tensions ('Bion's theory of thinking', 1981a: 177), and thinks, with Bion, that it is the basis for the baby's earliest communications, and for much of what is communicated in the consulting room. In a sense, all her papers can be seen as an extended exploration of projective identification; but perhaps her central paper on the topic is 'Words and working through' (1982). She remarks that 'A patient's talk is not simple. It is multiple in function', and says that 'the interchange between analyst and patient is wider than verbal'. As well as words there are other transmissions by projection – feelings like anxiety, sexual excitement or hatred, which are derived from projective identification. These enable a patient to 'bring his unevenly developed personality into analysis, using words not only as words to express meaning, but to engender projections into his analyst'. She illustrates these ideas from the treatments of two patients who tried to actualise with the analyst their primitive defensive phantasies. She says that the analyst needs to experience the patient's projections, while at not enacting them but instead containing them and expressing understanding of them in interpretations. In this paper she shows the gradual evolution in the analysis of what Money-Kyrle (1968) described as the frequent path of cognitive development from somatic event to concrete representation, to a dream, and ultimately to verbal thought.

O'Shaughnessy says that the mind is equipped to understand another mind. In this she follows Freud when he says: 'I have good reasons for asserting that everyone possesses in his own unconscious an instrument with which he can interpret the utterances of the unconscious in other people' (Freud 1913: 320). Countertransference is the analyst's main instrument for detecting the patient's projective identification. As such, it is a central preoccupation of O'Shaughnessy's, and she uses it with particular confidence and freedom of movement. She says, in her paper on Bion's theory of thinking, that 'the analyst's understanding rests on emotional experiences of knowing his patient in the original and deepest mode, i.e., through reception, containment and thought about his patient's projective identification' (1981b: 16). In 'Words and working through' (1983) she describes how the transference in one patient was divided between words and communications beyond words. As he spoke, she experienced feelings of enormous hatred that entered her during his sessions – though hatred from where, and of what, she could not explain. She began to think that he hated, but also feared hating, her and needed to split this hatred off and project it into her. Similarly, in her paper 'A 3½ year old's melancholic identification with an original object' (1986), she says that she did not always understand what her patient, Tim, was communicating. She used her countertransference feelings in understanding his non-verbal communication, as when she describes feeling 'acute pain which came over to me in enormous waves' (1986: 8). These communications are sometimes delayed in reaching the analyst. The patient described as using excursions as a defence in O'Shaughnessy's paper on 'Enclaves and excursions' (1992: 606) gave the analyst anxious, shifting feelings, just like the patient's own, but which reverberated in the analyst not in, but after, the sessions. These projections can be of many kinds: sometimes so that the analyst is filled with disowned and split off aspects of the child self, such as of hatred, rage, impotence; sometimes so that the analyst is put in the position of parental figures – variously willing, guilty, anxious, or powerless. An alternative classification, suggested by Money-Kyrle (1958: 300), is that the patient may be enlisting the analyst as a friend, a 'necessary adjunct', or as an enemy.

O'Shaughnessy suggests that such projections are both vivid and specific, and that this can enable the patient to bring to the analysis aspects of his history in ways that communicate the psychic truth of his experience, and which may contradict his conscious or verbal account of his history. For example, in 'Words and working through' (1982), to the patient's despair, interpretations seemed to him to be useless. O'Shaughnessy suggests that this was the transference version of his deep anxiety that his objects were powerless to help him. Patient

L in 'Can a liar be analysed?' (1990) seemed, in the analysis as in a dream he brought, to be identified with parents who were superior and ignored the child. His parents had in rather the same way ignored or walked past the him that suffered as a child both when he was at school and earlier. She thinks that connections with the patient's remembered history, or with their life outside analysis, should be made only when they are in the patient's psychic reality (see 'Where is here? When is now?', 2008).

The papers show a gradual change in her interpretative style from speaking to the patient in terms of anatomical part-objects (the breast, the penis, etc.) to speaking in terms of their psychological functions. The technique of many Kleinian analysts, though not all, evolved in a similar way over this period, as described by Elizabeth Spillius (1983, 1989, 1994). An earlier belief in the special immediacy of part-object language gave way to a realisation that the use of this language could become routine and stereotyped. Nevertheless, O'Shaughnessy, along with other Kleinian analysts, sometimes wonders if this change may in itself have gone too far, and that analysts can be too hesitant in naming anatomical part-objects.

Writing

One of the striking features of reading O'Shaughnessy's papers is the way in which she evokes patients and the particular atmospheres that they bring. Writing about clinical work with patients is extremely difficult to do: the written account is so different from the actual experience of the work with the patient that it takes especial skill to evoke the psychic reality of the patient and a session so that they have emotional resonance. Her writing has a particular combination of, on the one hand, intellectual precision and authority; and, on the other, poetic imaginativeness. One instance of the latter is her description of the 3½-year-old Tim 'slithering' under her chair, a session in which 'the atmosphere was sexual, hazy, idyllic' – evoking his wish to use his snake-like penis to invade the intercourse of the parents (1986: 176). This follows a closely written and lucid paragraph in which she connects Freud's account of melancholia, Abraham's theory of anal sadism and Klein's 1935 paper about the depressive position. This combination of intellectual clarity and imaginative evocativeness conveys, for the reader, something of the attitude that she implies is likely to be most helpful for both patient and analyst: to feel able to have great freedom in associating, and in experiencing one's countertransference, while this freedom is held within, and enabled by, a framework of clear thinking and firm boundaries.

O'Shaughnessy finds that an image or picture used by a patient can crystallise, for both the patient and the analyst, many elements in the internal reality of each of them, and in their interaction. In this sense, the picture can act as what Bion (1962b) called a 'selected fact'. This was an expression used by the mathematician Henri Poincaré (1905 [1952]) to refer to the element that gives coherence to a group of scattered data. Poincaré said: what 'we must aim at is not so much to ascertain resemblances and differences, as to discover similarities hidden under apparent discrepancies' (Poincaré 1905 [1952]: 21). Bion links this with an emotional experience that makes it possible for the analyst to move from a paranoid-schizoid position experience of fragmentation to a more depressive position experience of coherence and meaningfulness.

An example of this process occurs in 'Relating to the superego' (1999). A patient said that he had seen a dirty and lame homeless woman urinating in the street. He was about to be out of work, and had spent many sessions being silent, sleeping or chatting inconsequentially. O'Shaughnessy took his picture as an ideograph, in the sense used by Bion (1962a) and Money-Kyrle (1968) – a symbol (also called by Bion an alpha element) usable for thinking. She saw it as compressing the patient's view of the analyst as homeless both because of his projection into her of his own homeless, workless, situation; and because he had made her homeless by refusing for so many sessions to give her a place in his troubles. She interpreted his fear that she might be pushed to the brink of getting out of control, might hate him, and might suddenly pour a urine-like stream of words on him. He came alive at the point, and for the first time for many sessions there was real contact between him and her. O'Shaughnessy reports something similar in her paper 'Where is here? When is now?' (2008c). Her patient Mr X, who was referred to above, had remained in a state of inaccessibility, until

one day, unusually, he brought an image. He described how on the way to his session he had noticed a house and its garden outside. It was a tidy garden that had been swept bare, except, that in a corner, there was a plant with two blue, delicate flowers. What seemed to me foremost and new was that Mr X had *noticed* the house and how the garden was, and had been able to bring what he had seen to his session and tell it as a communication.

(2008c: 5)

O'Shaughnessy thought that this picture expressed in a single symbol

his new awareness of how he and I and his sessions were – we are to be like the two blue flowers in a corner, close and delicate with each other, while the session is swept bare of disturbing things – like his hostility, or his fear that I get irritated and restive and might not want to be a delicate blue flower with him.

(2008c: 5).

Summary

These brief vignettes, and others already referred to, convey something important about her writing, and about the impression it conveys about her work as an analyst. This is her capacity to allow ingress to very primitive and disturbing feelings: not to blank them off, but to take an interest both in the anxiety that they provoke and in what has caused it, and thus containing them. What O'Shaughnessy says about Herbert Rosenfeld (in 'Intrusions', 2008: 2) rings true of her: 'He had an extraordinary capacity to be where ill patients were, in schizoid, manic and depressed places, to understand their compressed utterances and interpret in strong plain words.' The last point is important to her and in her work: in the same paper about Rosenfeld she says that her patient needed her 'not to prevaricate about his hostility (2008: 15). She conveys strength, and also courage, in naming some of the most difficult and attacking things in her patients' communications. For example, in 'A clinical study of a defensive organisation' (1981b: 6) she persisted with her interpretation in the face of her patient's contempt during the phase of the analysis when she thought that the patient was exploiting his personality organisation for perverse, cruel, ends. The patient became angry and strode out. However, by standing up to what she calls the 'Alsatian dog' of his cruelty, she showed that his object could stand him and not give up on him. This strength goes together with her sympathy that she conveys for the mental pain of psychotic anxiety. Her writing conveys these qualities, together with her imaginativeness in understanding her patients' communications. Her papers are the product of a truly original thinker about psychoanalysis, and give a picture of a great clinician at work. It is this combination that makes her writing so valuable and, as she says about both Bion's thinking (1981:1) and about Klein (1987:13), so rare.

Note

The papers have been ordered chronologically, as have, in a separate section, the book reviews.

Part I

PAPERS

1

THE ABSENT OBJECT

The subject of this paper is the absent sustaining object. This first intrudes on the life of the baby in the form of the absent breast. The absent breast is an essential part of the breast relationship, since it is of the logical essence of a relationship that there be times when the one person is with the other and times when he is apart from that other. The unborn infant – being permanently in union with his mother – does not yet have a relationship to her, or to her parts: he enters on the condition for a relationship at birth. A relationship, moreover, needs to be distinguished from a simple association, which ends as the partners part. The feeding infant does not have a feeding association with the breast, like a strictly business association. He has a relationship to it, which spans presence and absence, which goes beyond the physical presence of the breast to the breast in its absence.

The first point of interest is that the character of the absent object is opposite to the character of the object when there. The object when present is *prima facie* a good object. Whatever the difficulties, the feeding breast sustains life. As against this, the absent breast is first experienced in hunger, when it is needed and is not there; that is, the absent object is a bad object which is leaving the baby to starve and die. Nevertheless, the absent object is an integral part of his life, and in the course of his development the baby must come to terms with it. It will be a major difficulty in the way of establishing the good internal object, since hatred will be mobilised against it because of its absence, making it hard to keep the good gained in its presence. However, as well as constituting a difficulty for development, the absent object is also a spur to development. By its harshness it forces reality on the child, and breaks the hold of phantasies which protect him from the realisation of his vulnerability and dependence. It makes him know reality.

In particular, the absent object is a spur to the development of thought. It is not an accident that this is so, since there is a logical connection between thought and absence. You can be asked to think of something that is absent, a painting in a gallery (say), but you cannot be asked to think of a painting you are already looking at; perception shuts out thought, in this basic and simple sense. You can think about – in the sense of reflect upon – anything, things present as well as absent, but before you can 'think about' you must develop the prior capacity to 'think of'. This latter is essentially linked to things absent; developmentally speaking, to the absent breast.

Psycho-analytical theory has, indeed, always posited that frustration leads to mental development. Freud remarks on 'the exigencies of life' to which 'the psychical apparatus owes the impetus to further development', and goes on to say: 'The exigencies of life confront it first in the form of the major somatic needs' (Freud 1900: 565). Freud himself did not say much more about the conditions for mental development, his fundamental concern being regression rather than development. And since Freud, there has not been agreement about the way frustration acts in the psychical system. Now, the nub of the question is: How does a baby *experience* frustration? When he has 'major somatic needs' what is his state of mind? In other words, when a baby has 'major somatic needs' what phantasy possesses its mind?

In his book *Learning from Experience* W. R. Bion (1962a) has investigated this experience of need in the baby and gives the following account of it. When the infant feels hungry and in need of the breast, he is aware of a need not satisfied. This frustration, the pain of his hunger, is what is present to him, and this, initially, is felt as a bad breast present. The infant has now to make a beginning on a critical advance. For the wanted breast is *in fact* not a bad breast present, but a good breast absent when needed. The infant has in the course of time to come to know this fact, which is a fact of both inner reality – his need, and outer reality – the missing good breast. That is, the infant has to advance from experiencing the needed absent breast in the phantasy of a bad breast present, to being able to *think of* the real missing good breast. This crucial advance in his development is hard, since the bad breast, which in phantasy is present, is felt *au fond* to be starving him to death, and it is only by tolerating the pain and terrors of his frustration enough that he can put himself in the position of being able to think

20

about them, to think, eventually, that what he needs is the missing good breast. Such knowledge, in thought, of the good breast will also help him to endure his state of need. Since tolerance of frustration is essential for thought to develop, the infant who predominantly avoids facing his frustrations and in phantasy simply gets rid of them, is employing methods actively antagonistic to thinking, so that the development of his mental powers will be, at the least, inhibited, and may be disturbed. Thus we may say that the absent object gives the child his first opportunity to know reality through thought, and also gives him the incentive, viz. to make frustration more tolerable.

The child in treatment re-experiences the early alternations of his objects as the presence and absence of his therapist succeed each other by turns. Therapy repeats life in this respect, and allows us to observe the child's feelings about his objects in presence and in absence. It can be observed that, from the start, the child reacts to any break which disrupts the accepted rhythms of treatment, as the Easter, summer and Christmas holidays do. Furthermore, from the start, the child is sensible of even the ending of a session; with several sessions a week his reaction is particularly sharp at the weekends. From the start of treatment, the presence and absence of his therapist is experienced as an underlying alternation of good and bad, the current recapitulation of his early feeling of the breast when present as, *prima facie*, good, and the absent breast as, *prima facie*, bad.

Further, since according to Dr Bion's findings, the way the infant deals with the absent breast is critical for the development of his powers of thinking, it will likewise be the case that the way in which a child deals with gaps in his treatment will be critical for its successful outcome. The question here becomes: Can he preserve, and use, under the strain of the absence of his therapist, the insight – the thoughts – he gains in her presence?

The oscillation between good and bad felt in the comings and goings, and the difficulty of bearing the pain of absence so as to be able to think about it to make it more tolerable, explain the phenomenon, familiar in treatment, of the heightened clinical picture before a longer-than-usual break. Strong defences disown strong feelings about the coming separation, and at the same time, there is increasing urgency of need, fear and hate in the infantile parts, which may burst the defences and make the child unsteady with their intensity. In more severe cases, where the child is not able to acknowledge the coming separation, he becomes increasingly impoverished as he splits off more and more of his awareness until his personality seems to dwindle away. The general nature of the primitive phantasies the child has about the absent object is well known. In phantasy the object is attacked by various methods for its hostility, neglect, or selfishness in being absent and attending on itself or enjoying itself with others who are preferred. More basic, however, than such envious and jealous perplexities, is the feeling that the absent breast has left him to die. Listen to a small boy in a session before the Easter holiday when he became frightened of me as a malignant absent object. He spoke to the frightened parts of himself to try to reassure them. 'Listen', he addressed himself, 'the lady wants to say something. She says you'll be saved: she'll give you a drink. She's *not* glad you're dying.' The fear of dying emerges during treatment as the basic anxiety stirred by the absence of the object.

I should like now to give a clinical illustration of a child who is unable to tolerate the impact of the absent object. It shatters his defensive phantasy that baby and breast are one, and exposes the reality of his separateness. The absent object is then experienced as a threat of death, and instantly – in phantasy – exploded away. In the course of the session which is given in detail, we see how the child stops expelling the situation. Instead, he begins to face it. He starts on the struggle to think about it, which makes him attack the absent object, as well as become aware of his own aloneness.

The session took place the day after I told John, a 12-year-old boy, about his first holiday break. He had started his analysis five weeks before Easter, four times weekly. From the first, he was frightened in the play-room, and stood in one place looking apprehensively round at the items of furniture, the walls, and the air between things. It was as if the room were filled with particles. He could not move. At moments he also looked very sad. Only in the third session did he bring himself to the open drawer, and he did so in a curious way. He placed his coat, satchel and gloves on the table to make a wall in front of the drawer, and then he bent down and crawled along behind the wall to squat by his drawer and finger something. He then crept back, and stared round the room. The impression was of crawling into something in order to get to the drawer. This impression was confirmed two days later, when, literally, he stepped out of his own shoes, left them at the door, and then entered the play-room, in phantasy stepping out of himself and entering a new medium, denser, because interior: the interior of the object, that is, which he crawls into to get at its contents. The following day he suffered an acute claustrophobic attack in the room, screaming and struggling, feeling he was suffocating in the object in which he was imprisoned. The next few sessions were concerned with his claustrophobic anxieties. This brief account brings us to his 11th session when, so that there would be a little time left, I told him that we should be stopping for a fortnight at Easter. He had been standing by the window, looking out. When I made this announcement, he swung round to stare at me, his eyes wide with disbelief.

The next day he brought with him an exercise book. Nearly filling the first page a large drawing was in progress, and he sat down to continue it. It had an inner circle, and four surrounding circles which were finely subdivided. At the top, it was as if a shaft had sunk to the centre, leaving a gap in the first ring, and a bit of each successive ring in the one below it. I asked about his drawing. In his customary halting speech he said, 'It's of England and France who were once joined. Then a volcano came, and they got separated. The middle bit got sunk, and now they're like this,' and he showed me with his pencil how each of the four rings was mismatched at the sunken bit. I said, 'You feel you and I are like England and France, that we were once joined. You felt us to be joined till I told you we should be stopping for Easter. Those words sunk into you like a shaft in the middle. And then you simply stared at me. I think when you stared at me you were seeing me as a bad going away breast, and then, with a volcano from your eye, you felt you dispersed this bad breast out of your sight and into me.' ('Bad breast' is used in this interpretation rather than 'bad mother' because of the nature of his relationship to me, which I understood as being on an early part-object level.) I went on: 'Now you feel we're separated, and we don't fit each other.' John was shading the centre circle. He said, 'There's a fire burning in the middle, because it mustn't get out the other side.' He inspected the other side of his page to see if his drawing showed through. He started to pass wind. I said, 'Your drawing pictures your inside. You feel you've got me inside as a breast with your volcano in it – this is now burning you up in the middle. You feel you mustn't let these burning gases get out your other side – but all the same, you feel they are leaking out in the smells from your anus.'

On a new page he drew three heads in profile: the first had a low forehead, the second a higher forehead, and the third a still higher forehead. He labelled the first head '−1,000', the second head 'Now', and the third '+1,000'. He said they were just people, and that – 1,000 meant a thousand years ago when they had no brains, and now, they've got more, and in a thousand years' time they would have still more brains. His own long hair gives him a low forehead, and I said, 'These people are you, really. You feel you've more brains now you understand what you did to me as an absent breast, and what breast you've got inside. This is unlike yesterday, when you didn't see anything of it, since you exploded it out of your sight. This volcano-method seems so far from understanding, that yesterday seems like a thousand years ago. This sense of long ago comes also from the fact that the volcano-method would be how you got rid of your mother's absent breast, when you were a baby long ago. I think, too, that your sense of having more brains now gives you hope of still more brains in the future.'

He had started another drawing. He drew a circle and said it was the moon. He drew four rockets round it. He said, 'The rockets are dropping darts of air into the moon. Then there will be enough air to live.' I said, 'When you erupted the absent breast out of your eye, you felt the volcano came from your eye and travelled the space between us until it reached me, where it entered, and made me a moon breast. Now you feel you've got to breathe life into me and the atmosphere round me, and then there will be enough air for you to live, too. I think you feel your words to me do this – they are the darts of air which give life to the analysis.' He turned the page over to see if his drawing was showing through. He looked worried and touched the marks that showed, and all the while he was making smells. I said, 'You are worried your smells, which are attacking me for going away, are undoing the work of reviving the dead breast and its atmosphere; you're afraid they are fouling it.'

He started a small drawing. He drew the earth and then a big moon. He put in the four rockets – not round the moon as before – but near the earth. In a despondent voice he said, 'They're going back now.' I said, 'The four rockets are the four days you come to me. And now, Easter, you must go back.' On the moon he drew some irregular shapes. He said, 'They're what you see in the evening, if you look up at the moon.' I asked him what these things on the moon were. After a long hesitation, he replied, 'I know what they are now. They're called craters,' and he turned back to the drawing of the three heads and made the third head bigger. He was in an uneasy state. I then said, 'You know now that you see in me the craters from yesterday's eye-volcano and to-day's smells. Perhaps when you speak of looking up at the moon, it's also a memory of the baby-you looking up at the breast, and seeing how you attack it and put craters or extinct volcanoes in it to rid yourself of what will otherwise extinguish you. Knowing this brings you despair, because you feel a cratered breast can't keep you alive. Indeed, you have become uneasy with me now as a dead moon breast giving out foul gas.'

He turned back to his first drawing. In its centre he wrote 'Fire'. In the top sunken bit he wrote 'Wet from Water', saying, 'The sea comes in.' I said, 'You go back to your first drawing, to yourself inside, because I, the outside breast, am felt as dead and foul, and as far away for Easter as the moon is; and you show me how you feel on fire inside with the volcanic breast, and that the baby-you feels left to get wet outside from the water of tears and urine coming in on you like a sea when I leave you.'

Much in this session is not emphasised or interpreted, because it seemed subsidiary to the content of his anxiety about the holiday and his mode of response to it. The words of the announcement had entered him concretely: they were felt to sink him in the middle. The 'volcano' that then came was not an attack of anger, as one might at first suppose. He did not get angry. His eyes opened wide, not in a glare, but in a shock of disbelief: he could not believe *this*. Then he continued staring at me vacantly for a long while. The unconscious phantasy occurring during these moments was that he could volcano this absent breast out of his sight.

He was having an experience which may lie behind the stare of a very young infant in similar circumstances. It is sometimes supposed that because an infant only stares when the breast has gone, that he does not mind its absence, but we may presume that, at times, he responds to the absent breast – which for him is a starvation breast – by staring it out of his eyes in the way John does when he hears in the session that I am going to leave him. We could put it that death stares John in the eye, and when he turns round to stare at me, he has the phantasy that he stares out the death breast, hurtling it into me. That is, he is using a primitive pre-thinking mode of response to evade the anxiety of his extinction.

We can see how difficult it is for him to think, to use his brains, rather than evade fear by 'volcano' methods. He manages to think a little in this session, and each step in thinking seems to him so huge that it is as if it takes a thousand years. It is of interest that twice in the session he feels he has more brains: once when he finds out something about his inner world, that it contains a volcanic object which is burning him up; and again, when he knows it is his craters he sees when he looks up at the moon, that is, when he finds out what he does to his object. This second bit of knowledge is harder for him to acquire because of the persecution and despair of being kept alive that goes with knowing the breast is cratered. We can see the coming Easter break will be an especial strain now he has, as it were, more brains. The fact that his analysis helps him to understand what, in his language, 1,000 years ago he couldn't means that the break carries, in addition to the strain of the object being absent, the strain of anxieties which before coming into treatment he had been unable to face, and now may dread facing alone. Indeed, it is a commonplace that patients may not be able to contain such anxieties during a break, and may break off treatment, or commit follies, or even crimes.

We see, too, in this session how his full aggressive powers mobilise themselves to get rid of the absent breast. He himself describes it so: 'A volcano came.' This means he is not only expelling extinction into the breast, but with such violence, that – to continue in his images – the volcano shatters and cracks the moon as it lands. This is an important happening. It means that the reinternalised absent breast is a breast in inner decline because destruction is felt now to lodge in it. Further, since the original situation of hunger in which the object is absent means starvation and death to the young infant, it is really this threatening extinction which is projected out, and which the re-internalised object will be felt to contain. The internal object is then felt to die from within, and the absent object, by projection, in its turn becomes a dead object. Furthermore, at an immature stage of development, any processes which make for improvement depend very greatly on the presence of the external object, so that in its continuing absence the child is given over to increasing fear and despair, like at the end of John's session when he turns back in on himself, feeling that his internal object is burning itself up, while he is in a sea of wetting and crying.

This fact, that the internal situation declines in the absence of the external object, poses a difficulty for development. The internal object must be kept alive, or else at each re-union so severe a setback has occurred as to make a continuous relationship impossible. Now, the task for the infant in the presence of the breast is different from his task when the breast is absent. In the presence of the breast, he has to take in the good, overcoming difficulties of temperament and circumstance. The task in the absence of the breast is to keep the good gained in its presence, the counterpart task for a child in treatment being to use and preserve his insight into himself, when he is away from his therapist. But often, he finds himself instead on his own in a declining situation. The pain of needing the object when it is absent may force him back to primitive mechanisms, like those illustrated by the case of John. Unable to face his situation, the child rids himself of those parts of himself which feel and know about his pain by expelling them into his object with a violence that is felt to damage it. He resorts, that is, to increasing use of projective identification. The result is, that the object is taken in again worse than before since it is felt to contain now these violent parts of himself, and he is further hindered from rallying because the external object is not there.

In her paper 'Mourning and its relation to manic-depressive states' Melanie Klein (1940) shows how the external presence of the mother is necessary to overcome such internal anxieties. It is not merely that when the mother is away she cannot replenish her child's stocks of food and love, but also that she is not then able to reassure him by her presence. When her child attacks her for deserting him, he internalises a damaged mother, so that her external presence gives him visible disproof of his internal state, and he can introject the external object to improve his internal object. The delight in regaining the absent object comes partly from this. Indeed, an inability to separate from the object may be due to a fear of being alone with an internally damaged object without the reassurance of its external presence.

There is another of the object's qualities which is lost to the child when the object goes away: there is no-one then to receive and care for his unwanted parts. This capacity of the mother, in her reverie with her child, as W. R. Bion calls it, to absorb from him what he does not want to go on containing, and to return it to him in better shape, is as important on the emotional plane as the giving of love, just as the removal of urine and faeces is as important as the provision of nourishment on the physical plane. When the child has no-one there to take his emotionally unwanted parts, he is left with the alternative of containing them in an unchanged state, or exuding them and then living in a space contaminated by them. Children who suffer an unduly long separation may get a look beyond being in decline, a look of having declined to a standstill. Internally this means that the flow in and out has ceased because of the continuing absence of an external object which can nourish and reassure, as well as receive his state of mind, so that the child feels overwhelmed by his condition.

What may add further to his distress is the absence of external control over bad parts of the self. Particularly if the ego is weak and destructive impulses are strong, is there need for external restraint. In the absence of a restraining object, the child feels himself at the mercy of his jealousy and envy which are aroused by the absence of the object, which is often felt to be absent because it is occupied with something else, another baby, or the penis, or selfishly, even its own insides. For instance, as a holiday came close, a boy of eight played several times in the following sort of way. He made a breast by placing a bowl upside down with a small red object on top for a nipple. He put some cars underneath inside the bowl. Then he brought wild animals to stand around this representation of a breast, and taking another car he pushed his way in among the residents of the breast, and battered them. Here we see a child's primitive parts gather round the breast which is felt to house others while away from him, and in phantasy enter it and savage its inmates.

These assaults on the internal object make it difficult for the child to preserve it and use it when the external object is absent. However, despite these difficulties which it creates, the absence of the object is an essential condition for development. As a small instance: The absent object shatters John's phantasy of living in a breast, and spurs him, in the interval between the two sessions – though he had not drawn, let alone prepared a communication before – to set down his state of mind on paper and bring the drawing to his analysis.

It is now necessary to take up again the discussion of the connection between thinking and non-presence, where it is shown that the ability to think must start with thought of an absent object. The absent object has the character of offering a 'critical' choice, in Dr Bion's words 'between procedures designed to evade frustration and those designed to modify it' (Bion 1962a: 29). John's 'volcano' method is clearly an evasion of the situation. He does not deal with it, and this is reflected in his own account of what happened. 'A volcano came', he said, which conveys how he felt that there was an occurrence in him, rather than that he exercised his mental powers. The first rudimentary thoughts, however, necessitate that the child face his frustration and exercise his mind to deal with it.

In the beginning stages, he may attempt to modify his situation by thought of an omnipotent kind, to save him from fully realising his situation of dependence on an object which is not there. An example is the preparations made by a 12-year-old girl for the summer break, in which she imagines herself the omnipotent possessor of all she needs. She constructed a calendar for the month of August, and illustrated it with a drawing of a tea-garden. Most of the picture was taken up by a table in the fore-ground on which were two tall glasses, filled with round ice-creams. From her associations we could understand that she was denying the separation from me, felt to be her mother, during August, by making herself in phantasy the owner of the tea-garden, that is, making herself into her mother with all her possessions, notably the ice-creams, her breasts.

During the holiday, the reality situation of being without me intruded into this phantasy, breaking it down, and a few days before she resumed her analysis she had a dream which she told in her first session. She was standing on the edge of the beach, and she had been advised to go out into the sea for a bathe. As she looked at the sea, it seemed cold, and already dark, and uninviting. So she decided not to try it. This was a prologue to a change of scene in the dream. She was in a hip-bath, together with another girl, a school friend. Her tummy was very big, and she was pregnant. There was a big knob sticking out at one place in her tummy which she thought must be the baby's head. Her associations, plus the general position of the dream in the analysis (coming, as it does, in the context of work on whom – when the object is absent – the patient feels she is), allow the dream to be understood in the following way. In the second part of the dream, she makes herself all at once the pregnant mother, the parental couple – she and her school friend, and the unborn baby – in a hip-bath. She becomes, by omnipotent phantasy, all that she is not, to deny the pain of what she is. Were this the only part to the dream, it would be an example of a patient omnipotently denying the absence of the object. The prologue to the dream, however, shows that in the holidays the patient is beginning to have insight into her omnipotence and to understand its purpose: it is to save her from going out into the sea, that is, to spare her the pain of coming out of phantasies of tea-gardens into the uninviting sea of reality, where she has to acknowledge that during a break in treatment she has not got her sustaining object with her. In the dream this is a cold state, already dark, so uninviting that she decides not to try it and resorts

29

to omnipotence instead. She also understands that her analysis is, as it were, 'advising' her to bathe in reality. This holiday dream in which she saw the purpose of omnipotent thinking to be a defence against an uninviting state, proved to be the moment from which her use of omnipotent methods was much lessened. It would seem that the interruption of the treatment had been a stimulus to progress to real, as opposed to omnipotent, thinking about the absent object.

It is of interest to see how the dreamer conceives of the absent mother. She feels she has been advised by her to go out and bathe in the sea, and it is apparent she feels she has been despatched to so uninviting, cold, dark and solitary an experience that she will not even try it. The mother who does this to her is bad. Indeed, the absent object, from the time when it is first met in a situation of painful need, is felt to be bad for withholding the benefits of its presence from the child. The child's natural greed for his object will make him further resent its absence and so will his jealous wish to prevent his object having a relationship to anyone but himself. There are also morbid functions for which the child may require the presence of his object, such as the continuous reassurance already mentioned. Also, in this morbid category, is the need for the presence of the object by children who have a chronic sense of something lost. A small boy, for instance, was described as always losing things, even minute things like a match-head, which he must then find. With this went a strong anxiety about separating from his parents. In his case, his need of his external objects as 'necessary adjuncts' – in R. E. Money-Kyrle's sense (Money-Kyrle 1958: 130) – was due to his feeling that they contained the lost parts of himself.

This raises the problem of how the absent object can cease to be a bad object. What follows is a brief sketch of what is really a most intricate and slow process. As against the forces of temperament, the requirements for normal development, and the excessive demands of a disturbed development – all of which drive the child to cling to his object – as against these, there is a need in the child for the absence of his object. Absence is a natural and essential condition of a relationship, which otherwise becomes a symbiosis detrimental to the separate identity of either person. Time away from the object is needed to get an emotional perspective on experience had with the object. Appreciation, too, is sharpened in absence. Indeed, the continuous presence of an object would be persecuting; the child would feel the object was intruding into his identity, and he would also be burdened by guilt for claiming the object for himself.

It is not that the child, grudgingly, in the end, tolerates the absent object, but that he has need of its absence. His own emotional growth will help him oppose the forces which make him cling to the object. Chiefly, it will be his concern for the object in its own right, rather than as an accessory to himself, which makes him give it freedom for a life of its own. A child always, in part, wants even to be weaned. Further, as he matures, and can better tolerate his guilt, his need to have a bad absent object lessens, and the object can be allowed to keep its good qualities when away. Also, if it is felt to be benevolent when absent, it can be trusted to return when needed. In other words, the history of the absent object is this: first, it is a bad breast present; second, it is thought of as a bad aspect of the breast; and third, it is thought of as a good breast missing.

In the third stage, the absence of the object is felt to be reasonable and desirable even while it is missed. It is allowed to rest, and follow its own interests, while the child himself goes on with his own life. Greed, jealousy, and envy will be less, and love more active in protecting the object against attack. This means that the object which the child re-internalises is not in decline, but is alive, and can sustain him from within in the absence of his external object. This stage is reached in treatment when, by himself, the child puts to use his understanding of himself.

Acknowledgements

A previous edition of this chapter was originally published in the *Journal of Child Psychotherapy*, 1964, 1: 39–43.

2

INTERMINABLY A PATIENT

A discussion of 'Expiation as a defense,' by Ruth Riesenberg Malcolm

As the clinical record shows, the analysis of Mr K was conducted by Mrs Riesenberg Malcolm with courage and persistence, ending painfully when, still very ill, Mr K could no longer use it beneficially. The author's main purpose in reporting the case was to focus on the handicapping effect of a particular type of masochistic defence, which she names 'expiation'. She shows, too, how Mr K's mode of functioning makes termination hazardous, since his defences lead either to disintegration or to suicide. I think her paper throws light also on another problem, since there is another possible outcome for him: if Mr K is neither to deteriorate nor to become suicidal, he must perpetually be, if not Mrs Riesenberg Malcolm's patient, then somebody else's. It is this contingency that I should like briefly to discuss.

Mr K, and patients like him, must of necessity continue to depend on therapeutic care because of the specific direction and disposition of their activity and passivity. Mr K is actively destructive and sadistic but only passively connected to help and care. His ego is in alliance with his destructive forces while his constructive functioning is delegated to his object. This is his abnormal resolution of the primary instinctual conflict between his life instincts and his destructive instincts. In this short commentary, ignoring the complex and unfortunate interaction of innate impulses, infantile anxieties and inadequate nurture that created such a resolution, I shall only try to describe in broadest outline Mr K's active and passive functioning.

32

Mr K has not been able to confront and deploy his instincts in the normal manner. In 'The economic problem of masochism', Freud (1924a) postulated that in the service of the life instincts the essential first step must be the deflection of the death instinct outward. Later, Klein (1932) postulated further that fear of annihilation from the death instinct within is the factor that initiates this outward deflection. This original deflection sets in train several important aspects of development, one being the normal frightened relationship to a hostile external object – a relationship noticeably missing from Mr K's world. He is not afraid to indulge his sadism, and he claims that the object is not hostile. On the contrary, he insists the object likes his mocking, his paralysing and destroying: 'It keeps the analyst on her toes.'

Instead of perceiving the death instinct with anxiety within and deflecting it outwards, Mr K has embraced it within. His ego is in a perverse alliance with it, identified with its impulses in a way that is the reverse of normal, since normally the ego identifies at its core with the life instincts. Mr K deflects instead – in the sense of allotment – his life instincts to his objects, on whom he then enacts excitedly and triumphantly his cruelty and destruction. His objects are to be corrupted and seduced into liking this arrangement; they are also to continue to care for and sustain the patient. Yet he does not feel identified with this care, but merely submits to it passively.

This constellation emerged clearly in the analysis. For long periods, Mr K was actively destructive of the analytic work and setting and sadistic to his analyst, while only passively accepting her care of him. It was she who had to worry, struggle and endure, provide a nurse to ensure safety, etc. Indeed, in the first week of the analysis, Mr K warned his analyst 'that he has always been very passive and wants to be told what to do'. In this respect, as the analysis verifies, Mr K knows himself. To some extent the analysis did help him with his problems of activity and passivity. It enabled a part of him to emerge that could cooperate a little more actively with the analyst as a helpful figure: as Mrs Riesenberg Malcolm reports, there were times when Mr K dreamt and reported his dreams to her and brought his material coherently. Furthermore, the analysis also brought Mr K nearer to the perception of the terrifying truth about the cruelty and destructiveness that he embraced, which he was able to express in his material about the torturing gang in the Blind Beggar pub. But Mr K, having been taken thus far by his analyst, could not go further.

His predicament is communicated in his two last dreams before he paralysed the analysis completely. The first dream was as follows: 'I was walking through a very dangerous path, probably mined, full of barbed wire. It was surrounded by police, just standing there. It was in Connaught Square, and I felt that if I managed to walk through, I would be free.' His dream says that the nodal moment has now come. If he is to reach freedom and safety, he must take an active step: 'if I managed to walk through, I would be free.' But his first association is ominous, containing an indication of his habitual underlying passive attitude to the analysis. 'Well', he says, 'we lived right next to that place. *Nanny used to take me there for walks* ...' (my italics). That is, he has been passively taken by Nanny, the analyst, to the place he has reached; he has passively submitted to the analytic process rather than actively allying himself with it. Now he must walk along a dangerous path, and brave his persecutors, represented by the mines and the barbed wire, instead of allying himself internally with them. But he cannot. It is not too much to say that this is the moment of his tragedy. His ego is too weak, the attraction of the easier and habitual perverse solution is too strong, and he is unable to take a step for fundamental change. In despair, he retreats and puts himself to sleep; for the potentially developing part of himself the sleep is now to be permanent. When he makes contact with the analyst again it is in his old mode; he is inaccessible to progress, he is actively sadistic toward and paralysing of the analyst, who is now, as the clinical record shows, the only one trying and caring, since Mr K is again submitting merely passively to her efforts.

Mrs Riesenberg Malcolm draws attention to the significant similarity between Mr K's very first dream on the night before his first session, in which 'he was in a village inside a ditch, and had to climb up to get to freedom. He had in his hand a kind of miner's pick. When he proceeded to make his way up, an enormous amount of rocks, earth and all kinds of heavy things fell on his head', and his very last dream before the complete stagnation of the analysis: 'I want to reach freedom and safety. To do so I have to dig a tunnel and go through it. While I am digging it, I see the gravel and rubbish piling up into a terrible mess that makes me feel that I will never be able to clear it up.' These dreams show how Mr K ends back where he began. Having been taken by the analyst to a vision of the freedom and safety that he cannot attain, he now closes himself away completely. Instead of being in a ditch, which at least is open, he is now shut in a tunnel. The dream also tells us that he is in a tunnel accumulating psychic debris, with which, I think, he will continue to require therapeutic aid.

In fact, Mr K has already communicated to his analyst that he cannot manage without treatment. He made an attempt to leave treatment but failed; he had to ask to be taken back because of his fears of collapsing, becoming very depressed, and falling to pieces. And indeed, before Mr K started with Mrs Riesenberg Malcolm he had already undergone previous treatment. Mr K's life pattern is, I think, to be perpetually a patient.

This, then, is one more factor adding to the pain of terminating a case of this kind. Along with the admission that the patient is irreparable, and that it is wrong to continue, there is also the knowledge of the patient's interminable need of therapeutic care. The analyst knows he is passing on his case to someone else. At this point, in my view, analysis would no longer be the treatment of choice, since analysis is a treatment for change, which, it has now been established, is not possible for Mr K. Better a therapy which is openly a treatment for maintenance. It would set limits on Mr K's field for cruelty, since his immobilisations would no longer be thwarting hoped-for progress, and would provide a less suffering and guilt-inducing framework within which Mr K could be once again sustained as a patient.

Acknowledgements

A previous edition of this chapter appeared in the *International Journal of Psychoanalytic Psychotherapy*, 1980–1, 8: 573–576.

3

A CLINICAL STUDY OF A DEFENSIVE ORGANISATION

Some patients seek an analysis at a moment when they hope not to extend their contact with themselves or their objects, but, on the contrary, because they desperately need a refuge from these. Once they are in analysis their first aim is to establish, really to re-establish, a defensive organisation against objects internal and external which are causing them nearly overwhelming anxiety.

The current lives of the patients I have in mind are permeated by infantile anxieties that have not been much modified. They are patients with a weak ego who, with more persecution than normal, arrive in infancy at the borders of the depressive position as defined by Klein (1935), but are then unable to negotiate it, and instead form a defensive organisation. The defensive organisation, however, proves precarious, since the combination of a weak ego and acute assailing anxieties that makes a negotiation of the depressive position impossible also makes it impossible for them to sustain a defensive organisation. Their lives oscillate between periods of exposure and periods of restriction; they are exposed to intense anxiety from their objects when the defensive organisation fails, and suffer restricted, though tolerable, object relations when it is again established.

This paper aims to show how a defensive organisation, established and maintained in the conditions provided by an analysis, can strengthen the ego and diminish the area of anxiety. In this way the oscillation between exposure and restriction is halted, and instead the patient is able – in the particular manner open to him – to proceed with his development. The paper aims also to examine the nature of a defensive organisation.

A long, 12-year analysis of Mr M gave me the opportunity of studying the several successive phases – four in all – in the evolution of his defensive organisation. In the first phase I could see the desperate situation to which he was exposed when his defensive organisation failed. Then, in the next period, when Mr M was able to re-establish his defensive organisation, I could study the restricted object relations on which his defensive organisation was based and the nature of the relief and benefit it brought him. Later, in the third stage, I could observe how he exploited his defensive organisation for the gratification of his cruelty and his narcissism. Finally, in the last phase of the analysis, when Mr M, now with some trusted objects, was able once more to go forward in his development, I could observe how his ego, while much strengthened, was also split in a characteristic way as a consequence of his protracted use of his defensive organisation.

To lessen the mass of clinical material, I report a full session only from the beginning and near the end – from the beginning to present fully Mr M's initial predicament so that his defensive organisation against it may be understandable, and near the end to contrast Mr M at the start with Mr M in the final phase of his analysis. In between, for brevity, I resort to descriptions aided by images from Mr M's dreams with only a brief indication of their working through by analyst and patient. The four phases of Mr M's analysis – presenting predicament, establishment of a defensive organisation, exploitation of the defensive organisation, and progress forward – are described in a way that makes clear their distinctness, which was very marked; I have omitted the forerunners of, and returns to, the other phases which, of course, were present in each.

Presenting predicament

Mr M was an only child born after a long labour by Caesarean section. His mother told him there were no more children because she could not bear again the experience of labour. She also told him she breast-fed him for six months while feeling very depressed. Mr M felt his mother to be burdensome but caring. His father was a well-intentioned but chilly and remote man with a grievance about lack of professional recognition. Mr M felt his father 'psychologised' about him.

Mr M recalled his childhood as unhappy and lonely, and sometimes terrifying. At night he needed a light in his bedroom and also insisted on a light in the passage leading to his parents' bedroom. He slept fitfully and was enuretic. At the age of 7 he became acutely nervous and suffered nightmares. This must have been a period when his defensive organisation was failing him. His parents took him to an analyst who treated him for two years; they were of the opinion that this childhood analysis helped him even if it did not remove his problems. In this view I think Mr M's parents were right; his first analysis seems to have helped him to reconstitute a much needed defensive organisation, though it did not alter his underlying predicament. Mr M continued his schooling, hating it, afraid of the other children. Isolated and unhappy, he started university. His father urged him to have another analysis, but Mr M was unwilling. Two years later, his father died suddenly. At first Mr M could not absorb the fact of his father's death. Later, alone at home with his mother, Mr M became depressed and increasingly felt ill and frightened. He was 22 when he sought analysis with me.

In the preliminary interview I saw a weak and acutely anxious young man. Mr M spoke of his fears of dying and mutilation, his plagues of sexual phantasies and his excessive masturbation, all of which, he said, were 'driving him nuts'. He told me, too, that he had tried to approach one or two girls at the university but was sexually impotent.

For his first session he arrived laughing to cover terror. He poured out garbled material about 'oral castration', 'homosexuality', 'impotence', 'lesbians', speaking like a confused psychoanalyst and as if his mind was under intolerable pressure. He could barely listen to the few interpretations I made about the pressure and confusion in his mind and his terror of me. At one point, however, I said that because he was terrified of me he was giving me 'analytic' talk and that perhaps there was something else he might otherwise say. At this interpretation his hectic speaking stopped. 'It's hard to daydream. I try to but I can't. People distract me. But in a daydream I get left by myself with my thoughts – then there is nothing except thoughts.' He spoke with intense yearning. This was his first expression, often repeated subsequently, of his longing for a peaceful undistracted relationship to me, a relationship in which he could have what he here calls a 'daydream'. As the psychologising father in the transference I had already made him distracted; I terrified him, he projected himself into me to gain control of me, and then got confused with me. His longing is to get away from such distracting people, but not to be alone and left with 'nothing except thoughts'. The defensive organisation which Mr M later established in the analysis achieved exactly this. It got him away from 'distracting people' and gave him the undisturbed relationship to me for which he yearned.

But in this first phase of his analysis Mr M was very disturbed. The impact of his father's death, held off for some months, had broken down his precarious defensive organisation and exposed him to confusion and nearly overwhelming anxieties. I should like to portray Mr M's predicament in more detail as it emerged very early in the analysis in a Friday session. At the start of the session, Mr M had seemed afraid to enter the room. When he did, on his way to the couch, he stopped, bent down and stared into the seat of my chair (I had not yet sat down). He was very anxious and breathing irregularly. On the couch he began: 'You've changed your suit again. It's got stripes. I had been feeling anxious when I was coming here.' His anxiety, already acute, was increasing. I spoke to him, saying he wanted me to realise he was very afraid. Mr M replied: 'It's my breathing, it's abnormal. In an abnormal rhythm. I can't get back to normal breathing. I had a dream last night actually.' In sudden tones of self-admiration he said: 'Some dream!'

He relapsed immediately into anxiety, speaking as if he were watching the dream he was telling.

> I was watching an old film or a film on T.V. The woman who was supposed to be the star disgusted me. She was too old. I felt it disgusting her acting this role. She should be younger. There were two men with her all the time. I saw her in bed with her breasts bared and these two men were on either side of her. They were going to make love or something. But suddenly the man said something in a peevish flippant tone. I was surprised at this. Then the man drew out a big knife and started cutting at the woman between her two breasts. It was horrible. Then I wasn't watching any more, but I had got mixed up with the man in the dream and was stabbing the woman. I was sort of drawn into him and he was writing his name on her flesh with the knife. She was screaming.

He stopped.

Before I could say anything he shouted out angrily: 'You haven't said anything. It wasn't worth it. I wasted it on you'. I said he was angry I wasn't quicker. He felt it showed I didn't value his dream

– the star production for me (Mr M gave a giggle) but also, and more important, was his fear that his dream had become real, and that an intercourse was really happening here in the session, pulling him to the seat of my chair to see it, getting into his mind in pictures and also getting into his breathing. Mr M was attentive. I went on to suggest that he had been afraid at the beginning that I had actually changed into the screaming mother of his dream – perhaps my stripes had seemed to him to be screams. Mr M gave a little laugh of relief, and his breathing quietened.

Then the next moment he was saying, thinly boastful but also desperate: 'That dream was very vivid. Usually I can't remember my dreams. They are incoherent. I tried hard to remember that one. It was very vivid', he repeated, desperate to get me talking further about his Sex dream, as I shall call it. I remained quiet. Suddenly Mr M said in a totally tired and dead voice:

I had another dream actually. I was trying to hitch a lift. There were lots of cars coming along. Then I saw two old people. They also needed a lift. But as soon as I was wanting a lift for them the flow of cars dried up. Then I was with a big Alsatian dog. I thought 'I will never get a lift with that dog with me'.

Later I knew that Mr M's dream about Old People was a recurring dream. On this day it had been occasioned by the end of the week, when the flow of cars, that is, the flow of sessions, was ceasing. I interpreted that Mr M felt there was a baby him who was making a hitching gesture, moving his thumb, and needing to be picked up. But his dream, and his sudden tired mood with me, indicated that he felt abandoned with old people who couldn't help him, who instead made him feel tired and dead and that he had to lift or liven them. I reminded him how just before in the session he had been wanting us to talk about his Sex dream in order to enliven both him and me.

It was almost the end of the session. Mr M poured out a disordered sequence: 'haphazard … it's your desk. My testicles could get crushed. I'm having a picture. Too far …' etc. He was agitated. He was fragmenting his thoughts, talking to rid himself of 'hazards', and to keep me away from him, terrified I was 'Old People', who couldn't either care for him or manage on their own, any more than could his widowed mother, with whom he would spend the weekend.

In this session Mr M is almost overwhelmed by anxieties and confusions. At the start, the room, the analytic chair and the analyst all frightened him: they appeared changed. They had almost become for him actually the world of his Sex dream. Inside his body, his abnormal breathing similarly alarms him: it is the concrete and physical expression of internal copulating analyst-parents. Though he is confused and tending to function in a disordered and concrete way, he has not altogether lost his hold on reality or his capacity to think, but he is terrified that he could. Noticeable, too, is how he has almost no respite. No sooner has he gained a little relief, as he did when his terror of the room and his breathing is understood and interpreted, than another anxiety supervenes. When his objects stop copulating they are inert, depressed 'Old People', who need life from him – an impossible demand when he himself feels he is abandoned and dying on the weekend. The mixture of persecutory and depressive anxieties stirred by his depressed dying objects rouses an enormous and uncontainable agitation in Mr M from which at the end of the session he tries to defend himself by fragmenting and evacuating it.

This defence, like the others his ego attempts during the session, e.g., his thin bravado ('Some dream!'), or his distancing of his frighteningly concrete and invasive Sex dream by seeing it as a film, or his use of the Sex dream for erotisation, fails almost instantly, leaving Mr M exposed again to multiple anxieties. His weak ego is throughout unable to sustain its defences.

Mr M's ego is also too weak to resist the pull of his objects. In his Sex dream, for example, he is drawn into the murderous copulation, as in the session he is pulled helplessly over to the seat of my chair. It is his ego's lack of cohesion that vitiates another important defence used by Mr M – projective identification. This was evident already in the first session when he arrived in a state of projective identification with a psychologising father-analyst, but confused and overexcited, and still terrified. The father transference was very important. Mr M often feared me as a cold, ridiculing, peevish father, a father depicted in many dreams as a monster.

Also in the session above is an interesting anticipation of an aspect of Mr M which emerged only much later in the analysis. This is the Alsatian dog which appears at the end of his Old People dream. It represents a treacherous, destructive, possessive side of him. When it appears it makes him despair – 'I will never get a lift with that dog

41

with me', he says in the dream, and later when it emerged fully it gave him, and me, cause for despair.

But in the present first phase it is not his impulses which trouble Mr M. It is the weak and confused state of his ego and his alarming objects which are causing him almost overwhelming anxiety, to the degree that he felt threatened by a psychotic condition. Mr M did not believe that his objects had the capacity to contain either their feelings or his, and he himself could not hold any one state of mind for more than a moment or two. Above all, Mr M felt a need for stillness and unchangingness, a need really to regain his defensive organisation against his borderline condition. He continued to voice his longing for his lost refuge in such terms as: 'I want to cry. I want to put myself away so as not to be troubled', 'I must regain my former calm', 'If I don't get calm I feel I shall never work again'. During one session he asked: 'Give me peace'.

Though Mr M was suspicious of interpretations, afraid they were trying to excite or mock him or were my outpouring of suffering or deadness or anxiety, he wanted me to interpret to him. This was the transference manifestation of his belief that his objects, for all their terrifying burdensomeness, were trying to care for him, just as he, for all his deadness, would have liked to be able to enliven them. It was particularly interpretations that recognised the extremity of his anxieties and feelings of disorder and confusion – if they could be formulated before Mr M shifted to yet a further anxiety, a task by no means easy – which gave him relief. Then he felt reached by an analyst strong enough to hold him, and in identification his ego strengthened, and gradually the level of Mr M's anxiety, though it remained high, began to drop. At the end of this first period, which lasted for 18 months, a change occurred in the whole nature of Mr M's relationship to me.

Establishment of a defensive organisation

Unlike before, Mr M now came on time to the second, pressing the doorbell hard. Also, unlike before, when he poured out constantly shifting anxieties about himself or the analyst, he was now oblivious of these. Nor did he bother about enlivening me; there was no more erotised 'stimulating' material. Instead, he spoke distantly, thickly, as though his head was muffled with sleep, dropping his words out in a deadened and deadening way which controlled and transfixed me. Mr M had split off his anxiety-laden parts and, in phantasy, projected himself into father's cold penis, which he used for making cold deadening speech that annihilated disturbance in the room, the couch and myself, all of which represented mother's body. In this way he made an emptied, unchanging place for himself in me as a mother-analyst. With a stronger ego he was able now to sustain his control of me and to stay in his state of projective identification without becoming confused, and to prevent the return and re-invasion of himself by unwanted split off parts.

Mr M had said: 'I want to put myself away so as not to be troubled'. He had now done so – almost. Mr M felt he formed me, in the sessions, into an object in which he could store himself and be free from 'trouble'. In place of the earlier lurching, agitated transference situation there was now a restricted, controlled relationship between Mr M and myself. He was in a sort of daydream state in which only the feel of the couch and the sound of my voice impinged on him. He had nearly no anxiety; and in this minimal way he had a sense of having what he needed. Mr M felt calm. His calm was an enormous relief; he felt he had been saved from an impending psychotic condition.

At the same time that Mr M was forming me into the undisturbing place he could tolerate, he was also splitting off and projecting into me his unwanted states of mind. His unchanging, cold, repetitive behaviour projected into me feelings of being dealt with by a relentless object, of being helpless, of being deadened, of being tortured to the point of madness, of having to endure what I did not like again and again. Mr M was projecting into me the suffering infant he had been, and also expressing, through what he felt he made me endure, his hatred and resentment. Any interpretation that he experienced as my forcing feelings back into him, or that seemed to him evidence of my anxiety or my curiosity (he aroused both in me by his mental state and the lack of almost all information about his existence) he could not take. It was a return of disturbance. Immediately, he flattened and deadened the interpretation to safeguard his new calm state.

Looked at broadly, Mr M had now formed a defensive organisation by the interlocking use of several defences, omnipotent control and denial, and the several forms of splitting and projective identification described by Melanie Klein (1955) to organise relations within himself and between himself and his objects. Clinically, he formed the controlling and static transference, characteristic of the operation of a defensive organisation in an analysis. He exerted intense pressure on me to form me into, and keep me restricted to, the object he required in order to remain calm. And for five years, analytic work was received by him within the broad framework imposed by this defensive organisation.

There is a matter of terminology. I should like to propose, though it is a departure from analytic usage, that the term 'defensive organisation' which was introduced by Willi Hoffer (1954) be reserved for the kind of defensive system Mr M established.[1] Unlike defences – piecemeal, transient to a greater or lesser extent, recurrent – which are a normal part of development, a defensive organisation is a fixation, a pathological formation when development arouses irresoluble and almost overwhelming anxiety. Expressed in Kleinian terms, defences are a normal part of negotiating the paranoid-schizoid and depressive positions; a defensive organisation, on the other hand, is a pathological fixed formation in one or other position, or on the borderline between them. Segal (1972) describes another such defensive organisation in a patient more disturbed than Mr M.

To return to Mr M's defensive organisation. In his material, oral and genital ideas were infiltrated by anal notions, and anal terms and processes themselves were very prominent. Mr M delivered his words making noises of being at stool; most thoughts and feelings had for him the meaning of unwanted faeces that he wished to evacuate; his highly controlled objects were felt to have been changed into stool. Mr M's functioning, and his relations to his objects, now often had for him a predominantly anal significance, and in this sense, his defensive organisation was also an anal organisation.

Mr M pictured the kind of object he needed in order to obtain his calm in the following dream.

He dreamt that he met a friend who led a hand-to-mouth existence, sleeping in a flat in a broken-down warehouse, which was disused – but his friend said it was safe.

The dream is of Mr M leading his 'hand-to-mouth' existence – he often put his hand to his mouth – sleeping in his flat sessions in a broken-down analyst-mother, who was barely able to move, and since Mr M had control of father's penis there could be no copulation and no babies, so that the analyst-mother was also 'disused'. I was both the warehouse-mother in which Mr M stored himself and also his 'aware' house, the container of his own unwanted awarenesses.

But though he had a calm based on the absence of disturbance, he had not the peace of freely relating to an object that freely accepts him. Storing himself in a broken-down warehouse-mother, while it had an affinity – which Mr M felt – with being in the womb, or peacefully lying in a mother's arms, was only the best alternative available to him for this. And though enormously relieved, Mr M still felt unsafe, ill and also 'bad'. He had always to be on the alert for anything that signalled disturbance; as he put it once, he was like a dog that must keep its ears pricked up. His splitting off of awareness made him sleepy, and the intrusion into his head of his intruded-upon objects made his head feel strange and thick. To get his calm, Mr M had to organise his object to give it to him: he had to break his way into it, annihilate its disturbing properties, and control it to make it fit his needs, to the degree that he almost converted it into faeces or destroyed it, and he was troubled by anxiety that he was 'bad'.

After some months he began to ruminate about a monster featured in the newspapers, the 'Abominable Snowman', a monster who had smashed into a house. This expressed Mr M's feelings of breaking into me each day exactly on time with his hard pressing of the doorbell. Mr M asked repeatedly: 'Is the "Abominable Snowman" a real monster?' He knew he was being abominable and coldly controlling but was he so monstrous out of fear that otherwise the object would, as before, cause him feelings he could not endure? Or was he himself really a monster? He could not decide and there were signs of a small monster, signs of what in the future evolution of his defensive organisation was to escalate: Mr M found he got a sadistic pleasure from my controlled transfixed condition and from making me endure the projections of his hatred. Sometimes, I caught a smirk hidden in Mr M's flat tones, but usually if I pointed it out a long silence annihilated both smirk and interpretation. Very occasionally he was able to let his awareness that he was not only defending, but also gratifying, himself get near. Once he brought a dream about a strange, damaged animal that was half a mammal, but which had evolved on its jaw a long snout. In the dream Mr M felt responsible for the animal and was very upset.

He associated the animals with piglets who like putting their snouts in the dirt. The dream was Mr M's picture of himself as a damaged infant who needed to protect himself by evolving a long snout, but an infant who was also getting a cruel pleasure from using his snout to control me and reduce me to dirt. The analysis of the dream made, unusually during this period, a lot of anxiety break through in the session. The next day, as Mr M needed to split off his upset about his piglet-self, I was almost suffused by the extent of the anxiety and depression he projected into me. But in the main Mr M succeeded in organising himself and his objects so that he kept the session almost flat and deadened, and himself, though on the alert, almost untroubled and calm.

It was important to Mr M that I understood, in its daily and detailed manifestation, his need to remain calm and destroy potential disturbance emanating from himself or from me, and sometimes interpretations about his holding us together in a controlled and deadened way because he was frightened of freer contact, enabled him briefly to bring material that was more alive. He could take in only those interpretations which he did not experience as forcing unwanted feelings into him or as criticisms of him for being a monster. Those interpretations he could accept gave him a different experience from his calm state. He reported that they 'cleared his head', made him 'feel different'. They were an experience of a much more alive relationship occurring between us.

By the fifth year of the analysis, Mr M's life had improved in several ways. He completed his university courses and obtained a job. After one failed attempt he succeeded in moving away from living at home with his mother (this, of course, he was doing instead with me in the analysis) and established himself in a flat. He found one or two friends. It was also evident to me – the overall unchanging character of the sessions notwithstanding – that his ego was definitely strengthening and I was much less frightening to him. But he did not, as I think I was expecting, use this improvement to begin to tolerate more integration of himself or his object. On the contrary, he used his improvement in a quite opposite direction.

Exploitation of the defensive organisation

One result so far of Mr M's analysis was the lessening of his fear of being flooded with disturbance from his object. He used me in the fixed form he needed, and he projected unwanted feelings into me, and he trusted me not to move overwhelmingly or to project back into him. Objects so used, can also be abused – and Mr M began to exploit this relationship. It became a venue in which he felt his narcissism and his cruelty could emerge and operate more omnipotently, unrestrained by complaints from the object or interference from himself.

At the beginning the paramount function of Mr M's defensive organisation had been defensive. This was now not so. His defensive organisation was now equally, at moments predominantly, a vehicle for the omnipotent gratification of his narcissism and his cruelty. His object relations now constituted a narcissistic organisation of the type studied by Rosenfeld (1971). In this new form his defensive organisation still served a defensive function. It defended Mr M from feeling small and slow, from the fear that he might never be able really to change or be well, and from all the fresh anxiety and guilt, that the use, and now also the abuse, of his defensive organisation aroused by his controlling, his separating, and his deadening of his objects, and now further by his triumphant and cruel robbery of them.

In the sessions he was often now openly cruel, refusing me material and producing any jumble that occurred to him, at times when I knew, if he cared to, he was able to communicate much better. Mr M got excited by his cruelty and my flounderings with his disordered material. He did not now ruminate about being an 'Abominable Snowman'. Instead, he omnipotently split off his superego. His triumph over me, felt to be dismayed and disappointed by his perverse use of his improvement, escalated.

Mr M felt increasingly attractive. He used splitting mechanisms to split off not only his superego, as described above, but also to split off realities that interfered with his narcissism. In his burgeoning phantasies he felt he was inside and had inside him not only his father's omnipotent penis, but all his mother's attributes – her breasts, her stimulating beauty, etc. He felt, almost believed, he was the penis, or the breasts, I desired, and that he could consummate his positive and negative Oedipus complex, and that he could stay in analysis for ever. The analysis was to be the fulfilment of what a recent writer has termed 'the golden phantasy' (Smith, 1972). In his current life, after one or two failures, Mr M was sexually potent and found at this time several girls ready to chase him and confirm his feeling of power and attractiveness. Now he felt no need of my work. He had contempt for interpretations which he dismissed as 'pedestrian' and a similar contempt for the aware and more realistic part of himself which he felt was also 'pedestrian' – a favourite word of his at this time.

His excited state is well depicted in a dream.

In the dream Mr M saw a fellow with combs sticking out all over him and thought: 'That fellow ought to be defused.' There were traffic lights going in the wrong order – red, yellow, red – and the fellow was also looking the wrong way.

After telling the dream Mr M paid it no more attention. He moved off quickly to new topics in a jumbled order that I could do nothing with. I tried to show him he was being the fellow of his dream, who, I suggested, was a coxcomb – the combs sticking out all over being his showy bursting excitement. I suggested he was living his dream in the session, feeling excited about giving me his material in the wrong order, like the traffic lights, and looking the wrong way – that is, away from his dream that told him about this coxcomb self, that he knew ought to be defused. Mr M did not want to look at these interpretations. I persisted, he got very irritated, and the session ended with his saying contemptuously, 'You annoy me' as he strode out. The smirky piglet had grown into an openly contemptuous and omnipotent coxcomb.

Increasingly at this stage Mr M did not want the part of himself that was aware of what he was doing and knew he was getting dangerously excited and should be defused. He wanted to be free of it. Mr M wanted to be 'free' from all 'trouble' of reality, sanity, anxiety and guilt. He made an increasing split between his cruel narcissistic part which he idealised, and the part of himself capable of awareness, feeling, thought and judgment, which he disowned. The split in Mr M's ego was of the kind described by Freud (1940) in his paper on 'Splitting of the ego in the process of defence'. In Freud's view such a split is 'a rift in the ego which never heals'. The split in Mr M's ego stayed, although the nature of the rift between the two parts changed.

At this stage his omnipotent part was dominant and constantly tried to increase its dissociation from his sane aware part, a process which culminated in an acting out at the end of the sixth year when Mr M became temporarily almost deluded. He quit his job and informed me he was quitting the analysis and not returning after the holidays. He made unrealistic plans for extended travel. In the last weeks of the term he was so insulated by feelings of excitement and omnipotence that I could make little contact with him. I continued to analyse his plans as an enactment of his omnipotent phantasies rather than as the expression of an intention to leave the analysis. At this moment he had deposited all his sense and sanity in me. After the holidays Mr M returned. He said his travels had been a disaster, his firm would not take him back and he had yet to find another job. His experiences during his holidays had defused and collapsed his omnipotence and excitement, leaving him very frightened. His more aware part had forced itself back into his mind again, and he now felt he had been 'crazy'.

He could not, however, bear to know this for very long. He split off his knowledge that his omnipotent feelings were crazy and gave himself a changed and twisted version of his return to analysis: it was his fulfilment of my desires. Soon, he was relating to me in the same overall defensive and highly pathological mode as before.

I worked on this repetitive and, broadly speaking, unchanging transference situation. There were times when Mr M brought me close to despair. My despair arose from my concern about the lack of movement in the analysis: I wondered if we should go on. But it was also Mr M's despair projected into me, which I analysed, that he would hold on to and possess the analysis – there was no more talk of leaving – that he would use it treacherously to inflate his omnipotence and narcissism, but never let it move and come alive, and therefore that he himself would never feel alive. This period saw the full emergence and analysis of what had been foreshadowed long before in an early dream, the Old People dream reported on page 40 (this volume). At the end of that dream, you will remember, an Alsatian dog appeared and in the dream Mr M says: 'I will never get a lift with that dog with me.' That I did not give him up and persevered in my work with him was, I think, proof to Mr M that his object could withstand the Alsatian dog in him, his relentless and treacherous possessiveness, without being destroyed by it.

Progress forward

Gradually, during the eighth year of the analysis, there were distinct signs of a more alive, less restricted contact between us, as Mr M's defensive organisation began to slacken. Instead of a total and perpetual organisation of his relationships internal and external to exclude all disturbance, Mr M began to use his defences more transiently and to allow perturbing perceptions and emotions to reach him. Other related changes occurred. His speech altered. He now wanted to talk. There was a broader area in the purview of the analysis: his current life now figured in his thoughts during his sessions. He began to see the beginnings of his return to grappling with those problems that lie on the edge of the depressive position from which his defensive organisation had been a much needed retreat. Mr M was not now almost overwhelmed by these returning anxieties: he was better

49

equipped. His ego was stronger, more cohesive, and more able to tolerate anxiety, and the area of anxiety itself had lessened – along with his old, dying, cold and over-impinging objects, he had new relations to warmer, stronger, more contained, alive objects.

With a characteristic configuration, Mr M began to confront his developmental problems. The configuration was a sequel to his protracted use of a defensive organisation in the sense given it in this paper, namely a pathological, static formation needed when development is arousing almost overwhelming and irresoluble anxiety. Mr M had a split in his ego: one part was capable of awareness and feeling and tried to progress even though anxiety loomed; his other omnipotent part preferred to stay in a state of projective identification with its object, and was obstructive and contemptuous of 'pedestrian' efforts to develop. But unlike before, Mr M's aware part was often now the dominant one, and it had started to scrutinise his omnipotent part, which like the defensive organisation of which it was the precipitate, still served Mr M as a defence. The existence of a split and deep opposition within the ego, and the continued use for defence of the omnipotent part, are, I think, the characteristic sequelae of a defensive organisation.

Before concluding I shall report a session from the ninth year which shows this characteristic configuration in operation. The session, when placed alongside the session reported at the start of the paper, also shows the change in Mr M, and, as well, returns us to, and throws new light on, his longing for peace.

It was a Friday session. Mr M began in a sneering, hostile tone saying he was bored. Then in a different voice he said he was tired (he had looked tired) and he now sounded it. He changed back to being sneering and hostile, saying he had to make obeisance, he had to sort of nod his head to the side as he passed the exit door (he had, in fact, nodded to the street door on the way to the consulting room). I commented on his opposite feelings: that he was hating me, feeling I forced him to acknowledge it was exit day, Friday, and also that he was feeling tired.

Straightaway Mr M talked about his weekend sexual plans, talking about having sex again with X – a married woman with whom he was having an affair, and then talking about Y – a girl whose magazine advertisement he had answered, and whom he would also see and have sex with at the weekend, and his tangle with the pair of them; and then he talked about Z, a young Jewish girl who was interested and friendly, and whom he had invited out on Saturday night. He was worried that he was going to lose interest in her. He sounded worried. Acknowledging first his worry that his activities with X and Y might destroy his interest in the young Jewish girl who was friendly and interesting, I linked her with an aspect of myself, who was interested in him and noticed how he felt. I pointed out that he had already, with all the sex talk to me, lost interest in his tiredness and depression that had crept over him on exit day, Friday. The interpretation seemed to reach Mr M and there was a silence.

When he spoke next it was with a lighter, more alive voice. He said he felt better now than when he arrived; then he hadn't felt well, but now he felt relieved as though some weight had been lifted off him. There was another long silence. Then Mr M said he was thinking how it was cold in his flat. He had got some draught excluders and put them round the entrance door, but the gap was too big, and the thing got twisted, it got bent. I suggested to him that he was explaining to me about his draught excluders, his sexual arrangements for the weekend, his talk to me about them in the session. These were his methods of excluding the flatness and tiredness that came into him at the weekend and he was telling me that these methods didn't really close the gap and also that they made him get twisted and bent. Mr M said thoughtfully: 'Well, yes. A perversion. I know.'

After a while he said: 'It's funny to think I have two homes – one here and one in A … I like A …' (recently he had inherited a property in A …). He continued: 'A picture occurs to me of the Jewish cemetery in A … which I often go past. Sometimes there are swastikas painted on it. There is a wide pedestrian' – at the word 'pedestrian' he said with a friendly laugh: 'I know what you'll think' – 'path alongside it along which I sometimes walk'. I interpreted his thoughts about having two homes as expressing the two ways he felt with me. When he first arrived he felt hostile, hating me for the way I force him out at the weekends and he painted me as a Nazi, and preferred his exciting weekend girls to boring Old People analysis. Now, in the middle of the session he felt at home with me, liked me and felt communicative. I also said that the 'pedestrian path' was important. Today he was not going past the 'Jewish cemetery'; he was on what he often thought of as the pedestrian path of noticing how things are. I suggested that by taking the life and sex out of me, as he had done at the beginning of the session, he felt he reduced me to a cemetery, which then got into his inner world, making him tired and depressed.

It was near the end. Frightened of depression and his exit, Mr M split off his aware part. Abruptly he was like a different patient on the couch. He spoke of his women, X and Y, and described excitedly a film about homosexuals. He sniggered and ended the session saying it had got good reviews and he would take one of them to see it at the weekend.

In this session Mr M was beginning to face, or at least to give a nod in the direction of, a number of disturbing problems: exit day, the persecution of being forced out, his perverse and destructive defences, and the tiredness and depression, really deadness, that stem from what he fears is a cemetery he makes in his inner world. We can also see the interaction of the two parts of Mr M. Both arrive and in the beginning they alternate. As the session proceeds his aware part becomes dominant, communicative and thoughtful about his twisted defences, acknowledging that he has a home he likes, and recognising the existence in himself of Nazis, dead objects, and depression. But when the end comes, Mr M is at this stage still too anxious. He needs to split off his aware part and his omnipotent part, defensive and twisted, completely takes him over, as it will partly do at the weekend.

The atmosphere of the session was characteristic of many in the concluding fourth stage of the analysis. Mr M was able to feel and show his hostility. He was also able to feel affection. His words and thoughts function very differently from early in the analysis, when they tended to become concrete and disordered. Mr M can now take his time. He was not frantic as he used to be at the start, nor dead calm as he was when he first formed his defensive organisation, nor dangerously excited as he often was when he later exploited it. I think Mr M himself expressed the change when he said: 'It's funny to think I have two homes.' It was his feeling of having a home, i.e., an object he could trust to accept him – in fact he felt he had two homes, one for each part of him, that was beginning to give Mr M a real sense of peace. This peace is different from the calm got by organising and restricting himself and his objects in order to remain undisturbed. As the session shows, this kind of peace is compatible with disturbance: indeed, it is based on having a home for disturbance.

The last years of Mr M's analysis saw an intricate conflict, and sometimes alliance, between his aware self and his omnipotent self. Gradually he faced some of what had previously been, in a phrase he often used, 'inadmissible evidence' about his object relations, including his terror and refusal of separateness that lay hidden under his omnipotence, and he was able, after his own fashion, to work through some of the feelings and anxieties of the depressive position. The broken-down, disused warehouse, Mr M's image of the mother who housed him, emerged in an important dream as a beautiful historic mansion that should not have been ruined and which the National Trust should restore. This, Mr M's increasing trust, partially did.

By the end of his long 12-year analysis, though his omnipotent part was liable to intrude suddenly into and spoil his relationships, and when he felt persecuted or over-guilty he was liable abruptly to lose interest in his object and become omnipotent and perverse, such states of mind were temporary. They were not seriously disturbing to his stable relationships, foremost among which was a marriage that brought him considerable satisfaction.

Summary

This paper is concerned with those patients whose lives oscillate between periods of over-restricted object relations based on a defensive organisation, and periods of exposure to almost overwhelming anxiety from their objects when their defensive organisation fails. The paper reports a 12-year analysis of one such patient, a young man whose defensive organisation had broken down. The clinical material shows how, in the conditions an analysis tries to provide – interpretive understanding, emotional containment, and analytic perseverance – he first re-established and then maintained his defensive organisation long enough to halt the oscillation between exposure and restriction, and to resume instead his forward development.

In the course of this clinical study, the nature of a defensive organisation is itself examined. I suggest that a distinction be drawn between defences and defensive organisation. Defences allow for the working through of anxiety and are a normal part of forward development. A defensive organisation is an overall pathological formation, a fixation of object relations when progress is impossible; its benefits come from the elimination of anxiety from object relations, and inherently, as the clinical material shows, such object relations offer the possibility of exploitation.

As regards technique, the paper shows the necessity of recognising the patient's need to be analysed for a long time within the framework of his defensive organisation. This allows his ego to strengthen and the area of his anxieties to diminish – changes which will enable him, often only after many years, to resume his forward development.

Acknowledgements

A previous edition of this chapter was published in the *International Journal of Psychoanalysis*, 1981, 62: 359–428.

Note

1   In fact, another and different proposal to rescue Hoffer's term from obscurity was made by Lichtenberg and Slap (1971).

4

A COMMEMORATIVE ESSAY ON W. R. BION'S THEORY OF THINKING

When W. R. Bion died in 1979 his own work, in his lifetime, had changed psychoanalysis. He made clinical discoveries which led him to formulate new concepts and original theories over a wide spectrum of fundamental psychoanalytic problems. Because of its close connection to new ways of working with patients, I have chosen as the topic of this commemorative essay Bion's work on thinking.

Bion formulated a theory of the origins of thinking. He posited an early first form of thinking, different from, but the basis for the development of, later forms. This first form of thinking strives to know psychic qualities, and is the outcome of early emotional events between a mother and her infant which are decisive for the establishment – or not – of the capacity to think in the infant. Bion's theory, which carries the interesting implication that knowledge of the psychological precedes knowledge of the physical world, represents a new understanding of thinking as one of the fundamental links between human beings, a link which is fundamental also for the forming and functioning of a normal mind. Throughout Bion connected his work on thinking to analytic technique and so made possible clinical advances with patients of all ages.

It is not easy to convey the rare originality of Bion's thought. He expressed himself in austere propositions with a high yield of exact meaning. They repay the reader's repeated return, as, for diversion, do his occasional and lastingly funny jokes. My plan is first to summarize some of the main aspects of his work on thinking and then give clinical illustrations of its use in child analysis.

What does Bion mean by 'thinking'? He does not mean some abstract mental process. His concern is with thinking as a human link – the endeavour to understand, comprehend the reality of, get insight into the nature of, etc., oneself or another. Thinking is an emotional experience of trying to know oneself or someone else. Bion designates this fundamental type of thinking – thinking in the sense of trying to know – by the symbol K. If xKy, then 'x is in the state of getting to know y and y is in a state of getting to be known by x'.

Bion's work on thinking began in a series of brilliant clinical papers delivered and published in the 1950s (Bion 1954, 1955, 1956, 1957, 1958a, 1958b, 1959). These papers record his investigations of thought disorders in psychotic patients who illuminated for him the nature of normal and abnormal thinking. In 1962 he formulated these discoveries theoretically in a paper called 'The psycho-analytic study of thinking' (Bion 1962a, reprinted as 'A theory of thinking' in Bion 1967a) and published his book *Learning from Experience* (Bion 1962b), in which he developed his ideas further, expounding them in terms of the symbol K. He never tired of acknowledging his debt both to Freud and to Melanie Klein, particularly to Freud's 'Formulations on the two principles of mental functioning' (Freud 1911a) and to Melanie Klein's theory of early object relations and anxieties, and her concept of projective identification. Bion developed their ideas and also combined them in a new way which formed then the foundation for his own discoveries.

In 'Formulations on the two principles of mental functioning' Freud described the aim of the pleasure principle as the avoidance and discharge of unpleasurable tensions and stimuli. In 'Notes on some schizoid mechanisms' (Klein 1946) Melanie Klein described something similar to the pleasure principle from a different perspective – an early mechanism of defence which she named projective identification. In her view the young infant defends his ego from intolerable anxiety by splitting off and projecting unwanted impulses, feelings, etc., into his object. This is an object relations perspective on the discharge of unpleasurable tensions and stimuli. In the course of exploring the nature of projective identification, Melanie Klein noted how its use varied in degree from one patient to another: more disturbed patients made what she termed 'excessive' use of this mechanism. Bion, from his work with psychotic patients, recognized that more than a quantitative factor was involved. He came to the conclusion that psychotic patients employ a different, abnormal type of projective

56

identification. Bion made another discovery. Projective identification, in addition to being a mechanism of defence, was the very first mode of communication between mother and infant – it is the origin of thinking. The very young infant communicates his feelings, his fears, etc., to his mother by projecting them into her for her to receive and know them. During a psycho-analysis projective identification as a mode of communication is an important and distinctive occurrence in a session. A 9-year-old girl, for example, while going swiftly and systematically from one activity to the next, at times projected into me a feeling of isolation. I felt the isolation intensely in myself, i.e., I contained and became momentarily identified with her projection. After thinking about what I had received, I interpreted that she wanted me to know her feeling of isolation. Such an event in a session is a primitive transmission from patient to analyst by means of projective identification, the transference version of the type of early event between mother and baby which forms a K link between them and which allows thinking to develop.

This is a very important finding. According to Bion, the infant discharges unpleasure by splitting off and projecting anxiety-arousing perceptions, sensations, feelings, etc. – such as in our example the feeling of isolation – into the mother for her to contain them in what Bion calls her 'reverie'. This is her capacity with love to think about her infant – to pay attention, to try to understand, i.e., to K. Her thinking transforms the infant's feelings into a known and tolerated experience. If the infant is not too persecuted or too envious, he will introject and identify with a mother who is able to think, and he will introject also his own now modified feelings.

Each such projective–introjective cycle between infant and mother is part of a momentous process which gradually transforms the infant's entire mental situation. Instead of a pleasure ego evacuating unpleasure, a new structure is slowly achieved: a reality ego which has unconsciously internalized at its core an object with the capacity to think, i.e., to know psychic qualities in itself and others. In such an ego there is a differentiation between conscious and unconscious, and the potential also to differentiate between seeing, imagining, phantasizing, dreaming, being awake, being asleep. This is the normal mind, the achievement of which depends on both mother and infant.

Failure to develop a reality ego may be due to the mother's failure to K her infant's communications to her by his first method of projective identification. If she fails, she deprives him of a fundamental need for an object unlike himself which does not evacuate the unpleasurable, but instead retains it and thinks about it. Failure may also be due to the infant's hatred of reality or his excessive envy of his mother's capacity to tolerate what he cannot. These lead him to continued and increased evacuation, both of the modified more tolerable elements returned to him by his mother and also of the containing mother herself, and, in extreme cases, to an aggressive attack on his own mental capacities. It is this last which brings about psychosis.

In Bion's view, psychosis comes with the destruction of those parts of the mind potentially capable of knowing. His classic paper 'Differentiation of the psychotic from the non-psychotic personalities' (Bion 1957) characterizes the divergence of psychotic from normal functioning thus: 'The differentiation of the psychotic from the non-psychotic personality depends on the minute splitting of all that part of the personality that is concerned with the awareness of internal and external reality, and the expulsion of these fragments so that they enter into or engulf their objects' (Bion 1957: 266). This is a disaster for mental life, which is then not established in the normal mode. Instead of thinking based on the reality principle and symbolic communication within the self and with other objects, an anomalous enlargement of the pleasure ego occurs, with excessive use of splitting and projective identification as its concrete mode of relating to hated and hating objects. Omnipotence replaces thinking and omniscience replaces learning from experience in a disastrously confused, undeveloped and fragile ego. Bion has described the grievous result of the psychotic's attack on his mind. The psychotic feels 'he cannot restore his object or his ego. As a result of these splitting attacks, all those features of the personality which would one day provide the foundation for intuitive understanding of himself and others are jeopardized at the outset' (Bion 1957: 268).

And further:

> ... in the patient's phantasy the expelled particles of ego lead an independent uncontrolled existence, either contained by or containing the external object; they continue to exercise their function as if the ordeal to which they have been subjected had served only to increase their number and provoke their hostility to the psyche that ejected them. In consequence the patient feels himself surrounded by bizarre objects.
>
> (Bion 1957: 268)

The psychotic is in despair, imprisoned in his bizarre universe. In analysis psychotic patients discharge a barrage out of terror of contact with either themselves or the analyst, who is experienced as a murderously punitive object. Their frail grasp of the normally distinct states of being awake, dreaming, hallucinating, perceiving, phantasy and reality makes for a confused, confusing and sometimes delusional transference. By continual use of projective identification, which may invade the analyst long outside the therapeutic hour, they attempt to evoke involvement and action from him, rather than K. Bion's hypotheses disagree with theories which view thinking as merely the emergence of maturation or as an autonomous ego function. According to him, K is hard-won by the infant ego from emotional experiences with a nurturing object, functioning normally on the reality principle.

But even when achieved, K is subject to hazard; it may become −K through being stripped of significance. −K is understanding denuded until only misunderstanding remains. Among its chief causes are excessive envy and inadequate nurture. Excessive envy changes the way projections are given. Bion writes: '... the infant splits off and projects its feelings of fear into the breast together with envy and hate of the undisturbed breast' (Bion 1962b: 96), and goes on to describe in his chapter on −K in *Learning from Experience* the infant's progressive denudation of his psyche which becomes permeated by nameless dread. From the mother's side, a failure to accept projections forces her infant to assail her and project increasingly, and he experiences her as denuding him. He then internalizes 'a greedy vagina-like "breast" that strips of its goodness all that the infant receives leaving only degenerate objects. This internal object starves its host of all understanding that is made available' (Bion 1962a: 308). Continuing mutual denudation and misunderstanding between mother and infant will leave only −K between them, a cruel, empty, degenerative link of superiority/inferiority.

So far I have summarized Bion's exploration of three phenomena: K, the emotional experience of trying to know the self and others; no K, the psychotic state with no mind able to know the self or others − the patient, in the psychotic part of his mind, exists in an unreal universe of bizarre objects about which he cannot think; and −K, the cruel and denuding link of misunderstanding the self and others. I want now to illustrate their application to the understanding and interpretation of clinical material in child analysis.

Bion places the capacity to know at the very centre of mental life. His work puts the pleasure principle and the reality principle on a par with the life instinct and the death instinct as the fundamental governors of psychic life. In Bion's symbols, K is as fundamental as L (love) or H (hatred). He links his theoretical regrouping to clinical practice. According to Bion, there is a key to each session. The key is L or H or K. When the analyst decides that L or H or K should be the subject of his main opening interpretations he has decided the key of the session, which can then 'act as a standard to which he can refer all the other statements he proposes to make' (Bion 1962b: 45). If Bion is right, K, or any of its forms of −K, or no K, is as likely as any of the forms of L or H to be the pivot of a session. The implication for clinical practice is that we must often work with our patients about K and that our attention should float as freely to the K link within the patient and between ourselves and our patients as it does to the L or H links.

This could be put by saying (although it would be quite foreign to Bion's view of analytic work to make rigid use of the idea): Ask of clinical material the question: Is the material in this session emerging as an expression of, or anxiety about, or a defence against, etc. ... L or H or K? (I shall omit L and H from further consideration as it is not the subject of this paper, and anyway more familiar.) If K is most urgent in the material there is a next question: What form of K? Is the child trying to know or is the child, e.g., too anxious to think about his internal or external object? In these cases the key is K. Alternatively, is the child misunderstanding or denuding his experience? If so, the key is no longer K, but −K. Or, is the child expressing in his material a psychotic condition in which he exists without the capacity to think? In this case the key is no K.

Suppose a girl of nine begins her session by drawing a house. The house is unexceptional; it has a conventional roof, a pair of windows with curtains, a central door. The neat drawing conveys order and emptiness. What, if anything with respect to K, does the drawing communicate? Is the child attempting with her picture of the house to tell her therapist that she knows her internalized mother is orderly but empty? And is she expressing also her feeling and her fear that the therapist who gives her regular appointments, has the same setting each session, and so on, is like that, too? If so, then the key to the session is K. The child is thinking about her internal object and strives in this session as against other times (she is, in fact, the child mentioned briefly on page 57 who projected feelings of isolation; she was at that time too anxious to think about the nature of her object and was instead being it) to know also the current and immediate external object, the therapist in the maternal transference.

But the communication might be different. Such a drawing may express a child's feeling that ordinary relations – and, in fact, this second child attends regularly, comports herself in an unexceptional way with the therapist – are empty of meaning to her. If so, and the total context of her other communications and the therapist's counter-transference feelings will decide, she is communicating that the session has no significance for her and that she will learn nothing from it, though she is there and does and says the 'right' things. The key to the session is –K, and an opening interpretation might be that she feels being with the therapist, like the house drawing, is empty and means nothing to her. The session will develop in one of many possible ways from there. The child may be relieved to be understood, perhaps her anxiety about the pervasiveness of such futile object relations at home and at school may emerge, or her fear that she cannot feel differently. More –K will almost certainly occur in the session, now in relation to the new K events of the hour (with some children it will occur at once in relation to the first interpretation) and the process of denudation can be caught in the immediacy of its happening.

There is a third possible category of communication in K. The child's drawing of the house may be orderly but empty because it is merely an inoffensive item to engage the therapist while the child is really engaged elsewhere. One such child produced neat conventional drawings and models for me while engaged in watching a hostile 'eye' watching him from the lock on the window – a terrifying bizarre object in Bion's sense. This third child had not the mental equipment to think thoughts about a house or draw a symbolic house, as could the first child – the drawing of a house was for him something quite different. He always took his drawings and models with him at the end of each session. Once, early in the analysis, he made an attempt to leave a drawing. An hour later I found him standing outside the playroom, panic-stricken, unable to go without his drawing, which he believed was a piece of himself he had extruded via his pencil onto the paper. To leave it was a self-mutilation. I was experienced as a terrifying object who must be appeased by drawings, models, etc., and from whom he must conceal his bizarre world about which he could not think; both because it would overwhelm him with terror and also because he had not the mind with which to think a thought. There was no K in his session. The key to his session, notwithstanding its apparent quiet and the patient's overt conventional activity of drawing an unexceptional house, is his state of being without K and his consequent despair about help with or rescue from the hate of the objects by which he felt surrounded – the hatred of the watching eye on the window, and the hatred of the therapist.

'The smile of the psychotic means something different from the smile of the non-psychotic', thus Bion, and the same can be said of children's play. In these illustrations, somewhat stylized for presentation though from three analyses each a type familiar to child psychotherapists, the drawing of a house means something different for each child. For the first it is a symbolic communication which expresses K. For the second in Segal's (1957) sense it is a symbolic equivalent of emptiness and meaninglessness, i.e., of –K, and another drawing or another sort of play would do as much or as little, just as at this stage analysis was an experience no different from anything else. For the third child, the drawing is a concrete extrusion of a piece of himself in a house-like shape to appease the therapist, without K in fear of H.

Bion's clinical insights have made possible quite new work with patients in each of the three areas of K, –K and the psychotic condition of no K. Consider, for example, the connection between K and splitting and integrating the ego. When K of her mother aroused too much anxiety in the first of the three children described above, she split off her memory and her judgment that her mother was orderly but empty. She defended herself from knowing by splitting and by being the object moving quickly, systematically from one activity to another. When she became less afraid to K, she was able to draw, and drew the orderly, empty house, integrating her knowledge of her internalized mother, and striving to know also her therapist/mother. Later in this session she communicated an intense feeling of isolation – which before used to be projected into the analyst as an unconnected event. This was a further movement of integration, bringing her the painful emotional realization that it is her orderly but empty mother who makes her feel so isolated. It is important, I think, to analyse both the relief due to integration as well as the pain K brings.

In regard to –K, Bion's work enables us to understand how delusional areas persist in children who nonetheless 'know' what the reality is, the clue being that such knowing is not K but −K. The second child knows in the sense of −K that she comes to an analyst and has drawn a house as she 'knows' she has a father and a mother. But it means nothing to her. She suffers from meaninglessness and futility. Split off, as Bion's work prepares us to find, is an alarming omnipotence and superiority to objects whom she does not know to be parents. There are no adults in her world; only objects who have pretensions to being 'grown-up' but who misunderstand, as she herself does. Between the child and her object, as Bion expressed it, 'The process of denudation continues till ... (there is) ... hardly more than an empty superiority-inferiority that in turn degenerates to nullity' (Bion 1962b: 97).

Perhaps the most original of Bion's contributions to psychoanalysis is his exploration of previously little known processes in the mind of the psychotic: his concrete experiences of invasion and manipulation in the head, his evacuations from all organs, the strange trajectories of his projections, and the bizarre objects which furnish his inner and his external worlds. Bion's understanding of what it is to exist without K has greatly helped analysts in their endeavours to reach children like the third one described above, who exist − it is not too much to say − in a horror chamber both internally and externally. Bion's papers illuminate in depth and with precision the nature and the difficulty of the analytic task for the psychotic patient and his analyst.

As well as advancing clinical understanding of K, −K and no K, Bion illuminates the interconnections between them. Understanding these interconnections can help the analyst with two situations of psychic movement as they occur in the playroom: the movement from emotional understanding to loss of that experience − the movement from K to −K, and the movement from being sane to being psychotic or vice versa − the oscillation between K and no K.

To take first the movement from emotional understanding to loss of the experience. The shift from K to −K is a problem of varying seriousness in different analyses. Sometimes all work done is denuded and −K spreads like a cancer over every link between patient and analyst. Sometimes the stripping of K until it is −K occurs only in pockets. Bion's work demonstrates the necessity for tracing the fate of meaningful interpretations, to see whether they retain vitality and their connection with the analyst. If they do they will be developed unconsciously; but if they become disconnected they will lose meaning and go dead. It is necessary to trace the particular processes which reverse the achievement of K, to ascertain whether the child believes they come from his object or from himself, for whatever reason of anxiety, perversity, pain or envy.

A brief example will illustrate what I have in mind. At a certain period of her analysis when real contact was made with an intelligent 16-year-old girl her relief and gratitude at this were evident. This was her initial response. Sessions later, however, there was a sequel. The very interpretations which had given her relief and made her grateful to the therapist were now produced as her own clever understanding without any knowledge of the fact that she had got them from her therapist. This was the emergence in the transference of a perverse process of phallic exhibitionism which was changing K into −K. That she was not keeping but losing what she gained crystallized for her when, following an unusually moving hour, she came the next day very late. She felt, as she said, bleak and flat. Just before the end of the session she remembered the previous night's dream. She had dreamt she was in her mother's house and her mother had died. She was wondering how to dispose of the old furniture. My patient needed no help from me. She said: 'That's how it is. Yesterday's session is old furniture.' Her moving experience of the day before had become useless −K. Such losses during treatment foreshadow the impermanence of therapeutic gains after the analysis is over. Clinically, in the hope of at least to an extent averting such ultimate loss, it is important that patient and analyst discover why the mother/analyst dies and the patient is left with interpretations which are merely useless furniture in her mind; in this particular case the pathological process was the patient's perversion of knowledge by her exhibitionism.

To discuss now the other movement – the oscillation between sane and psychotic states. To some children this is familiar and frightening: they know they 'change'. For example, a 13-year-old boy under threat of expulsion from school was provocative and violent to his therapist to a degree almost unmanageable. The therapist was frightened and felt impotent. Each onslaught forbidden was resumed at once with no sign of fear – exactly his escalating situation at school. He shouted at his therapist: 'I'll wipe you out.' In this state the child was not psychotic but using primitive defences of projective identification and splitting against massive anxieties. He was in a state of projective identification with frightening adult figures, like the headmaster threatening to expel him and so 'wipe him out'. Into the therapist he had projected himself – a child at the mercy of punitive grown-ups. Interpretations needed to focus on his terror of hostile grown-ups who drove him to split off from himself and project himself into them, with ever increasing fear and violence. The key to the session was H – above all, his terror of the H of the object, and his own H, and how H made all L vanish between him and his object.

At other times, however, as he violently broke each successive limit on the expression of H, his triumph and with it his sexual excitement escalated. Then he felt changed. His huge irresistible excitement destroyed his capacity to think and he had no K of who or where he was really. His penis became stiff – he undid his trousers to show his therapist. He had cut the link with reality, and could not think and was in a delusion of omnipotence. No K was then the key to the session, instead of, as before, H. The facts which now needed to be understood and interpreted were how his huge sexual excitement made him feel changed, how he did not know what he was doing, and the pleasure and the excitement of the change in which he knew no fear including the fear he was being mad, and how all his K was gone from him and existed now to be mocked at in the therapist. Though his excited psychotic states were often impossible to penetrate, there were times when such interpretations reached him and enabled him to move back into sanity; then he would know intolerable despair and fear which would almost overwhelm him and he would try with renewed aggression to raise his sexual excitement to attack his sanity and thinking again.

Bion has two central contentions. To develop a normal mind with a sense of reality an infant must learn from experience, i.e., he must use his emotional experiences with the object to try to know them. This means to notice them, assess them, understand their nature, remember them, i.e., to think. As well, the infant needs to be loved and known by his nurturing object. Of an infant's knowledge of the reality of his emotional life Bion writes as follows:

> ... a sense of reality matters to the individual in the way that food, drink, air and excretion of waste products matter. Failure to eat, drink or breathe properly has disastrous consequences for life itself. Failure to use the emotional experience produces a comparable disaster in the development of the personality; I include among these disasters degrees of psychotic deterioration that could be described as death of the personality.
>
> (Bion 1962b: 42)

Of the mother's reverie in which she knows the reality of her infant's feelings Bion writes: 'reverie is that state of mind which is open to the reception of any "objects" from the loved object and is therefore capable of the reception of the infant's projective identifications whether they are felt by the infant to be good or bad' (Bion 1962b: 36).

Often our patients are anxious about their ability to learn from the experience of analysis. This is the transference emergence of their anxiety about not learning from their experience with their early objects. They feel pessimistic, and worry that their analyst is obliviously optimistic. Consciously or unconsciously they know they do not think about and keep a truthful and real record of their relationships. In so far as it is themselves they fear, they fear K may become perversely twisted, or denuded into −K, or even get totally lost through an attack on their perceptions and memories: in this regard it is their own envy they fear the most. Envy leads them also to withhold information. Patients know knowledge is the analyst's lifeline as much as it is theirs. By withholding information about happenings in the session or current events in their lives they know they can make the analyst useless. Just as refusal of K often arises from an intense envious hatred, so conversely, the giving of K often expresses love and gratitude.

Patients are likewise anxious about the analyst's capacity to understand them. At depth this is anxiety about the analyst's capacity for 'reverie', in Bion's sense. A patient wants understanding based on actual events of emotional containment; he wants his analyst to be open to his first mode of thinking − viz., to communication by projective identification. Can the analyst receive primitive projected states and know what they are? Children do research on the analyst's capacity for reverie and bring material for the purpose of testing whether he can think, notice, remember, tell the difference between truth and lies, and emotionally understand − as opposed to verbally mechanically, or from books. Especially those children whose internal objects cannot K will have deep uncertainty about the therapist. Can he know me? And how does he do it? Anxiety-ridden research into the analyst's mind rather than into his own may be the focus of the analysis for a long time. The patient knows if the analyst cannot K he has no hope at all.

Each patient has a point beyond which he does not extend his K. Scanning an analysis for what K is present and absent gives a broad indication of the patient's level of development. Whole areas of knowledge may be absent from the analysis because the child does not emotionally K them. Sometimes the central pivot of the analysis becomes a disagreement between the patient, who believes it is better to be without further K, even at the price of deterioration or 'death of the personality', than to follow the analyst whom the patient believes to advocate more K. The patient fears that more K will bring not benefit, but intolerable conflict or uncontrollable emotion, psychotic states of persecution, mania, depression, or even total disintegration. In such analyses the patient's fear of, and antagonism to, the analyst and the analytic work is an antagonism to K.

This source of resistance and hostility may be missed, as I missed it in a 13-year-old girl. She was a sullen, heavy girl, the eldest of four children. Her parents were seriously caring of their children, but had also considerable psychological difficulties of their own. Her father had had two psychotic episodes since her birth, and her mother dramatized daily events and attitudes in a way that was at once foolish, frightening and exasperating. My patient was brought to analysis on account of her surliness and intractability at home, poor schoolwork, and unhappiness. Notwithstanding her suspicion and anxiety, in the first phase of the analysis she had communicated clearly and well, making it possible for me to understand her. This was evident from her response in the sessions and some betterment in her life.

In the middle period of her analysis, however, she became increasingly difficult to make contact with. Her sullen hostility, which had abated, returned increased. Session after session she set out farm scenes of figures and animals in a dull and surly way. These she fenced off in silence. Sometimes she sealed her mouth with a strip of sellotape. A pall fell over the sessions and I had to struggle to stay awake. She gave no response to interpretations I attempted, there was no shift of play, nor could I satisfactorily locate myself in the transference. Her material persisted with minimal variation and I became very worried that it was repetitious because not understood. Broadly speaking, I had taken the key to her material to be hate (H). I had understood her sullenness and silence as hostility, the emergence of H towards a persecuting object, myself, from whom she fenced herself away, and on an oral level, sealed her mouth to stop anything entering her from me. Bion's work provided an illumination: the key was not H, but K.

I approached her material differently. Her sullen resistance, which I had taken to be hostility I now understood to be a dulling and deadening of her mind. The pall which fell over the sessions was a deadening of awareness in us both. I tried to show her she felt a need not to be aware, to make us both unthinking – she should not know me and I should not know her. Within a few sessions she stopped the farm play and brought new material. She sealed her mouth with sellotape. Then she drew two knobbly misshapen figures, writing underneath 'Old Age Pensioners'. She raised her hand and lifted the sellotape off her mouth for a moment. I got a glimpse of a horrifying twisted smile before she covered her mouth again. The smile was her twisted excitement about her parents, old-age-pensioner-parents, knobbly, psychologically misshapen. I think she was terrified of a twisted, rampant, manic state seizing her if she let herself know her object's shortcomings. I think she also wished to spare her objects the pain of knowing that she knew them. Her dulling of her faculties and her deadening of any link between us was in order not to know, or be known to know – as I now tried to show her in an analysis that was moving again.

From the founding of psycho-analysis Freud held that K, knowledge, was at the centre of the therapeutic process. He wrote, for instance: 'We have formulated our task as physicians thus: to bring to the patient's *knowledge* the unconscious, repressed impulses existing in him, and, for that purpose, to uncover the resistances that oppose *this extension of his knowledge about himself* (Freud 1919 [1918]: 159, my italics). Bion's work returns us to Freud with a deepened understanding of what such knowledge is – both for the patient and for the analyst. The insight the patient gains in analysis rests on primitive introjections which are emotional experiences of psychic reality linked to his analyst. Equally, the analyst's understanding rests on emotional experiences of knowing his patient in the original and deepest mode, i.e., through reception, containment and thought about his patient's projective identification. Bion's conception of thinking, his work on the conditions of the achievement of K, its lapse into −K, and the psychotic's disordered 'thinking' with no K, will continue, I am sure, to be a rich source and a potent catalyst for developing work with patients for many years to come.

Acknowledgements

A previous edition of this chapter appeared in the *Journal of Child Psychotherapy*, 1981, 7: 181–192.

5

WORDS AND WORKING THROUGH

This paper discusses communication, its modes and its changes, between analyst and patient, and, more particularly, within the patient himself in the course of a psychoanalysis. In the form of spoken dialogue, communication has always been at the centre of the psychoanalytic method and there have always been puzzles and complexities about it.

A patient's talk is not simple. It is multiple in function as Freud showed when he differentiated three related processes – repeating, remembering, and working through (Freud 1914). Nor is an analyst's talk a simple conveying of information. James Strachey, in his classic paper 'The nature of the therapeutic action of psycho-analysis' (Strachey 1934) was among the first to review the work on, and himself notably advance the problem of, what a therapeutic interpretation is. An interpretation becomes the agency of change, according to Strachey, when it is specific about the point of urgency in the transference, i.e., the patient's impulses and anxieties at that moment active towards the analyst. Then it is a mutative interpretation, as Strachey called it, which enables the patient to change his archaic internal figures by introjecting the interpreting analyst.

Since Strachey's time there has been a vast discussion about analysts' interpretations and patients' communications. The investigations and the controversies in the literature have recently been summarised and reviewed by Langs (1976). From Langs's two volumes it emerges that, while some analysts endorse active, non–interpretive techniques for special pathology or situations of impasse, currently there is still agreement that interpretations play the key role, and that a mutative interpretation is a verbalisation of the immediate emotional transference. Analysts still agree, too, that their patients' communications involve Freud's basic three of remembering, repeating and working through.

Over the past 50 years, however, psychoanalysts have changed their view of their own method. It is now widely held that, instead of being about the patient's intrapsychic dynamics, interpretations should be about the interaction of patient and analyst at an intrapsychic level. It is timely to note in this issue of the *International Journal of Psycho-Analysis*, which commemorates the centenary of Melanie Klein's birth, that her work has been the most powerful single influence for this shift of perspective. Her view that object relations and also an inner world of objects start at birth precludes pre-object and objectless phenomena in development, and leads clinically to an object-directed, interactional view of the transference. From her first papers of the 1920s, Melanie Klein advocated a technique of interpreting positive and negative object relations between analyst and patient from the start of every analysis, adult and child alike.

It is also timely to recall our indebtedness to Melanie Klein for our much increased understanding of primitive defences and modes of communication. It is now generally accepted that the interchange between analyst and patient is wider than verbal; as well as words there are other transmissions by projection: feelings like anxiety, sexual excitement, hatred; mental images; sensations of drowsiness or rigidity; and so on. These processes remain mysterious, but an understanding of their defensive function was made possible by Melanie Klein's (1946) discovery of projective identification – her name for a group of early defence mechanisms in which the infant in omnipotent phantasy projects parts, sometimes even the whole of himself, into his objects, for his own safety or to control or to stimulate his objects, etc. Through highly original research, W. R. Bion (1962a) extended Melanie Klein's work. He found that projective identification is not only a defence mechanism, but is also simultaneously an infant's first way of communicating with his objects. Bion's theory is that projective identification is the earliest mode of defence and communication which needs to be understood by the nurturing object. From this primitive form of communication and understanding there develops, in his view, more sophisticated forms – ultimately language and verbal thought.

Clinically these are important findings. They explain and conceptualise the familiar transference in which words and what words unconsciously express are not all that is happening, when important events are also occurring beyond words, communicated in more primitive modes. In diverse modes of communication – verbal and more primitive – a patient can bring his unevenly developed personality into analysis. In the service of the less developed part of himself, a patient may also use words not as words to express meaning, but along with the other non-verbal aspects of the encounter to engender his projections in the analyst. In this paper I discuss two patients who need to communicate both by words and more primitive means.

My first patient, Mr B, illustrates one type of psychic predicament that unfolds in the transference in a dual way, divided between words and communications 'beyond words'. A man of 36, an only child, by profession a manager in a construction industry, he wanted an analysis after his girlfriend of several years left him suddenly. At the preliminary interview he seemed lonely and withdrawn. He told me he was depressed after his girlfriend's departure and unable to work properly, which surprised him because he had to admit he had not been that fond of her – not enough to marry her. A few days before starting treatment Mr B broke his arm.

At the start of his analysis he talked flatly about his ex-girlfriend, problems on sites, his state of mind, and so on. His talk did not arise from intensely felt experience nor convey much of an experience to me. In a minimal way it informed me of his life and his responses to starting a psychoanalysis. When I related his worries about the soundness of the builders to suspicions about myself, or when he told me how his girlfriend broke it up so suddenly, and I interpreted his fear that I, his new analyst, might suddenly get fed up with him, such interpretations relieved the real doubts and fears his talk expressed, but these were somehow minor. I sensed an area of latent anxiety and agitation far from his words and his awareness, which I did not understand at all. Moreover, during his sessions I often had an experience for which there was no evidence in his talk. There were no derivatives in his verbal material of an enormous hatred (I could not say of what or whom) which entered me during his sessions.

I began to notice that Mr B paid great attention to why I said what I said. He tried to find out how I looked at, and what I looked at, in his material that made me interpret in the way I did. He was very relieved when an interpretation was as he expected. I noticed, too, that Mr B was acquiring what he called 'new interests' like going to concerts, which were activities he believed his new analyst engaged in. As I tried to work, I felt almost as if Mr B was physically pushing into me: I felt watched in my head, uncomfortable, restricted in what I could say – only obvious familiar interpretations seemed to exist as possibilities. These experiences were my reception of Mr B's primitive communications and defences, the interaction between patient and analyst conceptualised and explained by Klein and Bion in terms of projective identification. I tried to put these experiences into words to Mr B. I spoke about his need to get into my mind, his feeling of being located there, his manoeuvring of me to give him familiar interpretations, and his relief at interpretations he knew would come. When he got these at first quite new and unexpected interpretations from me, Mr B made agitated endeavours to make them into old, deadened, 'familiar lines' as I called them.

Gradually Mr B's split-off activities became less dissociated, and his latent anxiety, inaccessible earlier, now erupted into his awareness. His material became entirely taken up with anxieties about a problem on a building site to do with joins. He spoke agitatedly, repeatedly asking the question 'What are the joins?' and saying 'I have to get the joins settled.' On the building site he countermanded the 'joins' he had ordered for the assembling of material and ordered different ones. I interpreted the joins on the building site as his representation of his problem of joins between him and me. Starting a psychoanalysis – now some 6 months under way – meant to him he had to find a whole new set of 'joins' for him and me to escape his acute anxiety when he got unexpected interpretations, which made him feel the joins between us were not settled and we were separate. Mr B kept distancing the problem away from the analysis back to the building site, needing not to know that he ever felt unjoined and separate from me. From my repeated experience of hatred arising in me during his sessions, I thought it was above all hatred that he feared and needed to split off and project into me. We began to see how he and I had a meagre, human, whole person contact through our talk, which was certainly without hatred, and how most of Mr B was still a frightened infant constructing and maintaining a unity of himself and myself, in his phantasy so joined, restricted and rigid that there was nothing to fear from it.

I say 'We began to see', meaning I and Mr B began to see. Over the months, as I tried to experience his verbal and also his more primitive transmissions and formulated these in words to him, I think Mr B gained some feeling of being known by me. He definitely looked less

72

lonely. That he was also himself gaining awareness was shown in a session to which he brought one of his rare dreams. Mr B began by speaking about one or two familiar themes and then fell silent. On this day his flat words conveyed so little of an experience to me that I said nothing. As I waited an enormous feeling of hatred washed into me. Then he spoke, saying he was pleased, he had had a dream.

> He dreamt there were two houses on adjacent sites, placed so that one was to the front and the other was further back. The most prominent feature was a gleaming white concrete strip between the two houses. The strip ran along the side of the front house and continued until it reached and ran along the side of the house set back, making a narrow path joining them.

Mr B's association was that the concrete strip was incredibly level.

I said to Mr B that we were the houses of his dream placed as we are placed in his sessions – he in front and I behind him, a little to the side. I said the dream brought his recognition of the familiar lines he tries to establish between us being a narrow path joining us concretely. In a quite alive way Mr B agreed. I then talked about his first association that the concrete strip was 'incredibly level'. I thought he meant what he said – he didn't believe it. I am not supposed to get higher by interpreting what he doesn't know, but of course I do. He gets higher, too; I reminded him I had sometimes caught a gleam of sexual excitement about his experiences of penetration and conquest of me. I went on to suggest, because of my experience earlier in the session of Mr B's split-off, projected hatred, that he feared there would be hatred between us if we were not kept apparently level. Mr B said 'Yes, possibly', still sounding thoughtful, but now also anxious. After a silence, he said he didn't know, but the concrete strip in his dream reminded him of a long thin bone. He then remembered the bone in his arm which was now mended, and then said a feeling of cold horror had just swept over him. I thought his horror came from the sensation of him and me internally as one long thin dead bone inside himself. Later, I pointed out that in his horror that he could only make 'dead bones' with people, it didn't exist for him that he could do anything alive – such as dream, or have an alive session with me as he was in fact doing on this day.

73

This was an important session and his dream was one of those dreams that becomes a reference point in an analysis. Starting analysis had meant to Mr B mending the break he suffered with his girlfriend, a break he had experienced as the snapping of a bone. Mr B's existence with me thus repeats his existence with his girlfriend, as she in her turn would have repeated his relations with previous objects. Mr B has been unable to develop; he exists in repeated ossifying unions with the minimum of human contact.

By this time he had been in analysis for nearly a year. A new phenomenon now emerged. Mr B would talk about something, and then say 'I presume that means such-and-such', 'such-and-such' being a stereotyped version of an old interpretation. These 'presumings' occurred more and more in his talk and began to persecute him, as I suspected from one or two remarks about 'boring concerts', did the 'new' interests he had acquired after starting analysis. Mr B was able to see how his 'presumings' came from a dead bone object inside him, which he could not stop from intruding with its repetitive unthinking bonehead speech, a meaningless echolalia, out of touch with itself and others. As to my talk, sometimes when he listened and wanted to know what I said, he was deeply disappointed. He would say 'Yes, that must be right. But what you say doesn't do anything for me.' He felt an increasing despair that talk could neither express nor convey meaningful experience. I think it is always the case in a transference with a preponderance of events 'beyond words' that at certain phases of the analysis the communicative properties of words are impaired as the talk increasingly reflects the entire primitive defensive organisation. To the patient's despair, interpretations cease to be mutative. This is the transference version of his deep anxiety that his objects are powerless to help him.

I have not considered the origin of Mr B's difficulties – the nature of his objects or his own endowment. I present his case to show how his primitive non-verbal communications brought into the transference a controlling, deadening form of projective identification, a defensive organisation by which he repeatedly and concretely evaded his infantile fear of any but the most minimal object relations which he expressed in his talk. In so far as I was able to experience, understand and put his emotional predicament into words that reached Mr B, it unfolded in the transference not as an 'acting in', a mere repeating between patient and analyst, but as part of a new process in which in successive stages Mr B was gaining increasing contact with himself. In the beginning,

Mr B's joining was mentally dissociated, an event completely beyond not only words but all awareness, internally a somatic event. Later, he was able to find a first concrete representation in the joins on his building site, and experience his anxiety about joining in his sessions. His dream of two houses joined by a concrete path was his first mental representation, the beginnings of true awareness. However, though Mr B dreamt and understood the transference meaning of his dream, the words about it were mine; at this stage he himself has not yet talked about 'joins' – a much later and crucial developmental step. The progression during a psychoanalysis from somatic event, to concrete representation, to a dream, and ultimately to verbal thought, has been described by R. E. Money-Kyrle (1968) as the frequent path of 'Cognitive development' in his paper of that name.

A second patient, Mr E, shows the psychic change which results as work progresses to the stage when the patient himself can express in words his former primitive communications and defences 'beyond words'. Mr E illustrates a different form – almost a polar opposite – of a transference divided between talk and activity detached from talk. Mr E, a sensitive man in his late forties, started analysis in an acute state of suffering – sexually impotent, confused whether his jealous suspicions of his wife were delusional or real, afraid of her and his own cruelty, afraid also of turning to homosexuality or even going mad. As a boy he had been seduced by an older boy, and later he had in his turn seduced younger boys. Still later, he married and had children, who meant much to him. In his sessions he talked narcissistically, with a patronising attitude that denied his need to be understood and to understand himself, and his desperate dependence on me to relieve him of his acute anxieties and confusions. His words were ambiguous, confusing, even contradictory, making it impossible for me to be sure of anything. Not during, but after, his sessions I was invaded for hours by feelings relating to Mr E of anxiety, confusion, guilt and need; since these occurred only after his sessions, as regards immediacy of interpretation and effective containment, I was rendered impotent. Mr E split off and projected his impotent, confused and anxious self into me, while he himself was identified with sadistic superego persecutors.

After about a year's work, when I suspected rather than knew – since he gave me no information – that Mr E felt much less mentally threatened, he developed an erotised homosexual transference to me, quite detached from his talk. That is to say, two different things were now happening beyond words: there was still the depositing into me in a destructive way of acutely painful states of mind, and, in addition, there was now Mr E's increasing state of erotisation, with a voyeuristic invasiveness, projection of excitement and stimulation of phantasy. Mr E was a strong personality, with more areas of illness, trickier, more omnipotent and difficult than Mr B, not least because too much happened too fast. From the first it had been a struggle not to seem to Mr E to have 'become' his projected, impotent self, and to find a way of interpreting so as to give Mr E the experience of being understood and contained. It now became also a struggle not to 'become' his excited partner. Sometimes, under pressure of his projections, I found I was expressing myself in a wrongly jokey way. Often he formulated his material with tricky, built-in pre-suppositions to get me to talk to him with some subtle difference that meant to him I was his intimate friend, a contemporary or junior, not a parent-analyst. Sometimes I would be tricked into participating unknowingly in private jokes, and experienced as an exciting seducing older boy, or young boy, or bisexual lover he had seduced. Mr E put enormous pressure on me to 'act in' − a subject explored by Joseph (1978, 1983) − and increasingly found ways of substantiating his phantasy that his analysis was a sophisticated affair with a collusive agreement between us not to get off our respective chair and couch and 'do' anything about it. Certain words and all kinds of non-verbal events, e.g., my necklace happening to match the colour of his tie, became exciting 'signs'. He was uncaring of his marital difficulties and used the analysis to stimulate his wife's jealousy. In any session, if Mr E believed he had seduced me into acting out erotic phantasies with him, his excitement and sense of omnipotence mounted; he believed he had entered me, and seen my corrupt erotic nature. He felt physically enlarged, the room itself, the entire neighbourhood, became the debased mother's body which he occupied and owned. His sense of omnipotence was enormous, as was his feeling of omniscience. He responded swiftly to what I said, talked profusely with a proliferation of analytic and other ideas he believed me to have, with a sense of knowing their source and direction completely.

Though alarmingly excited and feeling dangerously omnipotent (it was I, however, who felt the alarm and the danger), apart from brief delusional states in some sessions, he retained an awareness that we were patient and analyst alongside what had become a consuming passion, dangerous because it was so omnipotent and concrete and also because it was so confused; a mixture of communication, action, identification, defence, hatred and love, adult and infantile sexuality. It brought into the transference his identification with a series of persecuting over-stimulating objects – notably older seducing boy, mother and, on the part-object level, the breast which I think he had experienced as (and which very likely was) narcissistic and invasive and not containing. His excitement expressed his hatred through the destruction of the analyst as a sustaining parental object. It gratified his narcissism. But it was also for him a finding – in the wrong place on the wrong basis – of an object he felt he had never had, to which he would be able to offer happiness and tenderness that would be returned, as formerly in a confused way he had hoped to find an ideal object in the buttocks of boyfriends. Even though my talk at times was so stimulating and exciting to Mr E as to be useless analytically, I continued to put into words his feelings of excitedly invading me and knowing me, and my equally excitedly trying to penetrate him with interpretations. I talked about the code 'signs', etc. Gradually Mr E felt safer with me, was less wild, and concrete representations of various bits of his psychic state began to appear in his sessions. His excitement began to decline, ushering in a new phase, which I want now to describe in more detail. Above all, it was a phase in which words became paramount.

Less erotised and more hopeful, Mr E wanted to communicate. His proliferated talk, which until then he had narcissistically admired, he now began to hate. He had an outburst one day: 'Words are useless. They're very slippery. They're nothing. If I had to write with broken fingers they would be worth while, but they're two a penny,' he said with disgust and hatred. The next day he spoke about breaking through the 'language barrier' and, in spite of some wild fragments and sundry ambiguities and contradictions to nullify me, Mr E was really trying now to talk to me, and break through the language that had almost ceased, with its code words, intimacies and contradictions, to be an instrument for communication.

Arriving for his next session, he took out a cheque to pay me, holding up for a moment as he did so two theatre tickets. On the couch he said 'The couch felt the right size today. It was big enough. It fitted.' Then he paused and said: 'I could give that all a twist – it could sound like bureaucracy, everything fitting, everything in the right pigeonholes, and then there's the bed of Procrustes ...', but just as his speech was gathering momentum he made an effort and stopped himself. Equally I think he needed to test me to make sure that when he flashed his tickets at me I would remain the right size and would not with precipitate – to him excited – interpretations change into a 'boy lover'. Internally and externally he still had only a fragile feeling of a firm object. He then spoke calmly about paying his bill, showing me his theatre tickets, mentioning the play he was going to that evening. Then the thought of a 'real conversation' occurred to him. I think Mr E was at that moment having a real conversation with me. But it could easily cease either because prevented by Mr E out of meanness, or anxiety about being mocked, or a conviction that I was manipulating him, or, above all, because homosexual phantasies supervened again. His conviction of a homosexual affair could still be swiftly stimulated by a chance 'sign'. But whereas before his erotisation would be lived concretely and excitedly in the session, it was now for the first time communicated verbally. I want to report two consecutive sessions to show the changes that occur when a patient is himself able to put into words what before was enacted and communicated in primitive modes. Melanie Klein (1927: 314) remarks that words are the bridge to reality. I think Mr E's material shows how his ego changes as his omnipotence goes, as his sense of reality arrives once he can use verbal thought.

In the first session Mr E put into words, for the first time, his realisation that he is drawn into phantasies which he mistakes for reality. As I fetched him from the waiting room he got visibly excited. On the couch he talked fast, saying he had had three dreams.

In the first he was a teacher taking the register. He called a name and three boys put up their hands. They didn't do it to be disruptive; they just did it. In the second dream he was in a room which had water in it and he pushed off from one side, zooming and swimming across to the other side. In the third dream a tree had grown through the floor of a room.

Mr E's second and third dreams gave me a weird mad feeling. I interpreted that he was conveying to me his weird and mad experience on meeting me that day: he felt he zoomed across the room and swam into me, and that I, like the tree, shoved myself up into him. After a moment Mr E said: 'That's right.' He then talked more slowly and quietly about other matters, but increasingly sounded anxious and insecure. I though he was anxious that I would be critical of his initial

78

excited response and accuse him of being disruptive, which I said to him. I then interpreted the three boys who put up their hands as him responding eagerly with outstretched arms and an excited penis, and said he wanted me to recognise how the boy in him can be instantly stimulated and zoom into others and feel they zoom into him, and that he didn't mean to be disruptive, he is just like that. Though his anxiety subsided, Mr E made no direct reply this time. He talked on, becoming elaborate and ambiguous. He remarked on how he and his wife have a code. Eventually he said in a different and sincere tone that sometimes they don't mention that something is a dream but behave about it as though it were real. In his whole complex communication Mr E was trickily trying both to twist into a code our undoubted real contact at the beginning of the session, when he told me his 'dreams' – his instant phantasies, really, and I interpreted them and he felt understood, and at the same time Mr E was still also really talking. I said I thought he was now doing two opposed things: trying both to get him and me twisted together, claiming it is only codes between us, and also genuinely wanting to tell me that he realises he sometimes believes his very vivid phantasies – like his dreams of today – are real. Mr E responded warmly and straightforwardly: 'Yes. I know that.'

The next day was an important session. He began by saying he had a dream the night before from which he had woken in terror. It had taken him a long while to realise that he was safe in his bed and that his wife was there safe in hers, which was a great relief.

> In this dream he and L (his wife) were first in a school, waiting to see some list or other of some examination, perhaps results, it wasn't clear. He knew he and L had something to talk about, but it wasn't clear what.
>
> Then he and L were seated on the edge of a high mossy hill overlooking a precipitous drop. Far down below he could see a small pool, so far down the abyss it made him shudder. He was holding on to a slender pine tree which was not firmly rooted. It was coming away from the ground, and he was terrified. Even worse, his wife L was nearer the edge than he was. He suddenly realised he cared for her and that he must somehow slide forward and get hold of her and stop her falling.

After relating the dream he said again how terrified he was, adding 'It's my situation really.' Mr E is right. The dream, even the way

79

it is in two parts, is his situation really. He talked about how he and L were really on the brink of disaster, describing their current dangerous situation. Then he said: 'The pine tree must be you I have been holding on to – in the terms we'd been speaking yesterday, my taking it for real, I mean.' I pointed out that in his dream he recognises how dangerous it is when he believes he has really pulled me off the ground into his phantasy; then he has nothing to hold on to, and could go crashing down – could mentally crash, which I interpreted was part of his terror on waking. Mr E agreed.

The contact between us was straightforward and real. The session then changed in a similar way to the day before. Mr E became elaborate and ambiguous. His statements got vaguer. I reminded him then of the first part of his dream, so different in its vagueness from the second part, in which he knows he is terrified about crashing, and about himself and L. In the first part of his dream he apparently does not know any results of his examination in the analysis, as apparently he does not know what he and L should talk about. I interpreted that now there was another him to the fore, busy with vagueness getting rid of what he knows. There was a prolonged silence. Mr E said: 'I shall have to have what is vulgarly', he sneered, 'called a heart to heart talk with L.' He was again silent. He suddenly said 'I saw a programme on T.V. about refugees.' His voice broke as he went on 'I began to think that's all there's been in this century, ever since the thirties. Refugees, refugees. Pathetic. Evicted from their cities, leaving with their paraphernalia on their backs.' His words expressed and conveyed pain, distress and despair, this time reaching me in the session. Mr E cried brokenly for several minutes. He was crying for his lost omnipotence; its loss evicts him from his city, myself as mother's body. He was crying about his marriage. And he was crying with a deep realisation about himself as a pederast with his paraphernalia on his back, a pathetic refugee from a frightening world, who has been so all his life since his birth in the thirties.

In these two sessions Mr E is changing. He uses language for thinking and for communicating to me. He understands he is a refugee – 'refugee' is his word – and he feels the pathos of it. In the richly compressed way only language can achieve, he remembers his past, understands his current predicament in analysis and in his life and internally integrates himself. He is working through in words.

It is interesting to contrast Mr B and Mr E, so different, yet similar. Where Mr B (B is for Bone) is minimal, controlling and controlled,

Mr E (E is for Erotised) is maximal and almost out of control. Each needs to unfold his predicament in a mixture of words and primitive communications. In a dry way Mr B's talk informs me of the facts of his daily existence as he also by projective identification constructs and maintains a relation of narrow unity with me, to protect himself from a fuller libidinal life with its feared consequences of anxiety and hatred. Mr E's talk expresses his identification with a sadistic superego, conceals as it reveals, and is used to evacuate fear, impotence and mental confusion into me. Meanwhile, in omnipotent phantasy, he also zooms into me to make an erotised intimacy – multiple in function – to escape the fear and guilt of mutual cruelty and to evade also his despair about loving and being loved in real object relations. Both try to actualise with the analyst as partner these primitive defensive phantasies of symmetrical relations (Matte-Blanco 1975), 'incredibly level' relations, as Mr B calls them. The ossification and erotisation are repetitive, concrete and omnipotent – with Mr E omnipotence is paramount. Until Mr B's wordless ossifying and resulting impairment of the words themselves are analysed he will keep the analytic process so minimal that talk will be useless to bring about real change. He will stagnate, existing in a restricted state of projective identification with the analyst, repeating what he has always done with his objects. With Mr E the situation is more dangerous. The talk and entire analytic setting are in danger of becoming so erotised as not only to repeat his former homosexual relations to boys, but to run the risk, because au fond the analyst represents a primary sustaining object, of precipitating Mr E into a psychotic state.

The chief clinical problem in a dual transference of words and activities beyond words is to enable the patient's predicament to unfold by experiencing both what he conveys by talk and what he conveys by projective identification, while at the same time preventing him from living out his defensive phantasies with the analyst and so using the analysis as a refuge from life instead of a process which leads him to a fuller resumption of his own life. His predicament will unfold as part of an alive analytical process that lessens the underlying anxiety which drives him to omnipotent defensive phantasies only if the analyst avoids becoming identified with his projections and enacting them – a task not always easy – and instead contains and expresses them in interpretations. Then like Mr B he may in stages – from a dissociated somatic event of a broken and mended bone, progress to felt anxiety about a symbolic equivalent, and then to dreaming and working his dream through with his analyst – develop awareness of what he is doing and why he needs to. This is psychic movement though not yet structural change. At this stage Mr B still needed mostly to 'join' with me. I think change only comes, as Mr E's material illustrates, with the active functioning of the patient's ego in working through in words. This is the mutative moment, even though one only among the many needed.

In conclusion briefly: Why do words have a special importance in working through? Above all, the use of language is an activity of the ego. A patient hears interpretations, sees his dreams, etc., but he stays a passive subject of the analysis until his ego engages actively – as it does when he uses his own language for thinking and communicating. And, secondly, words break omnipotence. In the omnipotent mind of the infant, an impulse is the experience of its fulfilment. Omnipotence is always hostile to verbalisation because the moment a patient expresses himself in words he is restricting his omnipotence – words rest on a recognition of a gap between impulse and fulfilment, and an acknowledgement of the separateness of subject and object. (The connexion between the recognition of separateness and the formation of symbols has been extensively explored by Segal 1957.) Thirdly, words have multi-faceted meanings uniquely suited – this is no surprise since they are formed for it – to psychic awareness. In a few brief sentences, a patient, as did Mr E, can link in depth, connecting the past with the present, the transference and his life, as he tells his analyst his understanding of himself.

Summary

The paper discusses communication – its modes and its changes – between analyst and patient, and, more particularly, within the patient himself in the course of a psychoanalysis. Clinical material from two cases illustrates how patients may need to communicate to the analyst both in words and also – in order to bring their less developed self – by more primitive modes, which can be understood and conceptualised by Melanie Klein's notion of projective identification. As the patient feels understood by the analyst's words (the mutative interpretations) he may slowly become more aware of his primitive modes of relating, until, ultimately, his method of communication changes and he is himself able to express his understanding of himself in his own words. This brings structural change and a resumption of ego development, and is a mutative moment. In brief: mutative interpretations are not by themselves the agency of change. They put the patient in a position to change. He himself must do the active, mutative working through in his own words.

Acknowledgements

An enlarged version of this chapter was read at the London Weekend Conference of English-Speaking Psychoanalytical Societies on 3 October 1982. It was first published in the *International Journal of Psychoanalysis*, 1983, 64: 281–289. It was subsequently reprinted in E. B. Spillius (ed.), *Melanie Klein Today*, vol. 2, London: Routledge, 1988, pp. 138–151.

6

A 3½-YEAR-OLD BOY'S MELANCHOLIC IDENTIFICATION WITH AN ORIGINAL OBJECT

I shall describe a very short analysis of a child who is identified with a primal object which keeps reverting internally to a damaged and accusing condition.

Tim, as I call him, is 3. He has a 'big' brother, as Tim calls him, of 5 years, a younger brother of 2, and was faced by a new pregnancy which caused a crisis between him and his mother. When she saw me she told me that Tim, always a poor sleeper, was not sleeping at all. During the day he was obstructive, clinging, suddenly attacking, content only if the two other boys were away. She was depressed, extremely fatigued and unconsciously very hostile to Tim, but also affectionate.

She told me of a crisis which started when Tim was 2 months old and which ended in an early unhappy weaning. She was breast-feeding him, and being out one evening he was given a bottle in her absence. Next day he screamed and refused the breast. For weeks she struggled to breast-feed him and tried many formulae, all of which Tim refused. She felt very rejected. She and Tim 'worked each other up' – 'We still do', she added. Finally, she had managed to wean him to goat's milk. In the interview, her unspoken appeal was 'Free me. Take him.'

There is space for only the briefest sketch of the beginning of the analysis. Tim's feeling of being squashed under too many pressures, and his hatred of mother for having a new baby and for bringing him to me, rapidly emerged. Mother, told by Tim he had screamed and kicked me, herself screamed at me down the telephone, '*My child's not aggressive.*' Next, Tim communicated the content of the acute anxieties which were making him cling to his mother. In several ways he expressed his fear that his mother was fragmenting. For instance, out of blocks he made a table which kept breaking in pieces, to his great agitation. He seemed to feel totally identified with this breaking object and, in a state of acute anxiety for himself and his mother, he had to run to her, which reassured him, but renewed his anxiety that he was harming her by his clinging. He was anxious (I think with reason) about her state of mind that she would break when she gave birth to the new baby, and felt confused both with the breaking mother and with the baby coming out of her. Following his communication and my verbalisation of these anxieties and almost total identifications, Tim stopped running to his mother during sessions, and when she soon went to hospital for the birth of the baby, he stayed on his own.

The safe birth of the baby, a girl, at first relieved him. Then his persecutory phantasies escalated to such an extent they blocked out reality. He was terrified of shadows in the corners, and of little noises, hearing these as whispers to throw him away in the rubbish bin. He suffered sensations of invisible bits creeping up his arms or getting under his nails. I tried to help him to realise he was seeing and feeling his terrifying inner world concretely in the outer world which was lost to him. He felt unable to distinguish outer from inner, or self from object; for instance, he attacked and scratched my face, and felt for the scratch on his own face. Another time, he watched the tap running with water and said, 'Why is it crying?' as he wiped his own eyes.

With the first month's analysis and with the resilience of early childhood Tim recovered from his confusion of inner and outer, self and object, and his enormous anxiety subsided. In place of a total identification with his fragmenting primal object which had consumed almost his whole ego, his several identifications with his object were restored. Once he regained his more usual self, I could see Tim was a highly ambivalent, sensitive child whose superficial brightness covered misery and anxiety. What now began to unfold was his developmental impasse.

I give two sessions in illustration. Tim arrived looking cheerful and started saying, 'Mama, Mama' sounding her name happily. Suddenly he said, 'Mama poo-poo, Mama poo-poo', sniggering like a dirty schoolboy. He took a camel, pushed plasticine between its legs, saying, 'Poo-poo in your bum'. Then, growing very absorbed, he made the camel's legs stamp again and again on a lump of plasticine, saying, 'Making a hole. Making a hole.' Suddenly he gave an anguished cry, as from the deepest unconscious: 'San. Shan. It's too late. No, it's not too late'. 'San. Shan. It's too late. No, it's not too late' he called again in a voice of immense suffering (Shan links with O'Shaughnessy, and San is a condensation, uncovered in previous sessions, to do with Tim's family). I said he was making me hear something very painful happening inside him after he said, 'Mama poo-poo'; he feels he and I are hurt, he is in pain with it and calling out to me. Tim stopped stamping and making a hole with his camel and instead pulled faces, saying brightly, 'I'm a monster.' I repeated he felt there was a stamped-on crying mother and baby, calling out from inside him. He drew himself up tall, and in an angry, superior voice he yelled down at me, 'Poo-poo, poo-poo'.

The following day I heard him crying outside, not wanting to come in. In the playroom he still cried, making a rhythmic stamping sound, interlaced with an intense screaming in my direction. I said he was feeling stamped on inside himself, and was also screaming at me out of fear that I too will stamp on him for his angry pooing yesterday on my talk. He stopped crying and gazed at me for a long time, looking comforted, and then came to dry his eyes on my skirt. Suddenly he smeared spit nastily over my clothes, then took out the camel and stamped its leg on a bit of plasticine, calling out, 'San. Shan. It's too late. No, it's not too late.' He turned to me and said 'You're going to be sick for ever and ever'. I was so astonished that I asked him if he had heard someone at home saying something like that. He said scornfully, 'I'm saying it to you.' He crawled under my chair, pointing at my buttocks, calling them 'Camels'. Then he tried excitedly to shove plasticine under my skirt and down my shirt front. He scratched the door with a metal toy, and said, 'I did it' pointing to marks he had not done; he dirtied the wall with his boots, and washed where he had not dirtied the wall. His activities were so quick I had no time to think or talk about one before he was doing the next. Just before the end of the session, he became a cute little boy, appealing to me to take him to the toilet and to look at toys, so cutting us off from the rapid preceding sequence of disturbing events. I said to Tim that we were both meant to be far from how he lost me who had comforted him, and far too from the worrying things that had happened after that, and we were supposed to be nice now, but I didn't think he felt we were really nice together.

In the first session we can see how fragile Tim's relation is to the good aspect of his object. He arrived happily saying 'Mama' but then attacks her, first verbally, saying, 'Mama, poo-poo', behaving like a sniggering schoolboy – identified, I think, with his older brother – and then pushes plasticine between the camel's legs, saying, 'Poo-poo in your bum' after which he gets absorbed in the sadism of stamping and holding. Suddenly he is in a state of anguish, persecuted by guilt, suffering in identification with his object, veering between despair that it is too late ever to stop and hope that it is not too late to stop. He can't bear my interpretation about the suffering mother and child inside him, denies his guilt by claiming he's only a cute monster, and when I repeat the interpretation, he omnipotently denies all meaningfulness – I and the interpretation are 'poo-poo'. By the second session Tim is persecuted and suffering in identification with his internalised attacked and accusing analyst. He also fears that I, his external analyst, will retaliate and punish him. When instead I understand his fear, he regains me as a good object, becomes identified with it, and can comfort himself by coming to dry his tears on my skirt. But then his hatred erupts, why I do not know. He spits on my clothes, camel stamps, is excited by his anal sadism – plasticine up my skirt and down my blouse – scratches the door, dirties the walls, and he gives his impulse to reparation a perverse twist, cleaning where he did not damage. Only his last defence of massive splitting from object relations that will be 'sick for ever and ever' restores at the end tolerable though spurious and highly controlled relations with me.

In these two sessions, though Tim brought important communications, he shifted so quickly that nothing was faced or worked through. As I could see for myself, Tim's external objects also evade certain areas of psychic reality, particularly aggression and suffering, and they also – like Tim does with me – manipulate him into compliant behaviour. As well as his identification with blaming, suffering objects, Tim is identified with objects who do not try to confront and understand but who evade difficult object relations. As he externalised these internal objects into me in the transference, I felt a pressure when working with him to move on fast and ignore difficulties and join in a false relationship. From the point of view of technique, I think it was very important to try not to 'act in' with him but instead to interpret, for example at the end of the second session above, how he wants me to participate in a phony relationship and forget his rapid loss earlier in the session of a real good object who understood and comforted him.

Tim often repeated his play of stuffing plasticine between the camel's legs, then stamping with its leg on a piece of plasticine, and then in distress calling, 'San. Shan. It's too late. No, it's not too late.' When this material first emerged in the two sessions reported above, it seemed to me that by far its most intense aspect was its emotions: Tim's anguish, his object's suffering, and his oscillation between despair – 'It's too late' – and hope – 'It's not too late.' Not wishing to overburden him, I left the meaning of its anal elements 'Mama, poo-poo', 'Poo-poo in your bum' etc. for later sessions. As I understood it, this play expressed his ongoing preoccupation with various parts of his original object, Mother's breasts, belly, unborn baby, genitals, etc. which he attacks in fear and hatred, kicking them in and 'holing' them, stuffing them with faeces, so that they become buttocks or 'camels' as he calls them. Often when angry he kicked me, or lay on the floor to kick and dirty the wall, just as he might have bunched up his legs to kick out, or defaecate, in rage and distress as an infant, in phantasy penetrating and entering his Mother, so forming and then internalising a damaged object containing concretely violence, kicks and faeces. This object is a fundamental formation in Tim's inner world. In identification with it, he feels faecal, debased and depressed; in its violent superego aspect this primitive formation torments him, and in identification with this cruel superego, he in his turn torments his debased complaining object.

From a theoretical point of view, Tim is in a state resembling an adult melancholia, classically first described by Freud in 'Mourning and melancholia' in 1917 (Freud 1917 [1915]). Tim's object relations are ambivalent, his ego is identified with a lost good object and is tormented by a 'critical agency', as Freud termed it then, or superego. Tim loses his object mainly by anal sadism as described by Abraham in 1924 (Abraham 1924). In 1923, in 'The ego and the id', Freud described how in a melancholia, destructiveness is felt to become concentrated in the superego (Freud 1923), and 4 years later in 1927, Melanie Klein showed that the extreme and unreal destructiveness of the early superego is the result of the projection into it of the child's savage impulses (Klein 1927). Melanie Klein's psycho-genetic hypothesis formulated in 1935, that adult melancholic sufferings and anxieties return to and repeat early failures with the task she named the depressive position, places Tim's impasse in a developmental perspective (Klein 1935). Unable to overcome his ambivalence, when a good relation is achieved with his good object, he cannot maintain it and, unable to face his persecution and depression when he attacks his object, he cannot confront the damage or repair it. His parents, with whom he must work through his conflicts, though caring in many ways, handicap him externally by their inability to tolerate his problems; moreover, mother's persecution and depression and father's omnipotence do not provide the counter he needs to his inner states. Over and over he feels his internal object reverts to and remains in a damaged and accusing state and he is in despair that it is too late to save either his object or himself. He is in the early stages of a difficult depressive position and lives in the shadow of punishment and criticism. He often asked of a noise, 'What is it saying?' he answered, 'It says "I'm not doing it properly."' To try to find relief he resorts to false, omnipotent idealised relationships; indeed, as I shall now illustrate.

Tim arrived carrying an oversized elongated package, almost as big as himself, decorated with pink hearts, containing a small box of chocolates which he said was for me. He tried to push against me with his penis, and, very warm, he handed me some chocolates, urging me to eat them. The atmosphere was sexual, hazy, idyllic. I interpreted his sexual, feeding desires, and his feeling that now it was perfect between us. I explained that I did not, in my work, eat or take chocolates from any children. Tim moved away: physically to sit in his chair, emotionally to a more abstracted, more narcissistic contemplation of his phallus, his long hearts packet which he held over his penis, wagging it up and down. I said he had the feeling now of owning Daddy's big feeding penis that is so beautiful I must be a mother who admires and wants it. He appeared not to hear and urged me to eat his chocolates. I said when he feels warm and sexual he can't bear to know that he is still little and shut out from Daddy's and Mummy's sex. Tim said 'It doesn't matter' and took away the chocolates. Then suddenly, as if he had been kicked, he fell to the floor. Looking cold and nasty, he next slithered underneath the furniture rubbing his penis in a perverse way, cutting off from and projecting acute pain which came over to me in enormous waves. He stood up and said brightly, 'I didn't fall, did I?' I talked about the enormous hurt of my sexual rejection of him, so unbearable he tried not to know it had happened. He felt kicked out coldly which made him go cold and slide under the furniture and tell himself he wasn't stopped, he was in, but now it was different, it felt nasty and dirty like being in Mummy's and Daddy's bottoms. Tim made a crocodile slither towards him and became persecuted by invisible marks on his hands, desperately brushing them off (something which had not troubled him for many sessions). He left cold, fearful, hating, saying, 'I'll never come here again.'

Tim is not jealous young Oedipus, but, one might say, Oedipus Rex, by a projective identification with a father whose omnipotent penis flies him to a kingdom of no more problems. He experiences my refusal to fit in with his incestuous phantasies as a kick to the ground by a superego much more primitive than the prohibiting, loving father Freud showed is the heir to the normal Oedipus complex. Tim cannot bear this cruel rejection, splits off the pain, and in omnipotent phantasy enters and fouls his object which then retaliates and persecutes him. By the end, his sexual warmth for his mother has ominously turned to cold hatred, and he is back in his impasse.

Although it is so difficult for Tim to maintain or retrieve good relations with the good aspect of his object, there was evidence it was not too late for psychic movement. His mother rang me to say he was sleeping all night for the first time ever – he was a different child, she said. But often I could not understand or keep pace with him, or even if I could, he experienced me as too criticising, too damaged or too faecal to use what I said and sometimes he felt hatred of the very fact that I could analyse him; 'I'll scratch your eyes out', he said, and tried really to do so. You will recall that initially his mother told me that suddenly he would try really to hurt her. Once Tim yelled, 'I'll squash your throat' as I was talking, and hurtled a cake of soap at my larynx where it hit me painfully. Immediately he cut off, and asked coyly how one of the toys worked, after which he wrapped up the toy and cake of soap together. There was an uncomfortable false atmosphere of which I thought Tim was aware. I was angry, my throat was painful and he was miserable. I said I thought he knew we were not really friendly over the toy, we were only falsely wrapped up together. He thought I was angry and hurt from the hit with the soap, and he was miserable about it. Tim said, 'Three for sick.' I said 'Well, you are three and worried it's sick how you really hurt me and you are upset about it.' His face lit up: he had introjected an alive, understanding analyst and at once was identified with it. And indeed he had moments of great gratitude, e.g., lovingly hugging the blanket roll, which turned out, though he hid it in a muddle, to do with the change in his sleeping, which he eventually told me of himself, 'I do sleep in the night. No corners now', he said, glancing upwards.

Very soon I had to tell him of the first analytic break. The day I told him I gave him a card with the date. He clapped his hands and said falsely 'Hurrah!', but the next minute flew at my breast and beat it saying 'You did it in your study, with cigars and wine.' He took the holiday card and pinched and squashed it in the locks of his box. I said he had got a shock and was furious at the sudden holiday plan from me, which felt like a mother's breast suddenly joining with father to pinch him and squash him. He was now sitting miserably on the floor saying 'Dustbin. The drink is put away. Shan', distancing himself as he evacuated rather than uttered these words. Next he tried to wash the holiday dates off the card. Then he made a bed on the floor, lay face down and 'swam' himself along – looking up with a red face as if to say 'I'm in', after which he threw all the cleaning materials into the dustbin. When I tidied up and retrieved the cleaning materials, he drew himself up tall and said in a sarcastic superior way, '*I don't take things out of the dustbin.*'

The news of the holiday makes the baby in Tim erupt directly at my physical breast. Thoughts about his loss are intolerable and are evacuated as he splits off his love and helpfulness (expressed by throwing away the cleaning materials). He defends himself by projective identification into a superior penis who scorns to retrieve the situation – as in infancy, after the shock of a sudden bottle one night, not only was the good breast he had been drinking from altered so he could not take what he here calls 'a rubbish bin' the next day, but he kept refusing for weeks, you will remember, various substitute milks. In the month before the break, psychic reality kept breaking through his defensive identifications with an aloof superior object and with a false cute little boy. As the holiday drew nearer, the way – as his mother had stated in the initial interview – Tim and she 'worked each other up', dominated the transference. Tim would not help me. He ran out of the room, broke the floor, touched electric sockets, etc. so that I was ceaselessly pursuing him – to his excitement, and, intended for me, exhaustion and irritation. In this way, Tim expressed hatred and also worked us 'up', keeping us on the move, a manic denial of our real down condition: myself a failing rejected mother; for him, the immediately intolerable analytic break.

In the last week, Tim was fearful of the room, looked about at its shadows and corners, laid his ear to the ground, saying he could hear things. After I had interpreted his anxieties about the room feeling like a Mummy he knows is going, who frightens him with punishing looks and noises, he did a mocking act, saying, 'You'll have no drink. There will be no milk. I'm going to take it all away.' When I tried to speak he dived at the electric sockets, giggling, saying, 'You can't do anything, can you?' as I rushed anxiously to remove his fingers, feeling despondent at his hundredth refusal to accept that he should not touch the plugs. He took off his belt and started whipping me quite dangerously with its metal buckle, making faces, getting silly, and saying, 'It's my weapon', gradually though looking more and more unhappy. I said he was miserable because he knew he was trying to make me feel angry and hopeless – like a Mummy who cannot even get her child not to touch electric plugs, and here I cannot stop his mockery of what I say even when he knows it is true, and he wants me sick and tired and angry in a silly way with him – that's his weapon. Tim was quiet, he had his head down. 'Yes. It is,' he said. Then added, 'It's my old weapon', and looked very worried and thoughtful. In the last minutes he said 'Nobody loves me', sticking sticky tape on his hands and pulling it off, saying 'I hate plasters.' I said he hurt himself when he pulled off the sticky tape, like he hurt himself when he said, 'Nobody loves me', which he did not believe – he was making a false hurt to get away from his unhappiness about his weapon, and also to get away from the hurt and fear of no sessions in the holidays. This was the Thursday before the final Friday. For the last session he was 30 minutes late, was able for a while again to be thoughtful (it was very impressive) but could not stay that way and ended with a near tantrum.

In the break I saw his parents who said he was sleeping well, and nursery school looked possible, though he was more moody again. They were disconcerted when I queried whether the analytic break might be affecting him. Tim began nursery school. He was manic, having taken this step forward behaving like a rude schoolboy, a projective identification with his 'big' brother. In his sessions he was afraid I would undo his manic state and force back into him his split-off incapacitating fear and depression. He was also in acute conflict whether to identify with his parents or with the analysis. After a month mother telephoned to say his teacher said he was a normal child like any other, Tim did not want to come, and she had therefore decided to stop.

Conclusion

The paper gives a clinical glimpse, conceptualised along a line of theoretical understanding from Freud to Abraham to Melanie Klein, of a child who keeps losing through the eruption of his hatred his loving relation to, and identification with, the good aspect of his object. It was impossible in this short time to tell how much his hatred is due to frustration, grievance, persecution, fascination with sadism, or envy. His predominant identification is with a damaged object and he veers between despair that it is too late and hope that it is not too late to repair his inner world.

Tim is at risk because, as Melanie Klein put it, this impasse of the depressive position, unless it is worked through, is a melancholia *in statu nascendi* which augurs ill for his future. Already in childhood he has serious difficulties: family pressures can cause a crisis in which his melancholic identification with his mother becomes almost total and absorbs his ego, his sexual development is being distorted by his defensive needs, and since an identification with an original good object does not prevail, he tends to progress in his life by projective identification with father's penis or 'big' brother, both seen as cold and scornful of psychic realities.

His impasse is not yet a point of fixation, though many factors impede its resolution which will be difficult. During this short analysis, better internalisations and identifications were momentarily possible, as I hope my account has shown. Tim's melancholic situation is alive and active within him, his defences are not too rigid, and there are family resources in his mother's affection for him and his own tenderness. Later, I do not know how Tim will be. But now – it is not too late.

Summary

The paper describes a very short analysis of a 3-year-old boy. It gives clinical material to show his identification with a primal object which for inner and outer reasons keeps reverting to a damaged and accusing condition. I suggest that this constitutes a developmental impasse which can be understood in terms of Melanie Klein's theory of the depressive position as a melancholic identification which is affecting the child's current life and development, and which may put at risk his future mental health. The paper gives clinical glimpses of the cruel pressure of his superego, some of the forms taken by his underlying misery and anxiety, and the nature of his defences. In the brief time available (5½ months), though he made progress, his underlying melancholic identification was not really changed.

Acknowledgements

A previous edition of this chapter was published in the *International Journal of Psychoanalysis*, 1986, 67: 173–179.

7

THE INVISIBLE OEDIPUS COMPLEX

A current controversy about the Oedipus complex is whether it is indeed universal and of central importance, still to be regarded as 'the nuclear complex of development'. It is a clinical fact that there are long periods of analysis – possibly, some have suggested, even whole analyses – in which there seem to be little or even no Oedipal material. In trying to account for this fact, analysts have taken different ways. One way, taken by Kohut and his followers (Kohut 1971), is to set the Oedipus complex aside, posit a theory of self-psychology and advise a new clinical technique, which focuses on deficit and offers restoration. Kleinians take an opposite way. Their approach, when the Oedipus complex is what I am calling 'invisible', is that this is so, not because it is unimportant, but because it is so important and felt by the patient (from whatever causes) to be so unnegotiable that he employs psychic means to make and keep it invisible.

In this chapter I focus on one small area of the Oedipus complex: its first stages, when these are reached after a disturbed early development. When Klein (1928, 1932) added early stages and later linked the Depressive Position, on which in her view mental health depends, to Freud's nuclear complex, she expanded the emotional constellation from which the Oedipus complex of each patient takes its very individual form. The patients I describe are struggling to obliterate an early Oedipal situation, which feels continually to be threatening. As will become apparent, feelings of exclusion, problems of separateness and of being single in the presence of an Oedipal pair, and, above all, a distinctive type of sexual splitting are foremost in these patients.

I begin with a detailed account of Leon, who at 11 years of age is nearing puberty, but whose mental life is still largely occupied by defences against his disturbed relations to his primary objects and a traumatic early Oedipal constellation. His presenting problem was panic at any new prospect. A move to secondary school was looming when he began his analysis, and his parents thought he would never manage it. Otherwise, they told me – though father seemed not quite convinced – there were 'no problems'. He was 'just an ordinary boy'. Leon was their first child, followed closely by a second, another boy, conceived when Leon was 4 months old. Leon's younger brother was a head taller, rowdy and active, while Leon stayed in his room with a book, although he would go out to play if a friend took the initiative. Only with difficulty could his mother bring herself to talk about Leon's infancy, which she said was 'terrible'. He had cried for hours; she could not bear that, or the feeding. 'Not what I expected,' she kept repeating. This limited and, particularly on the mother's side, uninsightful picture of Leon – intolerable as an infant, and now, his anxieties unrecognised, with parents not expecting him to want or to be able to manage life – foretold accurately part of what unfolded in the analysis.

On the first day Leon placed himself near and opposite me, seating himself with a sort of screwing-in movement on a little bench in-between two cushions. Except for two sessions, during the first 18 months of analysis he left his bench only to go to the toilet. He watched me through two different pairs of glasses – one like his mother's, the other like his father's – checking the room or myself for the smallest movement or change. Any change made him acutely anxious. He seemed younger than his years, a depressed, lumpy, soft boy, who conveyed that he had almost no hope of being understood. His appearance could change astonishingly. He could 'become' and look like some version of his father, or 'become' and look like his mother; he also 'became' a small sick infant, and at times he looked strangely enlarged. These changing appearances were due, I think, to his projection into and almost total identification with his objects on an early feeling level. The figures he let into – or which he felt forced themselves into – his inner world, he experienced in a similarly physical and concrete way; they possessed him, and he personified them. Leon experienced analysis as a disturbance that he was both against and also for, sometimes gratefully so. He said once, 'I don't want you, I need you.'

In the beginning, after inserting himself between his cushions and checking the room quickly for change, he spent his sessions staring silently at the floor below or the door opposite him. I elicited that he saw dots on the floor, that they 'pulled him in' and 'made him dizzy', but that by looking away he could get out. About the door he said he 'saw patterns'. He pointed out what he called a 'pattern': distinctly a penis with testicles. He described how the door moved nearer and nearer, but if he left the room and came back, the door would be at its proper distance again. He reported these events in a matter-of-fact voice in answer to questions over many sessions, the anxiety that underlay these near hallucinations and his fascination with them totally split off. He seemed to be fragmenting into dots and patterns two terrifying internal objects and emptying them out of his mind onto the floor and the door. There he watched them, withdrawn from contact with myself or the playroom, trying to stay in control and to remain free of anxiety and emotional content. He could never succeed in staying mentally void and withdrawn for long. Momentarily, terror pushed into him, or a flash of hatred of me, or acute depression, or a sudden tenderness. He would quickly rid himself of these intense contradictory feelings, which pushed and pulled him about. He had an ongoing conflict whether to withdraw or whether to allow contact, a conflict indicated by his feet, which retreated under his bench, came out towards me and then retreated again. Sometimes he blocked his ears, more often he listened intently. After the first few months his enormous latent anxiety was greatly lessened, which brought him much relief. And, to his parents' astonishment, he managed the move to secondary school without panic.

This brings me now to the subject of Leon's Oedipus complex. It was possible and necessary to continue to interpret his fear of the smallest change, his need of an empty mind, his wish to keep me always curious and closely attentive, his chronic anxiety that I would not understand him, but come too close, or force his feelings back into him, etc., etc. But between whom and what were these processes occurring? What was the symbolic significance or equivalence of Leon's inserting himself between two cushions on the bench? What was the meaning of the movement and change he dreaded? What or who was I in the transference? In Leon's denuded universe I found it difficult to speak of meaning: it sounded artificial, and if I persisted it also aroused his anxiety and hatred.

To consider this more closely, if I interpreted that he did not expect me to understand him, he sometimes acknowledged such an interpretation with relief and, I came to notice, with more than a hint of a gloat. However, if I went a step further and spoke of myself as being like an inadequate parent, he became anxious. 'No! You're not like my Mum'. One issue that emerged was that he heard me as being disparaging of his mother and father and narcissistically implying that I was superior to them. This aroused his loyalty to his parents and, in addition, a fear of forming a nasty collusion with me against them. Beyond this, however, there was something more important. If I referred to myself as a parent in the transference, Leon became enraged and anxious; in contrast, if I interpreted his projection into me of a confused watching child while he felt he was being a cruelly indifferent father or mother (often, I thought, one of the dynamics in his sessions), Leon liked especially that bit of the interpretation in which I referred to myself as the child. He received it with satisfaction, as if to say, 'Ah, you admit it. You are a child.' Thus, while seeming to comply with the view that he had parents who had supposedly arranged for him to have something called psychoanalysis, a part of him privately held another view of the proceedings: he was big, his parents and I were little, and he had attractive superior activities – the dizzy pull of the floor and the nearing of the door – and from on high he watched our little goings on, sometimes even protecting us. In one of his rare spontaneous remarks he said to me loftily, 'I know all your little habits. I know the way your watch on your arm slips around. I know the way your shoe slips off.' These two selected observations are accurate. I thought their meaning was that he knew how my watch – that is, his mother's eye – had the habit of slipping round him and not really seeing him. And he also knew his father's habit of not staying in himself and slipping off, i.e., projecting himself into and getting too close and involved with Leon. But Leon did not want these 'little habits' to be transference phenomena with a dimension of meaning such as my watch to be linked to an eye. He cut the links between his inner world and his analysis, which he stripped of meaning, and he wanted me to accept and to adopt his disconnections and also to endorse his omnipotent phantasy of reversal – that he was big and I was little – and to join him in this as in other things.

I was also at this period drawing Leon's attention to how he mostly spoke softly, to draw me near to him to hear, and also how I had to come to him with questions, as he rarely spoke voluntarily. I interpreted that he felt that he pulled me so near that I became like the cushions next to him. I pointed out that he wanted me to stay very close, never disturb him, not make any connections or expect him to change, while he sat and looked on from on high, unmoving. Leon agreed that this was what he wanted. He also amplified with further freely given accounts of himself when I related what he let me see in the playroom to his daydreaming at school and his liking to stay in his room at home. But when I tried to explore the meaning (almost always there seemed to be some part of his ego for which meaning remained a possibility in spite of his continual stripping) of his high observatory, interpreting, however gradually, that with the movements he made when he sat down he imagined that he inserted himself into a home in mother's body, there to be the baby inside, or that he felt he held mother and father down on either side of him and so prevented their moving and coming together, or that sometimes he felt altered and big and saw me from afar as small, Leon was both enraged and disturbed. Often he rushed out of the room to the toilet, blocked his ears on return and told me, 'I hate your talking.'

At such moments, instead of being his cushions – he once explained he did not mind other little changes in the room, so long as the cushions did not move – he saw me exercising my analytic function. I then became parents who move and so destroy his phantasy of being inside. His rush out of the room expressed his momentary ejection from his seat on the bench, a change that made him hate me.

It is interesting to return for a moment to the beginning of his analysis, to the time when a change first occurred. By checking the room and knowing the fixed routine of his sessions, Leon was maintaining an overall phantasy world of no change, no separateness, and no separations – the gap between sessions or at weekends did not exist for him. This routine was first altered by my not working on a Monday Bank Holiday. He failed to arrive for the last session of the preceding week; during his hour his father telephoned in a panic, saying he had arranged to meet his wife and son at the underground and then bring Leon to me, but they were not there.

On the Tuesday Leon arrived, wearing no spectacles. At first he was terrified of being punished and pushed out of his home on his bench or even out of analysis altogether for missing a session, and he was relieved when I interpreted his acute anxiety. Then he tried to re-establish me as his cushion close to him, staying silent, making little movements to get me attentive and around him. After this he told me he had dropped his glasses during the weekend, and they had smashed. He then stared short-sightedly at the door on which he said there were 'waves', and the floor, on which he said there were 'bits not as nice'. I think Leon had found the changed routine unbearable, could not come, had smashed his sight and smashed also the objects of which 'waves' and 'not nice bits' were the residues, but so residual that it was impossible to know what he had fragmented and expelled.

After 8 months or so of analysis, Leon was more able to bear contact with the content of his psychic life, and then the nature of the change he dreaded became clear as over widely spaced sessions bits of his early Oedipal situation returned. First there was his move from the bench, to sit for the first time at the table. He took out a pack of cards, and we played a game. He was secretly enormously pleased to have moved. The next day he again sat at the table. He took out a different pack of cards. During the game he said, 'These cards are someone else's. They are nicer than mine,' speaking as if stating a fact accepted by him and me. He never brought cards again, and for ten months more never moved from his bench. Through this painful episode he gave me a glimpse of the trauma that the birth of his brother had been and still is to him, and of his belief in a family presumption that his brother was nicer than he. Leon showed me that he surrendered and did not compete; for a long while he never tried again in the playroom, just as he did not try at home or at school.

Following the two sessions with the cards, he resorted to various manoeuvres to find out the next holiday dates without actually asking. When I told him the dates, he gave one of his rare smiles and said 'OK', nodding his head happily. Then, with the approach of the break, several early Oedipal feelings pressed into consciousness.

On the last day of the week Leon brought a roll of sweets. He asked me if I would *like one*, slightly emphasising 'like' and 'one'. I interpreted that he wished to know whether I liked what he was offering and, really, whether I liked him. I went on to say that he was expressing his longing for me as a mother who had only him, rather than the mother who had his brother, too. Leon was furious. He pushed and pulled the knobs on his electronic wrist-watch very fast, saying angrily, 'I'm getting the time right.' I said he felt I had mentioned his brother at the wrong time, just when he was longing to have me to himself, and rage and disappointment were now pushing and pulling him about. I linked these feelings to his infancy, and how the baby that was still there in him felt that his mother, by becoming pregnant when he was 4 months old, filled herself with his brother at the wrong time, because he still needed to have her for himself. Leon continued to push and pull furiously at his watch, all his sweetness gone. He rushed out to the toilet, returned looking empty, and became very sleepy. However, when he said good-bye, he nodded his head, as if to say 'OK'.

On the Monday he was burdened, and instead of cursorily checking that the room was the same he kept looking curiously about. He spoke longingly of 'the chair with the cushion' at the far end of the room. This 'chair with the cushion' was more capacious, and he would be more comfortable, and as it is not opposite me he would not be closely watched or watching me. He said with great pain that it was 'far'. I am not certain what this 'chair with a cushion' meant to him, but it was the first time Leon had seen a place he wanted to get to and realised he could not, that it was at the moment too far for him. With insight into himself it was a widening of horizons.

He did not look at the 'far' chair in the next few sessions. He restricted the area on which he used his eyes to the small patch of the floor beneath him. Each time he was about to speak, he put his hand over his mouth and stopped himself. He became withdrawn and then despondent. When I spoke to him about the strong force in him that stopped him talking and moving, and how he felt hopeless about ever being able to reach what he longed for, he was very moved.

The last session of the week was again different. Leon came in without looking at me – not even when I opened the front door to him – and in the playroom he kept me entirely out of his vision. I interpreted that he did not want to see me because at the end of the week I was his going-away analyst. As if a shock-wave were passing through him, Leon's whole body shook. Then he kicked violently in my direction and made a rude gesture of 'up you'. He split off his feelings and became aloof. He said coldly, 'I am looking forward to the holidays.' I agreed that he was, that he wanted to be free of me, now a hateful disturbance to him. 'Yes', he answered with a cruel smile. I remarked on his cruel satisfaction, and he was instantly anxious, rushing out to the toilet; when he returned, he listened intently to my voice to assess my state of mind. When I next looked at him, I had a shock. Quite unconsciously he had bulged his jacket out like a pregnant woman, and his face had changed and become his mother's. He sat looking more and more suffering and unloved. I think he had incorporated and was totally identified with an analyst/mother whom he had cruelly called 'a hateful disturbance'. When I said that

101

he seemed to be feeling the suffering inside of him of his unloved pregnant mother, Leon's face worked in distress. For a moment it was real grief. Then he looked angry and anxious. Somewhere in the house a noise sounded. The word 'man' was drawn unwillingly from him: 'M-A-N', he said. It was his recognition of father's presence when mother was pregnant with his brother.

When the session ended, he was both trying desperately to pull me closely round him by his usual methods, and also repeatedly making three taps in a very menacing way, indicating how again and again there is a hateful, threatening three. As he was going, he prodded the wall as if feeling its solidarity and sensing the barring quality of a baby or perhaps a father who closes mother to him.

The end of this sequence was on the Monday. Leon looked different, for the first time like a boy nearing puberty, in smart trousers, such as a 12-year-old might choose. At first he was more communicative and active than usual, but as the session went on he was in increasing conflict – his feet coming out and going back under his bench – whether to continue to go forward or retreat.

In the last week he became a high onlooker from his position between the cushions. The sessions were immobilised, and there were no significant elements, dyadic or Oedipal. The coming holiday was idealised. He said he was glad to get away because here it was 'empty' and 'boring'.

His Oedipus complex was not the kind where sexual desire for mother and sexual rivalry with father are foremost. Leon started not with a parental pair, but with a menacing three – mother pregnant with a new baby and father. There was no rivalry; instead, as he showed in the sessions with the playing cards, there was surrender. Leon competed neither with his sibling nor with his father – he retreated. The onset of the Oedipal situation was so intolerable to him that he expelled his own and his parents' sexuality. When he started analysis, his internal sexual objects were ejected onto the floor and the door, and he looked sexless. On the floor was a confused vagina and mouth, minutely fragmented into dots that sucked him in or made him dizzy, which he saw as 'not as nice'. On the door was a more intact father's penis, alarmingly invasive, reduced to a pattern, which was what it was for Leon – his predominant identification was with his father.

In the earliest stages of the Oedipus complex the infant has phantasies of mother containing father's penis or the whole father, and of father combining with mother's breasts and vagina, all in a state of perpetual gratification. Leon's feelings of exclusion and frustration would have been enormously increased by a new baby in reality inside mother enjoying all that he phantasised was granted in mother's interior.

Foremost for Leon was the problem of separateness. At 4 months, his mother's pregnancy came at the wrong time in his development, when he still needed an exclusive relationship for the reception of his projections – all the more because of his disastrous start. He was still in the paranoid-schizoid position, on the brink of the depressive position, old relations to part-objects overlapping with emerging relations to whole objects. The perception of a 'going-away' analyst sent a shock-wave through him. He felt ejected and instantly made a two-pronged attacking entry of 'up you' on the pregnant mother. The sweetness there was in him on the 1:1 basis he longed for with his mother was gone, and his hatred turned cruel. Pregnant, she was unloved by him, and when Leon sensed her suffering, he felt a grief more than he could bear making him angry and anxious. His ego could not cope: it was pushed and pulled about by a succession of unmanageable emotions. At the first cancelled session near the start of his analysis he even had to smash his glasses and stay away. Now that his ego was a little stronger, he could allow elements of his Oedipus complex to return, to see mother, new baby and father, which affected his own identity. Instead of sexlessness and seeing the world through mother's and father's glasses because of being in a state of projective identification with one or other of them, he had a proper boyishness about him for the first time, even though he did not maintain it for long. He was soon again in conflict whether to go forward or retreat. As the break drew near, he dispersed his Oedipal experiences, which were invisible as he inserted himself in omnipotent phantasy into and between objects with whom he stayed and which were his cushions.

Leon's cushions are de-sexualised parents whom he holds apart and around himself – the comfortable remainders from which frightening components have been expelled onto the floor and the door. Because these expelled objects are so minutely fragmented or denuded into a mere pattern, the nature of the sexual splitting that has taken place is difficult to see. In other patients like Leon for whom the earliest stages of the Oedipus complex constitute a fixation point this is more possible. Melanie Klein writes, 'this (the combined parent figure) is one of the phantasy formations characteristic of the earliest stages of the Oedipus complex and which, if maintained in strength is detrimental both to object relations and sexual development' (Klein 1952b: 55).

In my view, a most important feature of this constellation is that the projective identification that aims to separate and attack the sexual parents fractures a combination. Because the emotional level is early, the objects of the fracture are in any case already distorted by unretrieved projections, but through their fracture and further projections their heterosexual procreative qualities are destroyed, and the patient has instead pathological sexual objects – distorted, incomplete and broken open. Often the father is seen not as father or husband but as a sadistic, phallic male, and the mother becomes a weak, open, masochistic female, both felt to be open to homosexual alliances against the other sex. These phantasies are so omnipotent that the patient believes he has achieved a separation of the sexes and will, for instance, have dreams about and make references to women, but always with women or girls, and men are again always with other men or with boys.

For instance, one of my patients saw the analyst who fetched him from the waiting room as female, over-sensitive and too eager to be empathic and nice to him. Once he was on the couch, he felt I had changed. I was male, high, aloof, and condescending, and he immediately projected himself into this figure, becoming totally like it.

A patient I analysed many years ago brought his fractured images in a dream.

> He was in a foreign country. There were two houses apart from each other, each with a tennis court. In one house, though there was no sign of it on the outside, he knew there was a woman inside with a corset and stockings wanting to have sex; the surface of the tennis court of this house was cracked. The surface of the tennis court of the other house was intact. There, two men were facing each other, playing very competitive tennis without a net.

This patient has split apart the early Oedipal couple and maintained separate relations to each. His dream illustrates how profoundly affected both his sexual life and his object relations were. For him, the mother was an evidently cracked and seductive female, wanting sex from him – one-half of his predominant perception of me in the transference for a long time. At the start of analysis he was himself highly erotised, feeling almost totally identified with a mad, promiscuous female – promiscuous sex with promiscuous women was one of his problems. During adolescence this patient had felt he was in a feminine body with breasts, a transsexual feeling so near to delusion that he had been unable to undress in the changing rooms at school or swim without a vest to conceal his chest. The seductive woman in the house in his dream was thus also himself inside his mother. Apart, meanwhile, males played a watchful, competitive face-to-face game, with no way of knowing the true score. This was the other half of his transference, which corresponded to the area of his life, his career, which on the surface was intact, although he was enormously envious and competitive with me (as he was with his business associates) and believed me to be so with him, both of us cheating to win. Often, in these cases, the analyst is made into a watcher, while the patient repeatedly acts out sexually with unsuitable partners in painful triangles, where possession of one excludes and makes hostile another of the combination.

Leon fractured the combined parent in a rather similar way to the patient who split me between waiting and consulting room. As we were able to see later in the analysis, as mother I was to be drawn away from father, come closer around him and coax him with questions, not only when he was anxious and needed me to, but also when he was hostile and chose not to relate to me. His feeling then was that I was no more a mother but a little girl, too soft, who does not confront his hostility but cushions it, with abasement and pleading that turns into a horrific masochistic sucking him in. The cushion on his other side was a caricature of father, stupidly idealising the practical and ordinary, cruelly aloof from meaning and marriage, and wanting instead to come too close and pair with Leon.

With respect to the early Oedipus complex following on faulty early development, there are two aspects that drive the patient to fracture and obliterate out of sight the combined Oedipal parents. The first of these is the stimulation of this primitive primal scene. Leon, for instance, felt pushed and pulled about by an onslaught of feelings beyond the limited capacity of his ego to tolerate. The second aspect arises from the fundamental fact that the primal scene excludes the patient. At this early stage, and especially when there has been an excessive use of projective identification to compensate for disturbed object relations, exclusion is experienced as ejection from the object.

The patient feels not only impossibly stimulated but also outside and alone – twin aspects I hope to illustrate with some brief material from Mr A.

Mr A, an intelligent and sensitive man, was married and a father. Earlier in his life he had had several homosexual relationships, and under pressure he still had strong homosexual inclinations. Among his reasons for coming to me for an analysis was tormenting jealousy of his wife. He thought she was betraying him sexually – but he was not sure whether she really was or whether he was only tormenting himself with phantasies. If he saw her speak on the telephone or make herself ready to go out, he saw her planning, and almost having, sex with someone else.

There were many strands in Mr A's analysis that I must ignore to focus on what is relevant to this chapter. In some respects Mr A was like Leon. He was affectionate, and he had a strong death instinct and at depth a conviction of fundamental non-acceptance by a narcissistic and otherwise preoccupied mother. Mr A lacked a securely internalised good object and used projective identification and omnipotent control as his main methods of operating with his objects. Unlike Leon, an early pregnancy played no part in shaping his Oedipus complex, for Mr A was the youngest sibling. The adverse external circumstance in his family was the degree of overt sexual disturbance. Father and mother seemed to have had some homosexual inclinations, and from the age of 13 an elder brother had had sexual relations with my patient. Since debased sexual figures were both the result of Mr A's projections and fracture of the Oedipal pair, and also really corresponded to his actual parents to some extent (and later to other real objects), Mr A was often confused and suffered a loss of reality sense; he became terrified there were no objects with whom reality testing was possible.

Unlike Leon, Mr A was psychically highly mobile, and during the analysis he was highly erotised. He aimed for instant penetration and possession to take him away from confusion and anxiety. The need to feel inside his object, not to be out and single, to be instantly recognised and form an excited pair was paramount in Mr A and was (in addition to identifications) the driving force behind his homosexuality. In the beginning he stripped the relation between patient and analyst of transference meaning – it was he and I, personal. I was an idealised 'new' object who would give him what he had failed to find before, and give it to him in a way he could tolerate, with no exclusion,

106

no waiting, without stimulating anxiety or guilt or envy or jealousy or wounding his narcissism. Mostly he was excited by homosexual phantasy in which he was inside a high phallus looking down on and in control of me – a boy who would admire and serve him. But if I disturbed him in some way, he turned cold and cruel. Sometimes he was in a state of projective identification with an effeminate, softer, more corrupt figure. The sexes were always split. This erotised homosexual transference and a conviction of perverse erotised relations obtaining everywhere was for a long time an enclave disconnected from his Oedipal situation. Oedipal figures were nowhere in view, in or out of analysis, and nor was the child in Mr A.

As his excitement lessened, he grew watchful. He started to see 'signs' in the room, or my clothes, speech, of intimacies, parties, sex, etc., which invited him or excluded him – he could not tell which. Confused Oedipal delusions and doubts about my sexuality were hidden in his material. Had I been, was I perhaps still, actually excited and over-involved with him, as he was with me? It was so painful a period of his analysis that I would say Mr A was in anguish as his deep Oedipal suspicions, delusions and confusions emerged. His paranoid feelings decreased gradually, and he allowed me more contact with his shame, disappointment, anxiety and depression about his objects and himself.

As his sexual delusions faded in the transference, he began sometimes to feel painfully exposed to an Oedipal pair who do not consummate his phantasies but exclude him. There were very considerable difficulties in his life at this time, and Mr A was more easily disturbed by 'signs' than was usual at this stage. An important detail is that on the day of the session I report I was more formally dressed than usual.

The instant he saw me when I fetched him from the waiting room he looked anxious and dark in the face. On the couch he was silent for a long time. Then he said he had had a dream, and speaking fast and sounding both desperate and excited he said he was in France, and he had gone to a restaurant, and he had ordered '*tête de veau*', and when the waiter brought it, it was on the plate without its eyes, black eye sockets, vacant mouth, black stuff, mushrooms, neck standing up. ...
He went on and on. He paused, waiting, I thought, for me to interpret something about a chopped-off head or unseeing eyes. However, the effect of his rapid relating of what he was calling a dream – which I think was really a swift flight into psychotic phantasy – had been to

project chaos and disturbance into me. Mr A continued: 'Then there was some string – do you say *'ficelle?'* This is what I ordered. Or was it 'cervelle ....' He paused again.

After a while he spoke about a frill on a chamber pot, or a cake oozing out over the edge, and so on. When he stopped, I interpreted that he had gone into the world of his dream and wished me to join him there, to get away from the chaos and disturbance that the sight of my suit had caused in him. He answered, 'I had my eye shut. I was thinking of analysis, anal Isis. Suit? What suit? Oh, you mean your suit ....' Mr A continued mocking me and falsely pretending not to know what I was talking about. I suggested that when he saw me and now when I spoke to him, he felt controlled, ordered to notice my suit and talk about it, on top of being made to feel so disturbed and chaotic by it, and that this was so offensive to him that it drove him to mockery and pretence.

At slower speed Mr A continued with his French 'dream' or theme with more variations, but his excitement was lessening. He ended saying in a bitter voice, 'Proust's Charlus ordered some rough trade and all he saw was his parents "doing it".' I said I thought he was describing his experiences in the session. The rough trade he wanted was having me join him in his world of homosexual phantasy, but what he became aware of instead was me at my job, that is, parents 'doing it', which made him feel bitter and sneering. After a long silence Mr A said, 'But why?' He paused, and said, 'We are not there together. I'm alone.' He began to cry, saying, 'It's ridiculous to feel like this.'

Melanie Klein writes, 'Sometimes the analyst appears simultaneously to represent both parents – in that case often in a hostile alliance against the patient, whereby the negative transference acquires great intensity' (Klein 1952b: 54–55). My suit is the 'sign' of a hostile primal pair, who are so enormously disturbing to Mr A that he is impelled to perverse defensive and destructive phantasies. Previously, Mr A would have immersed himself in homosexual phantasies for sessions; he would have become increasingly aloof and persecuted and ended with a masochistic depression. In this session, he and I could get through his fast, massive defences against Oedipal disturbance and stimulation, and he recovered his contact with me and himself. He was then aware of his parents' 'doing it', his hostility to their intercourse and his bitter feelings of betrayal. The boy in the man was suddenly on the couch, and he felt alone and cast out, and he cried.

Before I conclude, a brief word on technique. Mr A pressured the analyst to join him in rough homosexual trade, as Leon pressured the analyst to be a cushion in unchangingness and meaninglessness. Part of the pressure to 'act in' with the patient is the pressure to formulate interpretations that accept that rough trade or unchangingness and meaninglessness are all there is. The patient invites the analyst to ignore the mental work he has done, and which he is still doing in the session, to keep invisible an early Oedipal situation he is endeavouring to control and obliterate.

To give one small example from Leon's material: when he brought sweets and asked if I would like one, simply to interpret his longing to be my only one in this session would not take into account the full situation – viz., that he was trying to make invisible and induce me, too, to annihilate the fact of a weekend break which meant that I as mother shut him out because I had another baby. The fuller interpretation of his longing for a mother who was not also the mother of his brother enabled him to express rather than keep split-off his rage at a mother forcing a brother on him at the wrong time. With Mr A, there was the opposite problem in the session reported. His pressure was not, as with Leon, to go too slowly or not go at all, but to go too fast, to rush to interpret the content of his dream. Had I done so, I think he would have felt that he had fractured the combined parents and annexed me to himself homosexually in 'rough trade'. As it was, he felt the parents stayed firm, and were 'doing it' – i.e., that I had stayed at my job of understanding the emotional chaos and disturbance the Oedipal combination caused him.

Naturally, an analyst has to try to sense afresh in every session what is urgent and near enough to be potentially dynamic. In other sessions, the exploration of Leon's primal need for a 1:1 relationship, or the meaning of the details of Mr A's swift phantasies, may be where the emotional dynamic is.

Summary

Leon and Mr A belong to a group of patients whose Oedipus complex is not part of a normal developmental thrust with sexual desire and jealous rivalry foremost. Awareness of an Oedipal pair, because of their ongoing defences against their continuing early impairment, is forced upon them. It is almost intolerable, and they use further defences to make and keep it invisible. I thus disagree with the Kohutian view of deficit with no Oedipus complex in these cases.

Above all, because projective identification into the object has become their mode of coping with their disturbed relations to their original object, awareness of a combined figure ejects them from their projective home inside the object. In addition, the combined parents – a cruel structure in these cases – demand sexual watching, threaten invasion or suction into their perpetual intercourse, stimulate envy, and enormously increase anxiety and depression. Because the patient lacks an internalised figure that can contain and modify this nearly overwhelming state of mind, he feels alone with an intolerable psychic load and threatening chaos. To disburden his psyche and re-enter his object, the patient in phantasy inserts himself between the combined figure, pulls the couple apart, and projects himself into one or other of the separated pair. These exclusive relations, however, differ significantly from earlier pre-Oedipal ones. His objects, distorted already by unretrieved projections, now bear the marks of the defensive and attacking fracture of their sexual combination, so that the patient feels himself to be in a world not of Oedipal figures but of debased and damaged sexual objects. This form of splitting an object in the early stages of the Oedipus complex is so distinctive in its effect that it should, I think, be known by the special name of fracturing an object. Leon's sexless immobilisation and Mr A's homosexuality, both with at times near-delusional confusion, are two of the many forms this constellation takes; pathological sexual relations in a triangular framework are also characteristic.

Finally, because of their lack of an internal good object, these patients feel little capable of bearing singleness. They must be in a state of projective identification with another object. In Leon's analysis singleness is not yet even a dynamic, and Mr A, well on in his analysis, is still in distress when he perceives the parental couple and feels alone. For them the Oedipal story begins there – cast out. This, after all, is where the original myth began: Laius cast out Oedipus.

Acknowledgements

A previous edition of this chapter was published in E. B. Spillius (ed.), *Melanie Klein Today*, vol. 2, London: Routledge, 1988, 001 191–205, and reprinted in J. Steiner (ed.), *The Oedipus Complex Today*, London: Karnac Books, 1989: 129–150.

8

SEEING WITH MEANING
AND EMOTION

In 1989 Lynn Barnett invited a group of analysts and psychotherapists to a showing of a film, *Sunday's Child*,[1] which she had made about a mother and her baby. Members of the audience were asked to comment in writing on the film they had seen. Below is my commentary.

Everyone will have watched Lynn Barnett's film with a succession of intense feelings. I shall begin, not with something controversial, but by exploring something which is fundamental and, I imagine, accepted by everyone here — that emotions are not accidental but intrinsic to the observation of elemental relations between a mother and a baby. I call the psychological events we have just watched elemental because they are the elements of human development, the elements out of which all experience that follows will, in various and complex ways, be built.

At once we have a question. If elemental human relations must be seen with emotion, are we not at the outset throwing away the possibility of science? Shall we not be trapped in the subjectivity of individually variable, unconscious and sometimes irrationally motivated views with no possibility of deciding between different ways of seeing? Not so, I think — if understanding the diverse ways in which emotions enter into seeing is made a part of our science. Emotions enable and are essential to seeing but, oppositely, they may also impede seeing. This would mean a new paradigm for science, which traditionally has seen observers as dispassionate (a large subject in itself). It also means that the emotional seeing and its many problems are areas of investigation, relevant to understanding and settling our different ways of seeing.

I shall pursue the theme of emotional seeing by asking, in relation to the film, what do mother and baby see? I think Mother sees the baby with several feelings, with tenderness and persecution, to name two, and, as time goes on, it seemed to me, with less feeling and less capacity to perceive her baby. The presence of feelings facilitates the seeing of human beings, and mother's lack of feeling and lack of perceptiveness are among the things that most disturb us when we see the film. It calls for explanation. How is it she does not see a distressed baby being over-stuffed with spoon food, who we see?

The baby, too, has an emotional perception of his mother, in my view even in his earliest days, when he relates to parts and not yet to the whole of her. He sees not merely a physical breast or face, feels not merely a physical arm, hears not a physical voice only, but perceives a physical breast, face, arm, voice that are bearers of psychological qualities, i.e., various forms of love, hate, understanding, refusal to understand. He sees part objects infused with psychology and emotion – or the lack of it. From the first, the baby is one who looks and watches, who uses his eyes on the world.

It used, in the past, (I refer to it to get it out of the way today) to be objected that a new infant could not perceive psychological objects because what he sees, to take the example of visual perception, comes from his momentary retinal image, and the rest arrives later, it was claimed, by means of laborious constructions from experience. As we know, evidence has gone against such a minimalist view.

Developmental biologists have shown that it is a false hypothesis that visual perception, even initially, is caused only by the retinal image. Their experiments show, as from its clinical perspective does psychoanalysis, that the human perceptual system registers, not the low-grade information of retinal images, but, from the start, something altogether more complex that combines innate forms with external stimuli. Evolution has tuned infants to a human environment. Innately, the baby is ready for information which has survival value, which includes psychological and emotional information about the humans on whom he depends.

I see this baby, in the first film sequence, both hearing his mother's voice and being comforted by the tenderness in it. In the sequence in which he is in distress and she gives him, not herself, but the dummy, I see him as perceiving her physical gesture and its emotional rejection of him. I see his complex feelings as time goes on of disappointment and confusion, and his realisation that she cannot take his anger or distress. This is to say that the baby perceives his mother's psychological state, adapts to it and so survives and develops with her. That he can accept what she can give is his strength, as is his not getting angry with her much, though for his compliant adaptation he seems to pay with depression and anxiety.

I wish for the moment to return to his mother. After a receptive tender start, she feels ambivalent, and then depressed. She becomes unable to see, in the sense of psychologically perceive, any troubling aspects of her baby – his suffering, confusion, anxiety and depression. What is she blanking out? I am now in a dilemma, because the way I see mother's difficulties is influenced by mother's interview with Mrs Barnett before the baby was born. Today we have not seen this bit of the film. Unless I now break the ban on using anything other than what we've seen today, I cannot explain how I see the mother. So, with apologies: Mother told Mrs Barnett she knew her baby was a boy and she spoke of 'having had' or, rather, 'having' a younger brother. She went on to say that she is really good friends with men, 'matey' is her reaction to them. She expressed anxiety that one's state of mind affects the baby. She said she believed she would have a 'strong, healthy, perfect child', and she also said that she did not have a mental shape of a baby in her mind and that she was 'in two levels, one going on with the practical things, one blanking out a lot'.

Mother has told Mrs Barnett that she is blank about a new real baby. Instead, she has an image of strength, health and perfection. Soon the reality of a baby who is not perfect breaks down her first fragile defences. She resorts to stronger, more pathological defences and becomes narcissistically withdrawn from internal and external reality, as her elemental inner world begins to irrupt and overtake her. This impedes her love for her baby. There seem to be times when she sees him, not as her baby, but as her brother, the other baby of her infancy, whose grizzling and demandingness arouse in her a murderous hatred. In one filmed observation (which we don't see today), the cat pushes up to peep at baby. Mother says to the cat, as she pushes him away, 'You hate it, don't you.' Mother is struggling to ward off her hatred of a distressed baby brother, which is also self-hatred for being full of hatred.

These remarks are an attempt to link together and make coherent sense of a number of items we see in the film. Most of you will have some similar hypothesis calling upon familiar psychoanalytic theories of meaning, continuity in series from primary psychic elements, circumstances in which experience tends to arouse overwhelming primitive anxieties, and so on. Such hypotheses are not guesswork, but informed by theory and experience. They are, however, still only speculations made in these circumstances, i.e., from an observation, but they could be confirmed or disconfirmed in the special setting of therapy.

In regard to seeing with emotion and meaning, mother is evidence of two things: (1) intolerable emotions and meanings impede seeing; and (2) defending the ego by splitting off intolerable emotional sights and their meanings and the ego's capacity to see, leads, in the end, to a state in which there is no feeling and no meaning and no seeing. We all were babies with a mother once. To watch a film of a mother and a baby stirs emotions from our depths, which may help us to see what is happening, or which may impede our perceptions. We may identify with baby against mother, hate and judge her on his behalf and our own, or, possibly, though in this instance less likely, identify with mother and dislike the baby's needs when she manifestly feels strange and needs to be free of his impingement. Or we may deny the whole elemental sight (not likely in this audience!) – and say: What are you going on about baby brothers and meanings, and mother at a distance from her hatred of herself and her baby – she's looking after him! which she is. He's a good fellow – which he is. They are all right! Well, they are not all wrong, but they are not all right.

We have come to one of the central problems in meaningful emotional seeing: how to move towards an objective view of a primary pair, without denial and without identifying with one of the pair against the other, instead of seeing the couple. Our problem is how to see both mother and baby objectively in the whole new way of seeing introduced to the world by Freud. As we have been reminded by Mrs Alvarez, Freud's way of seeing has been developed in different directions. The problems of differences in this kind of seeing have to be explored in discussions such as ours, or in supervision of work and, fundamentally, through psychoanalysis, to help us to use our elemental experiences less for distorting projections, identifications and denials, and more as the basis of empathy.

I shall briefly comment on some selected aspects of the film in sequence. The first time we see the baby, he is 12 days old. He cries when undressed and washed, and shivers. Mother is responsive; she holds him physically and emotionally. She seems grateful he is there, that he has arrived and filled the blank for her. He likes being swum by her and he likes his feed, too. She is tender to him in distress and does not rush his feed, and he ends becoming a sleepy, satisfied suckling.

We glimpse something more troubled when the baby is 9½ weeks. There is a little happiness when he is carried and being changed, and he and his mother make talking noises to each other. But when he becomes unhappy and wants his mother, she does not want him. She wants him to use the dummy and not her, though in the end she can accept that he does not want the dummy. The baby is desperately impatient for the breast: it is what he wants and he goes to it, but it frightens him and he pulls off it. Throughout he is a very watchful baby. He sees the breast, not as a good object, but as a mixed, confusing object. Mother first laughs nastily when he pulls off, and then wants to comfort him. She cannot see she frightens him. 'Wind', she says, 'Honestly'. She cannot contemplate that his wind, in his mind, may have a connection with her. How could she see that he is frightened and confused about her, or that she can hate him or cruelly enjoy his distress, unless she had help to understand the complexity of what she is seeing – the past connected with the present – and help with her latent fear that she is harming him. Of course she cannot face any of this alone. She must cut off and not see what is happening between herself and the baby.

I move on to when the baby is 3 months and 3 weeks old, when he is being given solid food at the start of weaning. Mother is now very depressed. The baby has a cold, cannot sleep and is sufferingly compliant. For we who view the film it is very disturbing. Mother cannot see the baby now; she shovels food into him regardless, desperate to stuff him full to keep him quiet to leave her in peace. She herself is in considerable distress and needs to withdraw. The baby's first loss – where the spoon is, the breast is not – the strangeness of the new food, his depression and anxiety about himself and his mother, are not perceived by her. He even gets no hand; when his hand seeks for hers, he has to end by taking his own hand. Finally, mother has him in the swimming pool. Speaking as a film-goer, I would say there is murder in the air. She is also trying to cheer her baby and herself, dipping him up and down in the water, but dangerously.

Overall, the relationship between mother and baby has some good aspects and some very unfortunate aspects. Mother's cold, hostile depression has communicated itself to the baby, who is watchful and compliant. In some ways she looks after him well, but she shuts him out when he is not perfect. Mother had a blank about a real baby, and the baby, with no container for bad feelings, has a hole in his experience.

Then he finds the grater. There, in the outer world, is an equivalent of one of his already internalised objects: hard and smooth, shiny, cutting and having holes. His play with the grater is his intense investigation of its nature. We see here a beautiful example of how mankind gives meaning to his world, how from his internal elemental objects he proceeds outwards and invests objects in the world with significance.

Summary

As first commentator on the film, I have focused on a foremost characteristic of the way we — who accept Freud's way of seeing — see it: we see it with emotion and we see it as having meanings. These facts, I think, are as basic to the understanding of our differences in seeing as are our differences of psychological theory. Because the psycho-dynamic seeing of human relations is made possible, but is also prone to distortions and denials by the observer's elemental inner world, our science must include investigations into the instruments of seeing, viz. our emotional selves. Here we come upon a compounding of problems. Since the investigation of our emotional self is done by analytic discussions and psychoanalyses, which, *to an extent*, are informed by different theories, there tends to be a perpetuation of differences, in that different theories tend to make observers sensitive to seeing different things and/or formulating them differently. This complicates our already complex task of trying to settle our differences.

In regard to the film, I have told you something of how I see the relationship evolving between mother and infant, how I think mother and baby see, or do not see, each other, and how I see mother's past beginning to dominate the present. I have indicated how I see this determined baby adapting to and complying with his mother, and, as well, creating his first meanings, by proceeding outwards from his inner world to make symbolic equivalents in the external world, so initiating for himself the way of seeing with meaning and emotion that I have been talking about.

I look forward to the discussion of what I say and see, and, as our day goes on, of hearing other ways of seeing Lynn Barnett's film.

Acknowledgements

A previous edition of this chapter was published in the *Journal of Child Psychotherapy*, 1989, 15: 27–31, as one of a number of papers reflecting on Lynn Barnett's film *Sunday's Child*.

Note

1   Lynn Barnett, *Sunday's Child: the Development of Individuality from Birth to Two Years of Age*, Parts I–VIII. Part IX: 2 to 3 years, 1988. Part X: 3 to 6 years, 1989. Concorde Films, 201 Felixstowe Road, Ipswich, Suffolk IP3 9BJ, UK.

9

CAN A LIAR BE PSYCHOANALYSED?

Though common, lying has been little studied. There are many kinds of liars and lies, and this paper studies one sort, the habitual liar, to whom psychoanalysis has so far given little encouragement, since a liar who is characterologically a liar rather than a truth-teller seems so inauspicious a subject for a psychoanalysis.

Can a habitual liar be psychoanalysed? An analyst who considers this question comes at once upon a paradox. Psychoanalysis is founded on truthfulness, yet for a liar to be himself he must lie in his analysis, so that a basic contradiction appears at the outset which we fear may make analysis impossible. We have also the opposite response. Lying is surely, like any other symptom, a manifestation of disturbance, and, moreover, psychoanalysis has always recognised the human need for, and been ready to work with, a variety of forms of untruth – denial, disavowal, misconception, distortion, delusion. So why not the lie? There is in fact a little about lying in the literature – in connexion with the condition of pseudologica phantastica (e.g., Deutsch 1922; Fenichel 1939; Hoyer 1959), delinquency (e.g., Karpman 1949), the defence of denial (Anna Freud 1966), adoption phantasies (Sherick 1983), thinking (Bion 1970a). Blum (1983a) describes clinically a single central lie by a patient which 'surprisingly proved to be analysable', and Bollas (1987) describes an attempt to understand a habitual liar. Might we analysts not be like the philosophers who solved the logical Paradox of the Liar[1] with a theory of types and levels of discourse, and succeed in understanding and analysing a habitual liar, if we, too, could get the level – in this case, the emotional level – right? My view, even though, as I discuss later, our fears of a fundamental antagonism between a liar and a psychoanalysis are justified and the transference problems are grave, is that we can.

Because it presents itself in speech, lying might seem to be a relatively mature pathology. Analytic investigation reveals, however, that the fundamental problem the habitual liar is bringing to analysis by lying is primitive, and primarily involves not the truth and falsity of propositions, but the truth and falsity of his objects – their genuineness or deceitfulness. I shall illustrate my thesis with an account of the beginning of the analysis of M. M is a liar in identification with a lying object. His lying is linked to his deep doubts about communications which he fears must overwhelm him and his objects and express lies rather than truth.

At the preliminary interview M was quietly charming. He seemed not to want to talk about himself other than to say that he hoped he might perhaps, in the future, be able to train as a psychoanalyst. He accepted politely the practical terms, session times, fees, analytic holidays and date of starting. As the interview was drawing to its close, he asked in a light voice with a gesture indicating the room and the neighbourhood beyond: 'Are there communications here?' Consciously he meant: 'Are there buses, trains, etc.?', but when I looked at his face I saw that in place of the polite young man there now stood someone almost in a panic about whether communication was going to be possible between him and me.

The first sessions with M were a shock. The turmoil was a total contrast to the smoothness of the preliminary interview. M gave me fast and equivocal talk, and strained silences, both of which projected into me an almost overwhelming turmoil which lasted in and between sessions. M himself was bewildered by the effect of the analysis on him and terrified of his effect on me, as his emotional state oscillated between intense anxiety and intense excitement. I shall describe first his anxiety, which he communicated by his behaviour, his words and, above all, at a preverbal level by projections which were vivid and specific.

The turmoil took the form of a ceaseless churning round and round of M's communications, with painful attendant uncertainty as to their meaning and also acute feelings of insecurity and anxiety. In among M's ambiguous talk were a few clear desperate sentences that confirmed what he was communicating to me by projective identification. He said, for example, 'It goes on revolving', 'You can't like it', 'You won't believe my intensities.'

As opportunity arose, I spoke to him on the following lines. I spoke about his panic and bewilderment that had come with the start of the analysis and how it made him doubt that this treatment was good for him. I spoke about his need to get his intense feelings into me, so I would know them, and his belief that I couldn't like it and that he was damaging me by doing so. I also spoke about his fear that I would be overwhelmed by his feelings and would pour them out back into him, so that he and I would go on revolving without rest or relief.

With the arrival of each session I would find myself approaching M hopefully, willingly and anxiously, and feeling I was trying not to show my anxiety. From this continuing and consistent countertransference experience and many incidents in M's history, which he told me later, I am convinced that M's mother was a woman who wished to hold, but who lacked the capacity to hold, M's intense projections. She would have tried to conceal her agitation and present a good front to her child, who had not, however, been deceived – he had been aware of the contrast between her outer appearance and her inner reality. I said to M that he was bringing to the analysis what was still inside him from childhood – a child who felt his mother was agitated with him, and her agitation made him panic, exactly in the way that the analysis was now affecting him. I said, too, that he knew we were wrong together, but he thought that I, as mother, kept pretending even to myself that we were not wrong. Though I did not call it so, as his lying was not yet in the analysis, I was already in the transference M's primary lying object, the mother who cannot truly mother.

Every session M scrutinised me intensely, my face, clothes, voice and words. In the third week he brought a dream. He was inside a convent. He had his eye close to the small hole in the turning thing there is on convent doors. I interpreted his dream as his picture of his relationship to me as mother. He both feels inside and has his eye on a hole, which means to him no father is there, watching me churn round and round, which I linked to the way he was actually watching me closely in every session, to see through my external appearance to know whether or not I was internally overwhelmed by his intense onslaught. M was a difficult patient. His communications were evasive and obscure and he was anxious, excited and labile of mood. Sometimes he had fits of laughter, which collapsed into long silences, or changed into sly, mocking attacks. If he thought I said too much, he felt he had overwhelmed me and made me pour out through a hole, so confirming his fear that I was unable to contain 'his intensities', as he called them; if he thought I was too silent, it

120

became his conviction that I had stopped trying or had gone dead. In either case, I became, in another of his phrases, 'only a pretension' that made him despair. His fear that he had only a 'pretension' and not a real analyst was the emergence in the transference of his anxiety that his primal object was not a genuine or true one.

The nature of M's primal object relations was clarified further when his lying emerged openly in the analysis. This it did in the seventh week when he asked me to change his Thursday time a fortnight away, saying his cousin was arriving from abroad and he wished to meet her plane. A few sessions later he repeated his request, saying the woman was coming to England for an abortion. She was the sister of an old university friend, who knew no one here and he needed to meet and assist her. I noticed 'the cousin' had become 'the sister of an old university friend' (but, I thought, a cousin could be the sister of an old university friend) and I also suddenly remembered that, in the first week of his analysis, I had changed the Thursday time agreed at the interview for a different hour. I suggested that his wanting a time change might have to do with my having asked him in the first week of the analysis to change his Thursday time. M was silent. The next day he repeated his request in a threatening tone, adding matter-of-factly: 'The woman who wants an abortion has only one leg and people won't think it nice that a one-legged woman comes to London for an abortion.' He proceeded with laughter to do correct calculations of driving times to and from London Airport. By then I was bewildered. Was there a cousin really? Was it all lies? Was it a confusing mixture of phantasy and reality?

As the days went by, the time change grew into a fraught issue. He insisted he would stop coming if I did not change his time. I felt pressured and manipulated as well as confused. I did not change his time. I continued to interpret that he had an image of me changing his time in the first week of the analysis and he was being a sort of caricature of that image. He wanted me now to have his experience. I said he suspected it was a lie that I 'needed', as I had said, to change his time; he suspected I liked bewildering and hurting him by giving him a time and then throwing him out of it, so to say, aborting him. He had felt forced to accept my change then, just as he was trying to force me now. I also said to him that my impression was that he was so entirely now the one demanding a time change that it did not any more exist for him that it was he who had originally suffered a change of time from me. At this stage I did not know what he told me later, that he had had in the first few weeks of his life a difficult change from being fed at the breast to being bottle-fed. This fact of his history gives, I think, a deep resonance to the first analytic time change.

On the day of the requested time change, M did not come. I never found out whether a cousin or a friend's sister had in reality been arriving, and I still had not realised the central importance of his lying. M had now been in analysis for 2 months and I was focusing on another quality of his verbal communications – their ambiguousness, which was multiple in function. The ambiguousness projected doubts and confusion into me, made me feel uncertain and uncomprehending of what he meant, a state of mind, I interpreted to him, which was his own condition with his object, which he wanted me to suffer and know over and over again. He also wished to make it hard for me to understand him; even as he gave me material so that I could understand him, he also offered me the wrong material so I could misunderstand him, and by his manner of often sneering and laughing he meant to provoke attacking-sounding interpretations from me. Hostility, hope, fear and defence were highly condensed. He hoped I would understand him, he feared a wrong response to his communications, and he defended himself hostilely and masochistically by inviting it.

He had himself formulated his central anxiety in the preliminary interview: 'Are there communications?' By the third month he was able to express his anxiety in a clear dream.

I was feeding two pigs with some stuff; some of the stuff was food, some of it was rubbish. The pigs didn't know the difference between the real food and the rubbish. They ate everything. Then a black dog came in and, in the dream, I had an even bigger black thing to deal with the dog.

I started interpreting his dream by saying: 'The two pigs you feed stand for me, whom you feed with your talk. In this dream you are bringing your fear that I won't know the difference between your real communications and the other stuff, the rubbish.' M remained silent for a long time. When he spoke, he said with real feeling – and I could tell he meant it – 'I am astonished. I never thought that you would interpret the pigs as yourself'. I said: 'The fact that I did means to you that I am unlike the pigs in your dream who swallow everything. At this moment you think that I can discriminate the real from the rubbish, which is important to you.'

122

It was an important moment. It was M's first recognition of me, his new analyst, as different from figures which 'swallow everything' and it was from this point on, when M thought I might be an object who could understand him, that his lying became flagrant. He now assailed me with blatant lies, which threw into doubt such 'facts' of his history and current life as he had so far told.

His lies were delivered tauntingly to provoke me to get out of control, call him a liar and moralise at him. I had to struggle hard to hold an analytic stance and keep my focus on the experiences received as he lied to me. I interpreted that he was transmitting to me his experiences of deception, linking his lies with what had already been established in the analysis – and which we continued to see – his disappointment and suffering with objects that purport to hold him but instead agitate and confuse him, that purport to discriminate, but instead 'swallow everything'. I said that he felt these were all lying objects. M made me feel both deceived and in doubt about whether I was being deceived; at times I was so confused that analytic work was impossible, and I was made impotent. I did not (I discuss it later) at this stage try to analyse the hatred he was expressing in this way. I continued to talk to him about his intolerable feelings of doubt, threatening confusion and helplessness he was communicating to me.

M's flagrant lying continued for some months. Even the address and telephone number he had given me turned out to be false. On checking the street directory I found there was no such street and the telephone number, too, was of an impossible combination. When I told him, he ignored my remarks for many sessions. Then one day he snarled, 'I don't want to be rung up and told there is no session', revealing, as I said, his mistrust, his conviction that I did not want him. I also told him that I wanted his correct address and telephone number. He ignored my request and went on lying, watching closely how I responded, testing me to see if I could endure his continuing so blatantly not to conform to what I must want. Finally, in the eighth month, he announced through gritted teeth: 'Here is the true address and telephone number. I made the effort. I did it for you.'

M's material shows the primitive nature and the pervasiveness of a liar's predicament. His lie starts at the preliminary interview with his polite false facade to charm the prospective analyst, whom he suspects is a fraud who will reject him. He suspects and fears that, like his internalised primary object, the analyst will pretend, but will not be able honestly to know or bear the relationship he will make with her.

Once the analysis starts, M lies with excitement (which I have yet to consider) and externalises from his inner world his primary object relations. Intensely needy and very anxious, he invades and agitates his object, which receives his intensities and anxieties (it is not an impenetrable wall), but lacks the capacity to modify or contain them. No equilibrium is therefore obtained in M or his object, which tries to mask its inner state by a split between an outer facade and inner turmoil.

On the hypothesis (Bion 1962b; Klein 1952a) that an infant has an innate preconception of a good object, which will feed, clean, warm him, etc., and also receive and transform for the better his communications, that is, understand him, then, if actual experience falls too far short of expectation, the infant may doubt if the object is a true realisation of his innate preconception. In my view, M was unsure in this sense that his object, which did not relieve but increased his anxiety, was a true example of its kind. Moreover, he also knew his object to be not true in that it had a false facade. However, M is mostly in some part of himself able to know the facts, and a constant feature of his communication was its mixture of lies and precise information (recall the time change he wanted), i.e., while he experienced me as false for changing his time, he was also capable of knowing there could have been a genuine reason for doing so. In the same way, I think, M was aware that his primary object's false facade was an attempt at outward composure at least in part out of concern for him – not to agitate *him* further. His primary object was not in this and many other ways a total fraud. *That* claim was *his* lie – out of his hatred of a good object, and also in an attempt to get relief from the distress of his doubts, anxieties and guilt by pushing himself into the simplicity and righteousness of a paranoia.

From these several origins, his disappointment with his object's incapacity, his realisation of its false, masking facade, his attacks on its good aspects, his own refusals to help and his lies about his object's positive capacities, his object becomes for him a lie, a pretension – almost. Instead of basic trust, M has basic suspicions.

I mentioned before that I did not interpret his hatred in the first months of the analysis, but when, towards the end of the first year, he became less agitated and excited and his churning projection stopped, I began to focus also on that aspect of his lying which expressed his violent hatred. I interpreted his attacks with lies, contradictions, ambiguities on my analytic functioning, his feeling of power and success in getting into my mind and making it muddled and unsure, and his gratification in watching me become incapable of working with him. This was a recapitulation in transference terms of his history. He now told me his mother had been unable to get breast-feeding established with him, and then 'because of the war', as he put it, consciously meaning World War II, unconsciously meaning his war against her, she had been unable to find any substitute milk that was properly satisfactory to him. M was at war with me. He aimed to make a milieu in which I could not analyse him, and what became increasingly prominent was how he met instances of genuine communication and understanding between us with silences which were a refusal to acknowledge when I was good really. M is twice handicapped. His nature is intense in love and hate, but over-hostile; he is invasive; he does not easily tolerate frustration (of waiting and change in particular). And, in addition, the object who nurtured him seems to have been too weak to hold him, and would have increased his intensity, anxiety and excessive use of projection.

In terms of Melanie Klein's developmental theories, the lying object may be understood as a malformation of the paranoid-schizoid position, when normally an infant polarises his experiences into good and bad. M lacks good objects, however, and he splits instead between suspect objects and bad objects. M's problems are near to, though different from, other early pathologies which result from a failure to make a fundamental split between good and bad. For example, a schizophrenic, unlike M, is not uncertain whether the supposed good object is a fraud; he knows it is. He is convinced it lies, e.g., purports to nourish as it poisons, or looks as though it will help but meanwhile tortures. In that world there are only different sorts of bad objects. M's lying, I think, throws light on schizophrenic lying. A schizophrenic lies in identification with an object he knows is a lie. However, while a liar like M may temporarily convince himself of his lies, he does not, as in schizoid conditions, habitually sever his mental connexions. He keeps his links to the truth he is lying about; and the hostility of, and the damage he is doing by, his lies increase his felt fear and guilt. With anxiety running high, with guilt setting in early, and with objects who are able to facilitate little working through of persecutory and depressive feelings, M's early anxieties about himself and his objects have remained largely unmodified. In his depths he still churns round and round, and it is this nearly intolerable burden of his primary object relations which, once he starts his analysis, he releases into his sessions with doubt and anxiety that communication about these will be possible.

How does a patient like M manage in life? Like his objects he constructs a public facade. He dissociates himself internally from his turmoil and skilfully 'matches' (his word) externally what is required of him. Cut off from his depths, his facade is thin and lasts only while relations go smoothly on a superficial level. He soon tends to suspect his object of likewise having a facade, and gets anxious that he is unwanted, is being criticised, etc. Projections of acute anxiety begin again and, in phantasy, he invades his object to scrutinise its interior and control it to take what he needs from it. The whole cycle of irresoluble, over-involved object relations has begun again, based on a massive projective identification with a lying object in which M becomes the habitual liar who is chronically hiding behind and meeting his objects, not with communications, but with lies.

However, since he is further destroying his ego and his dubious objects by his lies, he would disintegrate under increasing fear and guilt were it not for the gratification and excitement he generates by his lies. To this excitement, evident in his analysis from the beginning, I now want to turn. M used the lie to achieve an erotisation of his object relations, which in omnipotent phantasy were then changed into a sadomasochistic partnership. Committing the outrage of lying in a psychoanalysis and forcing his analyst to be his partner made him enormously excited. The excitement buoyed him up and lifted him out of the reach of fear and guilt. Gradually, however, he would start to feel identified with his suffering object and then his need for masochistic gratification to relieve and evade his guilt would become imperative. His lying, because it violated his own instinct for truth, would then give him masochistic satisfaction. Also, he would lie to taunt me to call him a liar, eject him from his analysis, etc., and so make me become the sadist. M was often lost in masochistic phantasies during his sessions and he avidly sought to hear interpretations as sadistic beatings. This was the reason why I did not interpret his hatred in the initial stages of the analysis. His fear of a murderous superego made him instantly twist away from my one or two attempts to speak about his hatred and misunderstand what I had said as a concrete gratification of his masochism. I am not sure, though, that I was right to delay; not interpreting the hatred he was expressing with his lying made him fear I would not, or could not, recognise it, and increased also his conviction of my masochism.

For the moment I want to leave M and discuss, though in less detail, another patient, L. The following dream of L's shows how an exciting sado-masochism can be used to evade and change the liar's threatening constellation.

L dreamt he went on holiday with a friend. They were up on a high hill, overlooking a valley, and the entire scene was glitteringly beautiful. The point of the holiday was to watch a veteran car go past in the valley below. In the dream, L left the friend and was strolling with someone else, who was vague in the dream, along a special walkway high up on top of the hill overlooking the valley, waiting to see the car go past.

L is another habitual liar, though in a different style from M. L was truthful about matters of address, telephone number, history, even about his fraudulent business and personal relations, until he got to their emotional implications, when he would speak in a welter of misleading statements and bare lies, misregistering what he was saying. In the sessions before the dream reported above, L had been excited and also very anxious. His communications, in which the name of a crooked, risky financial associate occurred, were contradictory and full of lies. I knew he was troubled, but I could not understand him. Was a dangerous situation impending or not?

His dream is his picture of the transference at this time. He is high up on the hill with the excitement of watching me, the veteran car down below, going past what is happening to him. In the dreams he leaves his friend, who stands, I think, for his anxious self whom he abandons, and takes someone else (vague in the dream) who, I think, represents his analyst, on a 'walkway' with him – exactly as his contradictory lying material had been taking us away from his real situation of anxiety. The point, the excitement, the whole beauty is to watch his analyst go past.

This was his history exactly. L really had been ignored emotionally by his parents. For instance, he was brutally bullied with visible effects on his health at his first boarding school, but his parents took no action. He was rescued by the school doctor insisting they withdraw him from that school. His parents had, I think, failed him earlier by choosing to ignore his emotional difficulties as an infant and young child. L's dream revealed how the despairing situation of parents who see but go past his suffering is compounded by his own 'walkway' from his suffering self (in the holidays, for instance, he had lied to them about events at the school) and how this doubly ugly situation is turned into a perversely beautiful scene of exciting sadistic triumph, as he manipulates them with lies and watches and waits for their going past – exactly as he was doing with me.

With L, not registering implications honestly was the primal lie. He gave me countless instances, like recounting a defrauding business stratagem and then a moment or two later describing himself as taking honest care of his shareholders, or describing a co-director as cold, hostile to him, not to be trusted, and then adding that he knew he could rely on his warm friendship. He often complained that not in one of his company offices was there a reliable word-processor! His own word-processing failed to register the truth reliably; under any pressure he fibbed, 'glossed', lied, and he feared I, too, spoke to him in the same way. The foundation of my work with L, as it had been with M, was to try to analyse the ramifications of his relations to the primal lying object, in L's case an outwardly benign-seeming object which was inwardly uncaring, which does and says anything to evade pain or trouble. L's object is different from M's, which is weak, lacks the capacity to modify anxiety and dissembles its own anxieties. L's object is nearer to the criminal. It is brutal. It registers, but ignores and refuses, the pain and trouble of what it has registered.

For L and M their habitual lying has the meaning of an omnipotent tongue or penis, which opens their objects to their entry and control and so 'solves' their anxieties and sufferings with a sado-masochistic excitement. However, their lying tends to get out of their control and take control of them. M's conduct and speech at the start of analysis was infested with lies; he almost could not speak the truth. L came into analysis because, in a state of mounting excitement, he could not stop fraudulently overreaching himself and saw himself heading for a mental and financial crash.

L was familiar with anxiety states which drove him to start new 'schemes'. He was grim and depressed in the session following the one in which I, and I think he, had understood his dream of waiting to see the veteran car go past as his waiting in triumph for me to go past his anxiety. He said he had his familiar feeling of foreboding and he knew he wanted to 'go on a big spending spree' or 'start a deal'. He also told another dream.

He dreamt he had gone up to the top of a tower for a celebratory party. All the press and the TV boys were there. He felt suddenly he must get out of the party and go down to his car below, which he remembered he had parked with its headlights left on.

From L's grim and depressed state it was clear he was already down in the state of the car, which I linked to the veteran car of his previous dream, i.e. the analyst of the day before, now in his inner world, its battery flat, i.e., with no life in it. His dream pictures how when he is high, celebrating his triumph, he remembers his object and must come down to it. Once he is down, he feels totally identified with it, flat and grim, in a state of foreboding. But he does not want to know the connexion between his grim depression and his cruel tactics in the previous day's session. L ignored the series of interpretations which drew his attention to how there was a veteran car in the previous day's dream and a car in today's dream, connected their meanings and linked his depression to the emotional events between himself and his analyst. He was already doing a deal with himself, and trying to do one with me, too. He masochistically wants me to leave him to endure on his own his foreboding, his anxiety and guilt. His talk of going on a big spending spree is a lie, too. He never does, as we both know well; he looks for bargains, wheels and deals on the cheap, as he is trying to do between himself and me, to get on a sadistic high again – with M masochism was predominant, with L sadism predominated – without registering the true emotional price to himself and his objects of cruelly misleading communications.

The liar's perversion of communication involves a further lie. The lie is that the lying scene – in the terms of L's dream of being high on the hill watching the veteran car go past – is 'glitteringly beautiful'. This lie about lying is at the centre of the deterioration of his character. Like all 'bad character' liars, L has a narcissistic idealisation of its seductive destructiveness. L became narcissistically enraged, and beneath that terrified, at any exposure of his idealisation of lying, which was represented in his material by glitteringly beautiful scenes, 'high tech' furnishing, seductive eastern dancers, etc., and for a long time in the analysis he instantly walked out emotionally on such exposure, often with acting out against the analysis by publicly spreading lies about it. It must be added that in the analyses of both M and L it emerged that this idealisation was also a confused attempt to express their love for their primal lying objects by idealising their harmfulness.

129

The pathology of the type of liar I have considered, with its triad of a deficient primal object, a strong destructive instinct in the patient and a general perverse overlay, begins to look more familiar. His 'bad character' is the coalescence of his identification with lying objects and his own destructive impulses. He exhibits a particular form of the narcissistic organisation defined and studied by Rosenfeld (1971) in which the liar is the idealised destructive self which dominates the personality. His lying is a character perversion and a perversion of communication between people. It serves functions for the personality as described by, for example, Gillespie (1940) and Glasser (1979), affecting the analysis as described by Joseph (1981). (I leave on one side the problem of the relation between actual and character perversion.)

Can a liar be psychoanalysed? I return now to discuss this question in the light of the paper. First of all, to state the difference between forms of untruth familiar to psychoanalysis, like denial, disavowal, etc., and the lie. A denial, etc., removes a patient from contact with the truth and cuts him off from that truth in proportion to the omnipotence of his denial. In contrast, because a liar knows he lies, his lies are not cut off from the truth. While a denial, a disavowal, etc., expresses a psychic need not to know the truth, a lie is an acceptance of, and a perverse use of, a falsehood. I think this is the origin of what we feared initially, that there is a deep antagonism of perspective between a liar and a psychoanalyst, which must obstruct the forming of a therapeutic alliance and interfere with the analytic work, as indeed proved to be the case with M and L.

Nonetheless, the lying of M and L was the means of communicating urgently the fundamental truth about their early object relations. This, in my view, is paramount, and overrides the dilemmas which confront patient and analyst. The liar has to risk the abandonment of his present psychic structure with an analyst whom, as this paper shows, he will experience as a two-faced dissembler. He risks exposure to unpropitious truths about himself and his objects, and contact with enormous anxiety and guilt, as Bion (1970a) and Langs (1980) have shown. However, even as the analytic process is instituted it is also undermined by the lying. It damages the analyst's internal setting. Not only did M and L make me at times incapable of working by depriving me of needed knowledge, more seriously, they succeeded in getting me to take lies as truth, so that I actually became a partner in a perversion of the analytic relationship, unwittingly enacting it with them. They could watch how I was thinking what they said was true when it was not, and how they had corrupted me to respond with what in effect were lies, all of which heightened their excitement and sense of omnipotence. They then internalised a corrupted container, and, in identification, became less able to differentiate or contain their own states of mind, and their anxiety was further heightened by the hostility of their superego at their perverse successes. Moreover, since the lie is perverting communication between patient and analyst, the habitual liar is constantly undermining his belief in the analyst's words and destroying his essential tool, his own words (O'Shaughnessy 1983), for working through and changing.

The clash of basic perspective, the extreme anxieties of the patient which are behind this clash, the patient's actual intrusion into, and change of, the analyst's inner world to make the analyst act 'in' with him as a lying partner, and the patient's continual assault on words as truth bearers, all interfere with the analytic process. However, I think there is one thing in the liar's favour: since he knows he lies, he knows also there could be truthful object relations. Both M and L were deeply touched by, and appreciative of, the experience of being analytically understood on a level they had lacked and needed. This diminished their anxiety and their lying lessened. A liar will never stop lying entirely, since it is his basic defence and he will always resort to it. The extent to which a liar can change – a subject which needs a paper to itself – will vary with each patient's psychic constellation. If the fundamental level of the lie can be understood, that a liar lies in identification with a lying object, and, at the same time, if the patient's hostile lying, his different perspective in regard to truth and also his perverse excitement at using the lie to communicate with his analyst can be analysed in all their concreteness, I am sure at least of this: a genuine analytic process can be set in train.

Summary

At first glance a liar is an inauspicious patient for a psychoanalysis, a treatment based on truthfulness. Because it presents in speech, lying may seem a mature difficulty, but analysis reveals that it is primitive, linked to the habitual liar's doubts and anxieties about communication with primary objects which, from several causes, have become for him lying objects. As expected, lying makes for a series of problems which handicap the analytic process. Even so, the paper illustrates clinically the view that if the fundamental level of the lying that emerges in the analysis is addressed by understanding it as the liar's communication that he is a liar in identification with, and acutely anxious about, his lying object – in the transference the analyst – a genuine analytic process can be set in train.

Acknowledgements

A previous edition of this chapter was published in the *International Journal of Psychoanalysis*, 1990, 71: 187–195.

Note

1 A man says he is lying. Is what he says true or false? If true, it is false; if false, it is true.

10

ENCLAVES AND EXCURSIONS

I wish to call attention to two hazards for the analyst intrinsic to the conduct of psychoanalysis. I shall name these 'enclaves' and 'excursions'. In the course of clinical work an analyst may be at risk of so responding to his patient that he forms an enclave, or takes an excursion out of analysis, and thereby deforms the psychoanalytic situation so that the therapeutic process is interfered with or even halted.

I shall first illustrate what I mean by an 'enclave' by describing the case of Miss A. An attractive woman in her thirties, Miss A wanted an analysis because, though successful in her career, her relationships with men were impermanent and her biological time was running out. At the start of the analysis, she and I seemed well attuned. An intricate exchange took place between us about her feelings and thoughts about herself, the new analysis and her analyst. These explorations were, in their way, valid, though I was aware after a while of the lack of unconscious depth in Miss A's communications, and how very personal, even intimate, her generally appreciative relationship to me was, and that while she expressed also some aggression, it had no real punch – though my sense of Miss A was of someone with powerful feelings.

I found I did not know what Miss A's unconscious phantasies were, or who or what I was as a transference object, or what connexions there were between the analysis and her past history. I made some tentative attempts to speak of myself as a transference figure, e.g., I referred to myself as a 'mother-analyst' and I also tried to link events of the analysis with Miss A's history, by saying, e.g., that she felt now as she had when her brother was born. These interpretive attempts did not convince my patient and they led to no development. I stopped them as inauthentic and was driven back to interpreting in the denuded 'you–me, me–you' way.

Reflecting on this analytic situation, I saw that I had mistaken, just as Miss A herself does, over-closeness for closeness, and mistaken, too, a restrictive and restricting part object relationship for full contact between whole persons. My dissatisfaction with the 'you–me' interpretations that I had been making was now clearer. These interpretations were not part of a full interpretation, which in principle could eventually be completed, and involve internal objects, the interplay between unconscious phantasy and reality, and the reliving of the past. These interpretations were intrinsically denuded of such connexions. They were part of the opening interaction between Miss A and myself, which both constituted and facilitated the emergence of Miss A's characteristic relations to her objects.

However, had I continued to interpret in the same way, I would be in danger of making what I am proposing to call an 'enclave' with Miss A. More aware, instead of bypassing these problems with interpretations of myself as the mother-analyst or making at this point inevitably artificial parallels with my patient's history, I stayed with the uncomfortable fact that I could not see who I was in the transference, that there were no links available to Miss A's history, and that her and my outside life seemed not to exist. I tried to explore and analyse Miss A's limited and over-close relationship to me, and my own denuded functioning with her – an exploration which Miss A both resisted and wanted.

I think some degree of acting out by the analyst inevitably occurs as a relationship like Miss A's with her objects emerges in the analysis. Once the analyst is able to see it for what it is, however, the analyst's shift in internal perspective brings about a corresponding shift in the style and content of his interpretations, which helps to change the analytic situation from emergence of the patient's problems with unwitting enactment by the analyst, to emergence with potential for containment and transformation by the analyst.

With more awareness, I could help Miss A to see the true nature of her relationship to me. When there were relevant dynamic indications in her material, I spoke about her over-gentleness and over-closeness, her exclusion of other life, hers and mine, present and past, her control and impoverishment of me, and anxieties about herself and myself which seemed to lie behind her need for so limited and limiting a contact, which, as we now saw, stopped the analyst from disturbing Miss A and Miss A from disturbing the analyst. As time went on, Miss A found she was not entirely free of disturbance: she felt more anxious in sessions, and she was able to feel and express real disappointment and resentment.

Important unconscious phantasies emerged. She had a dream of homosexual seclusion, in which two figures, like a pair of erotised instruments, played and touched each other, so that there was no discord between them. Miss A's over-close, secluded relationship with me was thus revealed as a homosexual refuge, an erotised intimacy between similar, highly attuned instruments. Miss A was alarmed at the homosexuality, but very relieved by the interpretation of the mutual touching and playing in her dream, as the placation she felt was necessary between her and me for fear that, otherwise, we might become violent to each other.

For defensive and other purposes our patients need to make refuges of various sorts. We see at once that a delicate technique is called for from the analyst, a technique which both accepts a patient's need to make a refuge of the analytic situation, but, at the same time, analyses it. In this way the analyst averts the danger of so becoming what the patient requires that he deforms into an enclave what should be an analysis. Our patients feel, quite rightly, that the analysis of their refuge will change it, and bring exposure to what they fear they or their objects – in the analysis, the analyst – will not be able to bear.

As important as not enacting an enclave with a patient is not pushing and forcing a patient out of his refuge. Scrutiny of Miss A's dream tells us that within her refuge she has split off fears of seductive similarities between herself and her objects; the fact that she makes a refuge of symmetry and over-closeness tells us that she is even more afraid of differences and distance between herself and her objects. In sessions when acute anxiety threatened, Miss A worked to rebuild her refuge, subtly and powerfully controlling me to be over-close and to operate within its limits, and I had to struggle again with the difficult problem of how to interpret to minimise acting out with her.

At other times Miss A was ready to broaden her contact and to reach towards new areas. We know defensive formations change only with the strengthening of the ego, and that interpretations must not breach needed defences, but respect and acknowledge them. Nor, however, should interpretations lag behind what our patient's ego is ready for – notwithstanding the resistance we also know we must expect: to facilitate growth we must be timely with the new.

Interpretations made at the beginning of Miss A's analysis had two functions. They allowed for the emergence of her need for a refuge of homosexual seclusion, and the interpretations themselves gave her the restricted and undisturbing contact she required. However, had I remained unaware that Miss A was all the time drawing me into making denuded, undisturbing interpretations and had I continued interpreting in the same way, I would have gone on to provide Miss A, not with an analysis, but with an enclave.

According to Bion (1963), a psychoanalytic interpretation should have extension in the domains of sense, myth and passion. Miss A had needed me to make interpretations denuded of myth and passion, because of her fears of knowing her personal myths (her unconscious phantasies and world of inner objects), and of knowing her passions (her instincts and feelings). By keeping us over-close, denying our differences, obliterating the analyst's life beyond sessions and excluding also her own current life from her sessions (the counterpart in the analysis of how, in life, she dared not marry and have children) out of fear – all of which we gradually discovered – of the enviously depriving passions of her objects, Miss A constructed a denuded situation.

As a transference figure, I was an analyst who was no analyst, the denuded successor of a mother Miss A saw as no mother, and a father she saw as no father. She did not expect me to be willing to accept or to be able to stand her impulses, or to be capable of understanding her. Once I was more sensitive to the nature of the relationship Miss A really had made with me, I could try to analyse these unconscious presumptions and anxieties.

In sum: Miss A began her analysis by transferring into the analytic situation her restricted object relations. She communicated with words and non-verbal projections to help me to understand her and to control me to be the analyst with whom it would be possible for her to function. In accepting my transference role, I, to an extent, became the too well-attuned, over-close and denuded object she needed as a refuge from the fuller and freer object relations she unconsciously feared.

For me there was in this situation an inherent danger of being drawn too much into my patient's world and, in this way, letting the analysis actually become the symbolic equivalent of mildly erotised, symmetrical homosexual relations. I would then have made an enclave (as I propose to call it) of circumscribed contact, in which, though we continue trying to know about our interaction, our efforts stay within the restricted limits prescribed by the refuge. Until this situation is changed by the analysis of it, little therapeutic progress will be made.

An enclave deforms an essential feature of a psychoanalysis – its openness to possibilities of disturbance and the knowing of new areas. An excursion is different – not to do with limiting what is faced and known, but with totally evading emotional contact because of a terror of knowing.[1] Take a simple example of a threatened excursion familiar to every analyst: On the threshold of new emotional events, a patient quickly says: 'You mean, I can't stand separateness and dependence.' Though it is true he has problems with separateness and dependence, we all know how important it is not to discuss these at such a moment – that is, not to go on an excursion, but, instead, to draw the patient's attention to how, out of fear of the new, unknown emotional situation, he is trying to move himself and his analyst away to old and familiar ground.

Some patients besiege the analyst to go on excursions with them. I shall describe Mrs B who made repeated desperate attempts to move away from the incoherent experience of her sessions and take us instead on an excursion of pseudo-sense. A previous therapy had ended with Mrs B actually taking her therapist away on holiday with her. With me, there was a first 6 months of cautious enquiry, and then she let out into the analysis confused, ill, hyper-mobile areas of herself and her objects. These, for a long period, dominated the transference situation.

The pattern of her sessions was roughly as follows. In relation to some event in her life or the analysis, Mrs B would mention the names of a few persons and places of residence, and her feelings of anxiety or depression, moving rapidly from one item to the next. She seemed to some degree absent from what she was talking about. The identity of the people and places mentioned shifted in even a few sentences, so that her session was quickly cluttered and confusing. Though the same names and places tended to occur in session after session, it was nearly impossible for me to know who, in Mrs B's world, was who, what was internal or external, phantasy or reality.

I spoke to her about her anxious shifting, her need to communicate the flux and mental confusion she was suffering; her need, also, to keep out of contact with what she was talking about. Often after these initial interpretations I did not know what further to say, and I would fall silent and wait. Mrs B then became extremely anxious

137

and felt I was dismissing what she had said. Tension increased. She conveyed an urgency of demand for me to do something and I would review what she had told me and try to think, in relation to the atmosphere of that day, where her emotional centre might lie. Was she preoccupied with one of the people she had mentioned? Was it the state of the analyst? Or her own mind? Or the coming weekend? Etc., etc.

With a feeling of relief, I would select and pursue some theme. This brought relief to my patient also, but usually only temporarily. Mostly Mrs B would soon be on the move, away from the theme I was interpreting. I was then uncertain whether her movements away were because I was wrong, or were her rejection of my being right, or were less specific and expressed her pervasive mistrust of me. We often ended with a sense of nothing accomplished. After such a session, moreover, anxieties reverberated in me: I felt guilty of appalling work, I feared I had addressed the wrong issues, I feared Mrs B would not return (at the same time I knew she was not about to break off treatment). Then I shifted to another view: surely the session had not been so disastrous, had not this bit or that been in touch? And so on. That is, post-session, just like my patient, I had anxious, shifting states of mind.

After some months, I saw that this pattern was repeating itself and that there was no movement in the analysis. Contact with Mrs B was minimal and the minimal moments were not sustained. Nor was Mrs B contained; I and the sessions were too small for the scale of all her psychic operations. Many of her projections arrived in me, not in, but after, her sessions, when I endured the same anxious flux that tormented her. In sum, there was little contact and I, as analyst, was effecting no modification.

I began to think that the terrible tension which mounted at a certain point in Mrs B's sessions and which had driven me to find a theme to talk about was really latent panic, in me and in her, that I was unable to modify her mental state. Instead of going on what were really excursions into pseudo-sense with some 'theme', I started to focus on my failure to give her relief or effect any change. Mrs B was openly grateful when I understood this, even though it increased her anxiety, because while she felt understood, she at the same time experienced me as thrusting at her 'the fact' that analysis was useless for her.

Next, she had two dreams, followed by an important concrete proposal for mutual acting out. Her dreams, unlike many of her previous dreams, were significant in not being themselves a flight from psychic reality, but, on the contrary, a movement towards trying to know what was happening between us. In the first dream,

> Mrs B was in a city, trying to get into two churches, which were stuffed full with things of all sorts. In the dream, she was also always in the wrong place at the wrong time.

Her dream expresses her predicament. She is trying to reach and get into herself and me, represented by the two churches, but she is obstructed because both of us are full of clutter, as indeed we truly were. In the dream, Mrs B recognises how she is further frustrated by her own flights and absences of mind – she feels she is never in the right place at the right time in relation to herself or me. In her session Mrs B was well in touch with the validity of her dream and its insights.

A few days later she began her session by speaking with perplexity about her superior at work, after which she related a second insightful dream.

> She was in her garden. A lorry arrived to deliver a huge load of glass cloches. In the dream she felt total incomprehension, because the cloche frames were weak and their glass was cracked. She could not understand why cracked, broken cloches were dumped on her, since she already had plenty of cloches like that herself.

This dream portrays more images of herself and her objects. She sees her objects as being uncohesive (like a heap of cloches), and impervious (glassy), mad (cracked), and with feeble containment (the weak frames). They are like herself in these ways, and it is incomprehensible to her that they should unload on to her their psychic states, huge and identical to her own.

I first related Mrs B's dream to the superior at work she had mentioned at the start, about whom she felt such perplexity, and then I connected it to her view of myself and what I do to her when I talk to her. At first she was glad I was not glassed off about the meaning of her dream and thankful that I understood her incomprehension about the relations between heedless people, especially her panic about being projected into. Later a different idea took her over: I was dumping my cracked ideas of human relations on her. She lost her feeling of being understood and on succeeding days she was increasingly persecuted and anxious.

139

An intense session then took place during unusually lovely summer weather. Half-way through, with a mixture of uncertainty and despair in her voice, Mrs B said: 'What would you do if I stretched my hand backwards and touched you? If I said: "Come! Let's go and stand on the bridge and watch the trains go by. Let's get out of here into the sunshine".' Mrs B was in earnest. She was testing whether I would or would not accept her invitation to quit analysis. The session was intense as I talked about her fears that I was either in despair, or cracked and corrupt, and might really choose to enjoy the weather with her rather than work. I interpreted that her proposal expressed her despair, too, and, also her hope that we might not move out of analysis into the sunshine, but stay to try to know the meaning of her proposal.

Indeed, Mrs B's proposal was an aid to understanding, both in the session itself and also because I saw how invitations 'to go out into the sunshine' had occurred in subtler forms before, during those silences when tension rose and I felt an enormous pressure to do something with what Mrs B had told me. I realised even more clearly that when I found myself looking for an emotional centre in the content of Mrs B's material and chose a theme to talk about, though this relieved me and also gave Mrs B a little (usually temporary) relief, this was an excursion out of analysis into pseudo-normality away from the truth that she had no emotional centre, that her ego was in fragments, that she urgently needed its repair and feared I was unable to do it.

Now, at such times, I spoke about the atmosphere of mutual anxiety that we had come again to what felt like an impasse. I spoke about her fear that she and I were in the same uncohesive and cluttered state, and I addressed her panic that instead of healing her mind, I might make her worse by offloading my own state into her. I tried, of course, to analyse each of these areas in terms of the variable details of a given day.

Over a long period, Mrs B's level of anxiety dropped substantially; she ceased to be in continual flight from herself and her objects, nor was her mind in a state of perpetual confused flux; except for rare returns in special circumstances, post-session reverberations ceased in myself. Every analyst knows how stressful analysis is for such a patient, and how, though better, the patient continues to face formidable difficulties, as does, in a different way, the analyst.

To review the case of Mrs B: Mrs B was a patient whose chief defence – hyper-mobility to avoid contact – increased her distressed

140

state of flux and confusion. As psychic items were passed back and forth between us without being modified, she pressured me to move away from these incoherent object relations and make, instead, interpretations of pseudo-sense. In this way, Mrs B externalised into the analysis her mental world where there existed an underlying psychotic matrix that she and her objects were in terror of facing and kept avoiding. Once I realised that my resolution of crucial tensions between us by looking for normal themes in the content of her material was really an evasion of her panic that I was no help to her, and began to talk to Mrs B about this, a very important shift occurred which enabled her underlying psychotic condition to emerge in its full complexity. The real level of Mrs B's problems could then begin to be addressed.

It is obvious that had I continued, even in far less gross modes than 'going out into the sunshine', to succumb to her chronic pressure to go on joint flights, there could have been little advance in Mrs B's analysis. Her deep pathology would have been bypassed, not only by her, which was her right, but by me, which would have been my wrong. I would then have deformed an analysis into a series of excursions. Mrs B, you will recall, actually took a previous therapist away on holiday with her – a fact which shows the formidable force she exerts and which the analyst has to withstand.

Going on excursions with patients, or forming an enclave with them, are among the hazards intrinsic to the therapeutic endeavour. James Strachey, in his classic paper 'The nature of the therapeutic action of psycho-analysis' (Strachey 1934), called attention to how 'The analytic situation is all the time threatening to degenerate into a "real" situation.' He continued:

> But this actually means the opposite of what it appears to. It means that the patient is all the time on the brink of turning the real, external object (the analyst) into the archaic one; that is to say, he is on the brink of projecting his primitive introjected images onto him. In so far as the patient actually does this ... (the) analyst then ceases to possess the peculiar advantages derived from the analytic situation.
>
> (p. 284)

Strachey is referring to the very phenomenon which is the subject of this paper: the inbuilt risk of degeneration in a psychoanalytic situation. Strachey's notion of the patient 'trying to turn the analyst into an archaic object' is nowadays one aspect of accepted interactional clinical thinking, as over the years the psychoanalytic view of patient and analyst shifted away from exploring in isolation either the patient or the analyst and towards exploring in depth their interaction. Langs in *The Therapeutic Interaction* (Langs 1976) has summarised and discussed the writings of many analysts from different schools who have contributed to this overall change, and, though it is conceptualised variously, analysts over a wide spectrum continue to explore patient–analyst interaction.

This contemporary context is the general background of the present paper. Very relevant, for instance, is Schafer's (1959) important concept of generative empathy, and Ezriel's (1980) account of the tension the patient feels with the analyst between the required relationship and the avoided one. My more specific understanding of the way the patient interacts with the analyst is based on the concept of projective identification, as extended by Bion (1957, 1959) to encompass the defences and impulses described by Melanie Klein (1952a) and, also, his own discovery of projective identification as the earliest mode of communication. Spillius has a valuable discussion of projective identification in her introduction to the topic in *Melanie Klein Today* (Spillius 1988) while clinical studies of the patient's projective identifications into the analyst – both to communicate and to control him to act out a particular role – have been done most notably by Joseph (1989).

In my experience, because of the communicative and controlling functions of the patient's projective identifications, some acting out by the analyst inevitably occurs. Sandler (1976), with a different theory, has also pointed out how enactment by the analyst occurs as part of emergence in the transference situation of the patient's unconscious primary object relations. Carpy (1989) draws attention, with a different emphasis, to the importance for the patient of the analyst's partial acting out.

If the analysis is not to degenerate, it is vital that such partial acting out by the analyst is recognised, contained and analysed. These contentions disagree both with the view that if only the analyst were more quickly more aware he could entirely avoid acting out with his patient, and also with the view that acting out beyond the very limited and partial amount necessary for emergence, and to accommodate to what the patient can bear, can be beneficial. My two cases, plus some conceptual considerations, are offered as evidence of the existence of an inbuilt risk, with certain patients, of the analyst deforming the analysis into some type of enclave or excursion which will hinder or halt therapeutic progress, such risks being all the more insidious because some limited, partial acting out with the patient can play a valuable part in revealing what the transference relationship is. As Segal (1987) remarks: 'The same factors which are the crux of a potentially therapeutic situation also have a potential for an anti-therapeutic one.'

In addition to work during sessions, an analyst needs time to reflect on the overall interaction between himself and his patient, to consider the question of change and repetition, to think about his feelings for and his ways of behaving with and speaking to his patient. Also whether he and his patient are keeping out disturbances, and whether they tend to move away from, rather than towards, 'trying to know'. Such reflection can help the analyst to be more aware of the overall transference situation and to work with less acting out and more insight.

Miss A and Mrs B each illustrate one type of enclave and excursion. With Miss A, I was at risk of enacting the analytic equivalent of a homosexual enclave. With other patients, there might, for example, be the risk of turning the analysis into an enclave of mutual idealisation, or libidinised despair, or concealed psychotic phantasy. There are many sorts of enclaves and excursions and patients are not necessarily exclusively of one type or the other.

For excursions, I chose the case of Mrs B as an extreme and therefore vivid illustration. With her I was always at risk of evading her severe difficulties by moving off into pseudo-coherence and normality. With a less ill patient the risk of excursions occurs not continually but at times of special anxiety, when the patient may try to induce the analyst to foreclose with a pat interpretation, or give practical guidance or have an intellectual discussion; or the patient may unconsciously manoeuvre the analyst into moralising, disciplining or reassuring him, or into speculating about (as opposed to true analytic reconstruction of) his past. All of these exemplify excursions away from some point of analytic urgency in the session.

Before concluding I wish to discuss one seemingly interminable dispute: the debate about transference versus extra-transference interpretations. Naturally, but I think mistakenly, anxiety about

143

analysis being deformed into an enclave has fastened exclusively onto the use of transference interpretations; similarly, anxiety about analysis degenerating into a series of excursions has fastened exclusively onto the use of extra-transference interpretations. The thesis of this paper is that both hazards are intrinsic to the conduct of an analysis with patients like Miss A and Mrs B, irrespective of any particular analytic approach.

Many authors – for example recently Stewart (1990), but more extensively Blum (1983b) – have written of their concern that interpreting solely in the transference turns an analysis into an over-close enclave. Their presumption is that by focusing on what has sometimes been called the 'here and now', the analyst degenerates into a type of 'you–me, me–you' interpreting, which retreats from its proper analytic function and neglects events, even urgent events, in the patient's current life, and also ignores the patient's history, so that analysis becomes the patient's only life – really a retreat from life.

However, as illustrated by the case of Miss A, an over-close refuge between patient and analyst occurred, not because of my particular technique, but because it was the necessary externalisation in the transference of her characteristic relations with her objects. Had a different approach been used – say, of encouraging Miss A to recall and to recount childhood memories – she would unconsciously have attuned herself to that analyst, and controlled that analyst to interpret her history in a way that did not disturb her. She would again have established a refuge of restricted contact, homosexual in nature, this time in relation to her past.

This is not to say there could not be a poor interpretive technique which fosters what Blum calls 'a *folie-à-deux*' and what I call 'an enclave'. Indeed, one of my chief points is exactly that. If the analyst remains unaware of the nature of the archaic relationship his patient draws him into, and continues to enact it and not analyse it, there will, indeed, be a *folie-à-deux*. As remarked above, in a parallel way, the fear of going on excursions has historically attached itself exclusively to the technique of extra-transference interpretations, whereas, in fact, this hazard is intrinsic to all analytic situations in which a patient is in terror of knowing and desperate to take flight from contact.

Whatever our different psychoanalytic techniques, we share a concern not to deform an analysis into an enclave or a series of excursions. In practice it is often on these grounds that we reject one way of interpreting and choose another. When we discuss different ways of talking to our patients, I think it more useful, rather than asking whether an interpretation is a transference or extra-transference interpretation, to explore the interaction between patient and analyst, so as to see the nature of their contact. We should ask, importantly, whether the analyst's technique wards off rather than permits the entry of what is new and disturbing, and whether the type of movement being made by patient and analyst is towards or away from 'trying to know'. This, I think, is more in keeping with our contemporary interactional perspective.

A last word. Enclaves and excursions differ in a fundamental way. A patient who makes an enclave feels there is some way he can relate to an object – provided he finds an already suitable object or reshapes an object to fit what he requires to keep out aspects which threaten him with too much anxiety. Such patients find some way of making contact with their analyst. The patient who goes on excursions is different. He believes no manageable contact is possible with his object and the level of his anxiety is horrendous. Contact must be evaded, a new situation constructed, which characteristically in its turn becomes untenable. These patients are hyper-active, their talk proliferates, as, typically, do their dream images.

Mrs B is an example of a patient threatened with anxiety so acute she is all the time near to panic. Hers is a psychotic matrix, i.e., a matrix of object relations in which she believes no amelioration is possible. In analysis she is impelled to perpetual flights from herself and her analyst. Even in its less severe manifestations, a patient's impulse to pull the analyst on a joint flight away from attempts 'to try to know' signals terror about the state of the self, or the analyst, or both, which means that potential contact is very dangerous indeed.

Summary

This paper describes and names as 'enclaves' and 'excursions' two deteriorations of the psychoanalytic situation, which occur when an analyst exceeds the limited, partial acting out inevitable in clinical work. Under pressure from his patient an analyst may unwittingly turn the analysis into a refuge from disturbance, i.e., an enclave. If he succumbs to pressures to move away from, instead of towards, knowing what is psychically urgent, an analyst may turn the analysis into a series of flights, i.e., an excursion. Unrecognised, these deformations interfere with or even halt the therapeutic process, which requires that the analyst find a way of working which accommodates both the patient's communication of, and need for, a refuge or flight with the analyst, while at the same time analysing it.

Acknowledgements

A previous edition of this chapter was published in the *International Journal of Psychoanalysis*, 1992, 73: 603–614.

Note

1   Balint (1959) distinguished two defensive character types, the ochnophil who clings to his objects, and the philobat who avoids them. Although our distinctions are not quite congruent, Balint's ochnophil is similar to the patient with whom the analyst risks making an enclave, and his philobat is like the patient with whom there is a risk of turning the analysis into a series of excursions.

PSYCHOSIS: NOT THINKING IN A
BIZARRE WORLD

Bion often mentioned his indebtedness to Freud and Klein for the foundations of psychoanalytic thinking on psychosis. As an introduction to the exposition of Bion, I shall give the briefest of sketches of them both. Central to Freud's view of how psychosis differs from neurosis, and how neurosis in its turn differs from more normal states, is the ego's relation to reality. In its normal condition the ego is largely governed by what Freud called the 'reality principle', reality, 'internal and external, being made known to the ego by the senses, by consciousness and by thinking'. In Freud's words:

> one of the features which differentiate a neurosis from a psychosis [is] the fact that in a neurosis the ego, in its dependence on reality, suppresses a piece of the id (of instinctual life), whereas in a psychosis, this same ego, in the service of the id, withdraws from a piece of reality.
>
> (Freud 1924b: 183)

That is, in neurosis the relation to reality is retained at the cost of instinctual repression, while in psychosis the relation to reality is lost. The psychotic ego has a need to find some substitute for the reality it has lost – for example, in a delusion – which Freud sees as an attempt at cure. Moreover, as a result of his researches, Freud also became convinced of a proclivity for psychosis in us all. He writes:

> From the very beginning, when life takes us under its strict discipline, a resistance stirs within us against the relentlessness

and monotony of the laws of thought and against the demands of reality-testing. Reason becomes the enemy which withholds from us so many possibilities of pleasure.

(Freud 1933a: 33)

The loss of reality, delusional attempts at cure, and intrinsic hatred of thought and reality are Freud's main ideas.

Klein approaches psychosis via anxiety. It is her view that our earliest anxieties are psychotic in content. The normal development of infants, she writes, 'can be regarded as a combination of processes by which anxieties of a psychotic nature are bound, worked through and modified' (Klein 1952a: 81).

However, in an abnormal infant the processes of binding, working through, and modifying do not take place, and the result is that primitive anxieties and terrifying figures remain unmodified and threaten to dominate the psyche of the infant and adult psychotic, so that the ego is driven to an excessive use of the otherwise normal defences of splitting and projective identification.

All these fundamental notions of Freud and Klein enter into Bion's theories: our hatred of reality and thinking, the ego's loss of reality in psychosis, its dominance by unmodified primitive anxieties, its use of the defences of splitting and projective identification, and its desperate search for cure. Bion put these discoveries and ideas in a different framework, a much more extreme version of the difference between psychosis and neurosis which had so struck Freud. According to Bion, in psychosis there is a difference in the entire condition of the mind and a difference also between the very constitution of what for the psychotic is the world.

Bion opens his paper 'The differentiation of the psychotic from the non-psychotic personalities' (Bion 1957) with this statement:

The differentiation of the psychotic from the non-psychotic personalities depends on a minute splitting of all that part of the personality that is concerned with awareness of internal and external reality, and the expulsion of these fragments so that they enter into or engulf their objects.

(Bion 1957: 43)

According to Bion, the psychotic personality has its origin in the fragmentation followed by the expulsion of the *means* by which the

148

ego knows reality; that is, the fragmentation and expulsion of the senses, consciousness, and thinking. This is the hinge of the difference. What could bring about such an eradication of the very aspect of the mind that is central to the institution of what Freud called 'the reality principle'? Bion thinks there are two preconditions for the psyche to institute psychotic functioning: first, a highly adverse inborn disposition, and, second, its interaction with an adverse environment.

Such an adverse disposition will have the following features: a preponderance of destructive impulses, a never-decided conflict between the life and death instincts, anxiety at a horrific level so that, in Bion's words, 'there is a dread of imminent annihilation' (Bion 1957), plus a total intolerance of frustration. All these features are interrelated. At the outset of life frustration is concretely experienced as bad objects present. An infant with the endowment described will have bad objects of a terrifying order which raise anxiety to an horrific level for an embryonic personality which has anyway problems of toleration. The predicament of such an infant is very different from an infant with a better inborn disposition who faces and knows his frustrations and uses primitive precursors of thinking to modify them; for example, cries for his mother until she comes. The less fortunate infant, instead of facing his situation, evades it, in extreme cases completely. I have in mind an infant who lay in his pram in the garden from eight o'clock in the morning to late afternoon, not crying but gazing at the leaves of the trees. In his case a departure from functioning according to the reality principle has already set in. Instead of beginning to develop a mind for thinking, it is likely that such a psyche has become an apparatus for ridding itself of bad objects. It does this by the minute fragmentation and projection of incipient thoughts, sensations, and also the sense organs which threaten to bring awareness of internal or external reality. The infant in my example perhaps used his eyes as channels for projecting the unwanted fragments of his personality into external objects. On this model we can understand how the infant under the trees is free of hunger and terror because his psyche is in fragments in the leaves.

At this point a natural question arises: Why does his mother ignore him all day? Bion thinks that such an infant's situation is worsened by a mother who allows no ingress to projections. The infant experiences her refusal to take in his projections as hostile defensiveness, and will, Bion thinks, assail her with increasing hostility and frequency until in

149

the end the meaning has been taken out of his projections. I believe a process of this sort was demonstrated to me by a psychotic adolescent boy who brought a boomerang to his session. He threw it, but it never returned to him and seemed to land nowhere in particular. He threw it ever more violently, with increasing despair, and I saw that the shape of the boomerang matched exactly the set of his mouth. The boomerang was a mouth, a cry which landed nowhere and brought him no return; thus he acted out his feeling that there was no object to understand and respond to his cry. Such an object, unavailable to receive projections thrown out by the infant, will be experienced as an additional external source of destruction of communication and awareness. My surmise is that such a mutually hostile and despairing situation had arisen between the infant who lay all day under the trees and his mother – a situation which the infant survived by instituting a psychotic state of mindlessness. It should be added that a constructive interchange even between a mother who accepts projections and an infant with a highly adverse endowment is intrinsically nearly impossible because all frustration is intolerable to her infant. Only her continuous presence will satisfy him, and in addition she will have to tolerate projections of an abnormal and violent kind.

However, were such an infant to have an object capable of receiving these projections and retaining what Bion called 'a balanced outlook', his situation would be to an extent ameliorated, although it will still be serious since the psychotic infant is then likely to be, in Bion's words, 'overwhelmed with hatred and envy of the mother's ability to retain a comfortable state of mind although experiencing the infant's feelings' (Bion 1959: 105). The infant's envy then distorts her capacity for receiving projections into a greedy devouring of his psyche, and he misrepresents her balanced outlook as indifference.

So far I have outlined Bion's hypothesis of a pathological matrix of adverse endowment with adverse nurture, which leads to the forming of a psychotic personality at the outset of life. From then on there will be an ever-widening divergence between the psychotic and the non-psychotic parts of his personality, and Bion thinks that we will not understand psychosis until we recognise this. In that part of the personality which is psychotic (which to a greater or lesser degree is in everybody) the mind is neither thinking nor perceiving. Through the processes described the psyche has been altered. The objects it now desires and which it will experience as good are those which assist the process of expulsion. Bion sums it up:

The model I propose for this development is a psyche that operates on the principle that evacuation of a bad breast is synonymous with obtaining sustenance from a good breast. The end result is that all thoughts are treated as if they were indistinguishable from bad internal objects; the appropriate machinery is felt to be, not an apparatus for thinking the thoughts but an apparatus for ridding the psyche of accumulations of bad internal objects.

(Bion 1962b: 112)

Once the psyche is no longer a thinking, perceiving mind, it uses projective identification not only excessively, which it does, but also differently. Instead of being used for normal communications with objects, as when a normal infant cries to and for its mother, projections are used to evacuate and to eradicate the awareness of the self and the object. They are loaded with enormous hostility; they are weapons – boomerangs which destroy the foundations for intuitive knowledge of the self and object. In such a psyche, impressions from within or without cannot be converted into the type of elements normally in the mind, which can then be repressed, or be dream-thoughts, or be conscious, or unconscious, and allow a state of being awake and being asleep. In the non-psychotic part of the personality, perceptions, a delusion, a dream, or a phantasy, are what they are partly through contrast with one another. In psychosis these mental differentiations do not form and all elements have equal value. All are the same and one is as real or unreal as another. Nor is there depth to the mind. Items are spread out, flat, or in some other shape. Of course, a psychotic patient has been taught and he knows words like 'being awake', 'delusion', but in so far as the use emanates from his psychotic self, they refer to phenomena which are different from the normal.

The world in which the psychotic exists has also departed from the ordinary. It is more bizarre even than the primitive world of part-objects full of projections, which Melanie Klein described as the universe of the normal paranoid-schizoid position. The difference is due to the sadistic splitting attacks on eyes, ears, indeed on all organs of awareness, and the hatred with which the fragments are projected, in Bion's phrase,

to penetrate or invest their object. In the patient's phantasy the expelled parts of ego lead an independent and uncontrolled existence, either contained by or containing the external objects;

151

they continue to exercise their function as if the ordeal to which they have been subjected had served only to increase their number and provoke their hostility to the psyche which ejected them. In consequence the patient feels himself to be surrounded by bizarre objects.

(Bion 1957: 268)

Bion gives examples:

If the piece of personality is concerned with sight, the gramophone when played is felt to be watching the patient; if with hearing, then the gramophone when played is felt to be listening to the patient. The object, angered by being engulfed, swells up, so to speak, and suffuses and controls the piece of personality that engulfs it: to that extent the particle of personality has become a thing.

(Bion 1957: 268)

And he concludes: 'The consequences for the patient are now that he moves, not in a world of dreams, but in a world of objects which are ordinarily the furniture of dreams' (Bion 1957: 269).

Moreover, because frustration is intolerable and all frustration involves waiting in time and finding in space, space and time too are destroyed and do not exist. In such a universe it is always now, and self and object become increasingly bizarrely confused. The psychotic feels that his ego and his object are incurable, and that his psychotic state of mind is a prison from which he has no means of escape.

At this point I would like to offer an illustration of psychotic functioning by describing a few events in the analysis of a 5-year-old boy, Matthew. I told him that there was a Whit Monday coming and there would be no session on that Monday. Matthew arrived for a following session with a black and red bruised eye, a most shocking sight. He desperately needed comfort but could only scream, cough, and spit.

The next day began with an improbable attempt at seduction. He pushed down his trousers, showed me his bottom for a moment, confusedly calling it 'my wet po po' with a gesture of 'You like this.' Then he was as the day before, crying, screaming, shouting for his mother, coughing, and spitting. In among his screams I heard the word 'five'. I said the four days next week were a shocking hurt to him. Matthew cut in shouting and crying, 'Not four, three times,

152

five, not seven, not four, seven'. He screamed even more piercingly. I thought the whole house and all the neighbours must be hearing him. His distress was enormous, or, rather, my feeling of his distress and also my disgrace with the neighbours were enormous. At one moment Matthew screamed and said, 'I am going to come right near you and make you stop, stop, stop talking!', and he pressed himself on me. I made one or two interpretations which just made him scream more. But then, when I interpreted that with his screams he felt he was getting bad tearing pieces out of himself and into me, there was a dramatic change. He was quiet. He became abstracted, twiddled his hair in his fingers, and touched various places on his head. He held his fingers near to his face and gazed at them minutely and fixedly for a long while. He then looked out of the window at the road below and said in a shaky but ordinary, very depressed little voice, 'Cars. A brown car, a blue car, a white car, a car with a sunroof. Not all cars have sunroofs', as if chatting to me. He altered again. He began repeating, 'Twit to whoo, twit to whoo'. I questioned him and he made a frame round each eye with his fingers and peered through it. He was still saying 'Twit to whoo' which slowly became 'Two it too, do it to, do it, do it, do it, do it', insistently and excitedly. He clutched his penis. I said that he felt that his eyes were in an owl, the night bird, seeing sex on Whit Monday and he couldn't bear waiting to see it and wanted sex to happen now. Matthew agreed, very excited. Then he asked me anxiously, 'Is there more time?' He took several pencils out of his box and said, now in a lady's anxious voice, 'Oh, my nerves, my nerves'. He tried to keep the pencils bound in one bundle by trying them round with a bit of string to stop them falling apart. I said that he was trying to help himself, me, and his mother, all of us, he felt, ladies falling to pieces. He said, 'My pencils are in a mirror box at home.' It was almost the session's end. 'I'm going to make yellow butter. I must have a yellow bowl the same colour as the butter.' He rapidly found paints, yellow bowl and water, and stirred a yellow mixture quickly very smooth. He was shaky, but in control of himself.

Matthew's departure from the normal is tragically evident. The cancelled session on Whit Monday is completely intolerable to him. He cannot and will not bear it. The no-session is experienced by him concretely as sexual intercourse which is a physical blow to his eye. There is no time – it is not next week, but now. Nor is there space – his eyes, projected in phantasy into a night owl, are at the sex. Eyes

153

out of his head, his mind feels like a head pierced by tearing pieces, and then, when relieved, is empty and still.

Matthew is full of hatred. After I said four days were a shock to him, he rages at the 'four'. 'Not four, three times. Five, not seven. Not four, seven', he screams. His greedy demand is for seven, for no frustration at all. He and his objects are smashed to pieces. He said, you remember, 'I am going to come right near you and make you stop, stop, stop talking!' His states are split, without links, merely successive, whether his head is tormented, or he is the owl, the anguished lady, or looking through the window at the cars. All had to him the same reality or unreality. There are bizarre formations, the most striking being his damaged eyes in the owl and the Whit Monday in the twit-to-whoo call. He is confused with all his objects. He is the owl, he is the anguished lady, even his bottom is mixed up with a po po, his word for his chamber pot.

As to the therapeutic interaction, I felt shattered by his screams, ruined in the eyes or ears of the household or neighbours, wrong in my approach to him, and, if right momentarily, soon wiped out, exactly, I suspect, as his mother felt. It is significant that the only interpretation which helped Matthew was the one about screaming piercing pieces out of himself into me. That is, only when I had experienced emotionally his enormous persecution and could verbalise that he was trying to evacuate bad fragments from his head, was I, for him, a good object. He was then quiet and still for a short time and could look out at the ordinary world, shaky, depressed, but with normal, if remote, perception of differences restored to him. He saw the different colours and noticed that not all cars have sunroofs.

However, his projective identification with a perceptive object is not retained. Before he goes, hatred and intolerance of separateness supervene. He annihilates colour differences, the perception of which had come at the only moment when he felt I understood him. He makes 'yellow butter', pulverising any remaining gritty fragments: all is the same, no object relation is left.

The difficulty of working with Matthew is evident. Only one interpretation reached and changed him. I think, though some may disagree with this, that it is important to get to where the projected parts of his personality are located – for example, to where the owl is, seeing sex – to be with him, even if he misunderstands me in this instance as my being excited and therefore sexually stimulating to him. I think, or I hope, that he will even so feel a little less isolated.

Mostly, however, I have to say that his psychotic process proliferates too fast for even this minimal contact to remain.

I find Bion's theories of enormous help in the struggle to find a way of working with a patient like Matthew. Much of such an analysis remains obscure and very uncertain in all ways. Before I discuss the question of the analytic treatment of psychosis, I want to quote Bion's description of a malignant figure which he thinks is characteristically resident in the inner world of the psychotic and which affects the therapeutic outcome. We return to the adverse matrix of mother and child, the matrix too, I think, for Matthew and his mother. Bion writes:

> If the mother cannot tolerate … projections the infant is reduced to continued projective identification carried out with increasing force and frequency. The increased force seems to denude the projection of a penumbra of meaning. Re-introjection is effected with similar force and frequency. Deducing the patient's feelings from his behaviour in the consulting room and using the deductions to form a model, the infant of my model does not behave in a way that I ordinarily expect of an adult who is thinking. It behaves as if it felt that an internal object has been built up but has the characteristics of a greedy vagina-like 'breast' that strips of its goodness all that the infant receives or gives leaving only degenerate objects. This internal object starves its host of all understanding that is made available. In analysis such a patient seems unable to gain from his environment and therefore from his analysis.
>
> (Bion 1962b: 115)

The prospects for treatment, given all this, cannot be propitious, and yet in Bion's view, and that of many analysts, psychoanalytic treatment is relevant and possible. Anyone who has tried to work with a psychotic personality knows the anxiety and invasiveness which must be expected and carried by the therapist. We can all be fortified by Bion's opinion that these are not necessarily due to our bad work, but are inescapable if we are doing our work, as is the obscurity of many of the patient's communications and the amount of incomprehension we have to try to tolerate. A psychotic patient is instantly in a state of projective identification with his therapist and maintains this state tenaciously. He forms what Herbert Rosenfeld calls a 'transference psychosis' (Rosenfeld 1954: 117). Rosenfeld, of

155

course, is the other psychoanalyst who developed the work of Klein to advance greatly our understanding of psychotic states, but in this chapter I focus on features of the therapeutic process which can be understood more directly through Bion's work.

During treatment the patient's projections into the therapist, the room, and elsewhere construct a bizarre environment which, from fear and hostility, he tries to keep secret. He relies on his therapist to exercise the functions he has ejected and is still devoted to destroying. Under the load of anxiety and the barrage of splintered hostile projections, the therapist has to find a way of working, while meeting constantly the kind of ego-destructive internal object in the patient Bion described. The analyst or therapist also has to remember that, as a transference object, from the patient's point of view he is most of the time part of some split or bizarre formation. Also manifest in the transference is the patient's desperate need to get relief, which I think we saw with Matthew, and his hope of a cure. The problems which face him are vast: his ego and his internal objects are splintered and projected into various objects and lie in confusion in the psychic, organic, and physical world. Given his present condition and his adverse disposition, the therapeutic process will inevitably, I think, be far more distressing for him than for a more normal patient.

Bion points out that the psychotic patient who is able to attend for therapy will have also a non-psychotic personality, and this is, for us, a gain. He contends that, provided we recognise and analyse the abnormal functioning of the psychotic personality when it is operative, something worthy of the name of progress can take place. Though again, and I think that this is one of his most important contentions, such progress differs from the progress of the more usual patient. He describes it in the following way. If the patient's projections are received and understood, he may begin to feel less isolated and persecuted and his splitting may lessen. This may lead to an attempt to think, which is an essential part of the repair of his ego. This involves permitting entry to perceptions and projected bits, a process often experienced as an assault: the patient feels struck in the eye, or jabbed elsewhere, twitches, or may get a headache. Return of some awareness brings a new condition internally and externally. Internally, among other figures, there is his ego-destructive superego, more menacing now because internal and also because less splintered and more whole. Externally the patient now faces his neurotic conflict, and, although he feels more human and more real,

156

his inordinate superego anxiety and his intolerable conflicts with his objects will again drive him to free himself from psychic reality by splitting and projecting all means of awareness. That again will bring anxieties about insanity, a state which he will try to evade and to conceal. Then he will be driven once more to attempt to repair his ego, and return to reality and neurosis. Such is Bion's illuminating description of a forward movement to an aberrant depressive position which then impels retreat to the aberrant paranoid–schizoid position characteristic of the psychotic person. Bion thinks that such shifting back and forth can gradually lead to the patient sustaining a more human contact with whole objects and an increased ability to think and use verbal thought in place of action and projective identification. He stresses that the foundation of any improvement is the patient's own recognition of his psychosis: once he gains insight into the fact that he is ill he may begin to get well.

Although the difference between psychotic and non-psychotic functioning is so total, it can in practice be difficult to detect. I would like to illustrate this difficulty by describing another patient, Mrs L, whose material shows how easy it is to mistake psychotic functioning for normal.

Mrs L is a patient who has struggled with a large, often dominant, psychotic area in her personality. For the past few weeks she had been feeling less confused and frightened and less incapacitated. She has had no occupation for a long time, and once or twice recently she wondered during her sessions what she could think of doing now. She also told me that because she was feeling better her husband was going away for a fortnight. She feared this, thought it cruel, but felt she should accept it because he had stayed with her during the period when she was unable to be alone. I want to describe some events in a recent Friday session, the day after her husband left.

Mrs L arrived bleak, low in self-esteem, and very anxious. She spoke for a while, and when I interpreted that she felt very anxious because of a weekend with no sessions, alone in her house, a prey to strange figures and thoughts, she said, much moved, 'Of course'. Then she referred to various lectures she had been to in the past week. After that Mrs L said, 'I attended a lecture at the National Gallery this morning. I even asked a question.' She added doubtfully, 'It seemed all right. The question was a simple one, although the lecturer didn't know the answer. He thought it was thirteenth century, but he was at least one hundred years out.' Then very contemptuously: 'Anyone

157

with any general knowledge should know that! How can someone lecture and know so little? The lecturer had a speech defect. I, of course, have never had any of these little sinecures like teaching at the National Gallery. I have no need financially, of course, though I do have wide knowledge.'

By this time Mrs L was sounding 'big', and my thoughts were something like this: from past sessions I knew she thought I had defects both of accent and enunciation. She had also told me recently that it was evident that I knew nothing of literature, history, or the arts generally. Because of her repeated mention of lectures I found myself wondering if she had perhaps seen a poster advertising a lecture I was to give, and was feeling that if I could, surely she could be a lecturer and an analyst. Such were my thoughts, and at the same time I felt very unsure about what to make of Mrs L's communications. I was anxious, and I felt I must try to understand them, and must not just ignore them. So I said, 'You feel big in comparison to me who seems small, and as I, with my defects, am an analyst who has patients and gives talks, you feel you could.' Mrs L said: 'I agree with you about the big and the small. I am very big compared to you.' She spoke in a tone of stating an evident fact. Then, in a most pleased voice, as if I had showered her with compliments, she said, 'I think I could do it! But really I wouldn't like to be an analyst.' She continued in the manner of one refusing a gratifying invitation. I said, 'You heard me as inviting you to be an analyst, rather than that I was speaking of your feelings and phantasies.' Mrs L answered me, totally bewildered, 'But I don't have feelings and phantasies.' She repeated angrily, 'I don't have phantasies,' and then, very anxious, she withdrew from me and spoke coldly of entirely other things.

Quite evidently I had misunderstood and distressed my patient. She is bewildered, angry, cold, frightened, and she has to correct me. She tells me that she does not have phantasies. What then does she have? And how have I gone wrong? When she said, 'I don't have phantasies', what does she mean? I think she means what she said. Phantasies imply a distinction between real and unreal, between a wish and its fulfilment. She knows she is not functioning in that ordinary mode at that moment. Really, she had already given an indication of this when she agreed with me that she was big and I was small, and spoke as if these sizes were fact. I think here we capture a glimpse of the occurrence of the process Bion calls 'transformation in hallucinosis' (Bion 1965: 137–46).

The situation Mrs L dreads of being alone on the weekend and being unable to hold on to her mental improvement is already occurring in the session. She is reverting to abnormal modes of functioning as psychotic panic threatens. As a defence against the panic she starts to expand and to use her sense organs as apertures through which to squeeze, diminish, and then evacuate persecuting feelings and objects. In the end Mrs L has 'made' her persecutor into a small object outside of herself, which is then the analyst. This process of hallucinosis makes my smallness and her bigness a fact in her bizarre world.

Mrs L belongs to a particular group of patients described by Bion who cannot bear the dominance of the reality principle, but who do not completely evade frustration either. He thinks such a patient finds a resort in omniscience. Mrs L feels she has wide knowledge and moral superiority – she would not treat a patient the way I do. In this condition, she wants objects primarily for purposes of projective identification, that is, to be in, in order to cure herself, and when I said that she, not me, should be the analyst, she heard me as issuing an invitation, inviting her into me. My saying afterwards that this was only her phantasy was from her point of view a sudden horrifying ejection. She felt sadistically played with, seduced in and treacherously thrown out. For her psychotic self I think that it is even worse. Being an analyst was not a phantasy, as she said, it was a delusion which gave her at that moment an identity. It contained and repaired her dispersing personality, so that when I said it was her phantasy, I think she felt I was smashing bits of her repaired ego.

Now, why did I blunder so? One thing I did wrong was to attend to her words only and ignore what Mrs L had transmitted by projective identification. Had I instead given the priority to her projective identification, the whole situation would have looked rather different. My counter-transference, you will remember, was that I felt anxious and uncertain of what it all meant, did not know what to say, yet felt that I must try to make something of it. I think Mrs L was communicating exactly this: that she must try to manage, even though she feels anxious and very uncertain that mentally she will stay well enough. She feels she must try very hard. And she is trying hard. She managed to go to a lecture that morning, and she even asked a question. She was moved, you will remember, at the beginning of the session, when I understood her dread of the weekend, and had I continued with this theme I might have kept contact with her, but as it was I lost her. She very much wanted to

159

negotiate the weekend without analysis as an ordinary patient would, but she feared that waiting for Monday was going to be intolerable. Internally, her conception of me as benign is disappearing: I am seen as defective because I know her needs and dreads and yet persist in leaving her. Thus accused, I am destroyed as a good object, as I suspect her husband is too. Thus internally she is alone with persecutors. As she talks, Mrs L only partially uses verbal thought. She also uses words to disperse her ego and to escape contact with objects and feelings too persecuting and too full of dread to be borne. This mixture of psychotic and normal is part of what made it difficult for me. When I failed to understand and analyse any of this, I was actually a defective analyst.

The blunders were mine, but one further factor of great importance was that Mrs L meant me to blunder. She was speaking to communicate and disperse anxiety, and simultaneously speaking with great, if very quiet, hatred, to mislead. She used our shared knowledge of what had transpired previously about her longing to work, about my defective accent and so on, to control my attention. She led me away from the acute anxiety roused by her ego–destructive superego saying to her that she is no better, that she is incurable, that she will not manage the weekend. Perhaps too I found it easier to attend to her neurotic conflicts about working than to face how fragile her ego still is, and how, under pressure, psychotic functioning becomes dominant.

To return to the session: the situation was that Mrs L had withdrawn from an analyst who was out of contact with her, a defective and highly persecuting object, and I had to try to work from there. However, in my own time afterwards, what Bion has called the analyst's later 'reverie', I tried to reflect on how and what had gone wrong, much as I have done here. This case of Mrs L illustrates some of the characteristic shifts and extreme conflicts and anxieties which face a patient, and the difficulties which confront and confuse an analyst, when a patient with a psychosis is making progress.

Bion's new conceptions of psychosis have made it more possible, I think, to work with patients like Mrs L, and even Matthew, who is more ill than Mrs L. In brief, Bion's theory is that in psychotic states there is overall divergence from the normal due both to what the mind has lost – the power of thinking, the capacity for awareness, sense organs for perceptions, mental depth and contrast – and to what the mind has become – fragmented, its elements concrete and without variety, its sense organs become apertures, its chief functions

160

splitting and evacuating of bad fragments, an abnormal projective process which makes the world bizarre.

These are Bion's ideas. For me they are that truly rare thing – new scientific ideas. They have thrown light on the obscure territory of psychosis, and they will, I feel sure, illuminate it still further in the future.

Acknowledgements

A previous edition of this chapter was published in R. Anderson (ed.), *Clinical Lectures on Klein and Bion*, 1992, London: Tavistock/ Routledge, pp. 89–101.

WHAT IS A CLINICAL FACT?

Abstract

As a preliminary to the question, 'What is a clinical fact?', the author asks the wider question, 'What is a fact?', answering that facts are double in aspect: they both say how the world is, and they also depend on our species, our language, theory, etc. A claim of fact in any empirical discipline – in the natural sciences or in human studies with their different methods – is a truth claim which is not infallible or unique to the fact, and also a claim that must offer itself for verification. Using the clinical record of three sessions, she then tries to answer the question, 'What is a clinical fact?', offering the starting formulation that clinical facts, under the unusual conditions of an analytic hour which give an analyst access to a patient's inner world, manifest themselves in the form of immediate psychological realities between patient and analyst. On the way, the author discusses the analyst's anxieties about making a claim of clinical fact; further striking features emerge about clinical facts in the three sessions, and some unsolved problems, i.e., the variety of analytic theories, subjectivity and objectivity, are noted. Even while they bear the perplexities of their problems, clinical facts are of great significance to the study of the mind. They extend the domain of psychology to the area of the mind's interiority, with its human experiences of subjective meaning, conscious, and especially unconscious.

Clinical facts, materially transient, are unexpectedly durable – think how the clinical facts about Dora, the Wolf-Man, and the Rat Man have lasted. Yet important current critiques dispute their nature and even their existence (see, for example, Eagle 1984; G. S. Klein 1976; Schafer 1983; Spence 1982; and, for a masterly review, Wallerstein

1988). Such critiques reflect the present tension in psychoanalysis between the conviction that psychoanalysis discovers facts about the mind and the unease generated by the variety of existing clinical and theoretical views. Furthermore, issues of subjectivity, and the overall difference between physical science and human studies, also lead many to question whether it is *facts* that analysts find in an analytic hour.

At the outset allow me to state that there are scientific clinical facts. To support this view I shall offer, firstly, three sessions in which I claim clinical facts stand revealed; secondly, something of a philosophical enquiry into what a fact is; and, lastly, a discussion of the contribution that clinical facts make to the scientific study of the mind.

The clinical facts

My patient, whom I call Leon, will soon be 14 years old. At his request, his analysis is ending. Only 15 sessions remain.

Session 1

Leon puts the large box containing his drawings, paper, pens, etc. up on the table so that it forms a barrier between him and me when he sits down. He looks tense and fearful. He has brought with him a carton of Ribena, a children's drink, on which, in big print, is written 'FIFTEEN FREE EXTRA'. Through a straw he starts sucking the drink. He looks no more a schoolboy, but every bit a baby as he empties the carton, which is collapsing in a grotesque shape. Desperately, he sucks for the last drops. Then he hurls the carton violently away into the rubbish bin. I speak to Leon about being near the end of his analysis, of how he feels like a baby whose drinking causes such collapse and ugliness that he must get free – and free of me he will be in 15 days. I also speak about how he is not satisfied, and desperately still needs and hopes for something more, 'extra'. There is a long silence. Then, very anxiously, he peers round the box to look at me, retreating instantly. I speak of his terror that I am like the collapsed Ribena carton, and of his being so afraid that he cannot see how I really am. His breathing becomes distressed and he starts to wheeze. It is most distressing to hear. He transmits to me absolutely rending pain and anxiety. And suddenly he falls asleep – it is so unendurable.

Session 2

The next day Leon was different – every inch a schoolboy, a highly-defended one. He again made a barrier with his box, and then pulled out a pile of books from his schoolbag and spread them out ostentatiously. He read out his homework assignments loudly. For a brief moment he began to wheeze as if his lungs were again collapsing in agony, but he threw it off, and went on reading continuously in a loud voice bits from various schoolbooks. There seemed no way to make contact with him. I found myself feeling hopeless; I could do nothing but endure his loud blocking reading. I spoke of his need to free himself of a helpless baby who has to endure fear and pain by getting rid of it into me. Leon's response was to print his name on a sheet of paper in big letters and tear it in half, and continue even more loudly with his blocking talk. However, when I later interpreted his terror that I would make his schoolboy self disappear and be lost to him, a striking change came about. Leon was quiet and he put away his schoolbooks.

Hidden by his box, he stayed silent for a long time. I asked him what was happening. He was about to answer, then did not. I spoke of his fear that I would use what he might tell me to say something that would disturb him too much. He then started pushing his chair into view so he and I could see each other and then moving it away so he was again hidden by the box, doing so several times. I was reminded of something he had told me two years before – how he felt half-human and half-bird, that is, half like a human who stays in touch with humans and half like a bird who flies away. When I spoke to him in these terms he was visibly moved. He agreed it was so and then took down the box barrier.

Session 3

He made no box barrier this time. He sat down, openly hard and nasty. He took off his watch and started to draw it. In an exaggerated, mocking way he measured everything with a ruler. I first spoke about the watch being time of which he was so aware in these last days. His nasty performance continued and I then spoke about how he was giving a caricature of me as a cruelly measuring watcher. I went on to say that I thought he knew it was a false picture. Leon continued in the same spoiling way. Suddenly he announced with sarcastic emphasis

164

'I was going to draw it *exactly*, but I have decided not to', and he stopped. He drew the watch now in a straightforward way, and he started to bring his lips gently near to his hand several times as if to touch it with a kiss. I understood him to be showing the affection he feels when he thinks I know he needs me both to be gentle and not force him and also not to be weak and let him take bad advantage and make a mockery of me. He said 'Yip'. Then, with an effort, he said a clear 'Yes', going very pink.

This is my record of the clinical facts as I saw them.

But are they facts?

The claim of fact causes disquiet on a number of grounds. There is the nature of the entities themselves, insubstantial and unrepeatable, 'immaterial' facts as Caper (1988) aptly calls them. Moreover, a different analyst might see different facts in these three sessions. Is not a claim of fact incompatible with diverse clinical views about entities like these? I shall argue that, once we understand what a fact is, the special features of plurality, subjectivity and the immateriality of psychological phenomena, though they pose unusual and difficult problems, are not barriers to empirical fact. Indeed, in other forms, these problems are not entirely alien to other sciences, as Wallerstein shows in his important paper 'One psychoanalysis or many?' (Wallerstein 1988).

We tend to think of a fact as stark, out there, independent of theory, language and person. But investigations have shown such ideas to be naive. By the eighteenth century the great philosopher Kant had already demonstrated that objective reality is known only through the structure of the knowing mind. Kant was speaking of physical nature as known through the mind's categories of space, time and causality. In the nineteenth century, the remarkable hermeneutic thinker Dilthey added to Kant's categories others for human studies: categories of inner and outer; part and whole; the category of power between people, which helps or frustrates desires; and, overarching all, the category of development, which has a meaning for human beings that needs interpretation. Dilthey surely speaks to all of us and, as is well known, several psychoanalytic thinkers have applied his and other hermeneutic ideas with illumination to psychoanalysis (e.g., Gill 1983; G. S. Klein 1976; Schafer 1976); (for good discussions see Duncan 1992; Steiner 1992; Strenger 1991).

With this illumination, however, has come the temptation to adopt a relativism in which interpretations, readings and narratives are said to exist, each valid within its own nearly-closed scheme, but no facts, including clinical facts, can ever be known. Such a view, I think, is flawed. That reality is known through the mind's categories is no ground for lamenting that we can never know the facts. This lament is for non-existent entities. Rather, that facts are bound up with the nature of persons brings us a better understanding of what a fact is. And, indeed, psychoanalysis itself has discovered further categories that structure our perception and experience of reality, e.g., a psychically aware breast, a potent penis, an Oedipal situation, etc. (The full set of the mind's categories through which reality is known has yet to be found by philosophical, cognitive, psychoanalytic, or other studies.)

In our own time landmark work in the philosophy of science by Kuhn (1962) has shown further that scientific facts are not research method or theory free; and since facts are stated in language, whether folk or scientific, neither are they language free. This means that the same fact can fall under many different descriptions, and that no one statement of fact ever completely encompasses a fact. As the philosopher Thomas Nagel (1986) expresses it: a view of the facts is *always* a *partial view from somewhere*. With these regrettably cursory preliminaries, I now come to the nub of the matter.

What is it to make, as I wish to, a claim of fact? A claim of fact has two essentials. When I make a claim of fact, I make a truth claim, and I imply a readiness to submit my claim to verification. As others are speaking on the topic of verification I shall focus here on the truth claim; though, as truth and verification seem sometimes inextricable, I shall occasionally look at both.

First of all, when I make a truth claim, I do not claim to know *the* truth, or *all* the truth, but only *a* truth. Other true formulations are always possible. In a variety of vocabularies analysts make different, similar, or even the same statements about the clinical facts. Sometimes formulations seem complementary, e.g., Leon in the third session certainly gives what can be called 'a narrative performance' when he draws his watch in a nasty, measuring way. I wonder if Roy Schafer would agree to link his theory of narratives to the theory of internal objects, by letting it be said that Leon's nasty narrative performance is an attack on the better state of his internal objects? Variety of vocabulary aside, there remain nevertheless in our plural psychoanalytic scene real and complex differences of both theory and perceptions of clinical fact that are guided by theory. In my view, all psychoanalytic schools make a claim for truth – which is why, I think, our debates are so impassioned.

And secondly, when I make a truth claim, I do not make an infallibility claim. I might be mistaken. Here is where anxiety enters. Anxiety starts with the patient when I offer him my understanding of the clinical facts. Along with numerous other anxieties intrinsic to clinical work, there is always the anxiety that the clinical facts are not as I see them; yet, if I am to work, I must risk that I might be wrong. The patient is the first person to check an analyst's statement. Our patients say 'No' for many reasons, but the 'No' that tells the analyst that he is wrong is of immeasurable help. It may be said in words, or shown in other ways. You will remember how, after being overcome by an infantile state, by the second session Leon regained his schoolboy self. When I interpreted his need to free himself from a helpless baby and project it into me, he renewed his splitting – he tore his name on a paper in half – and his school talk became even louder. Leon showed I was wrong by an immediate increase in anxiety and defensiveness. Mistakes are an everyday risk for the analyst, hence the need for constant inquiry in the session into the patient's response to interpretations, explored in the present series of papers by Britton and Steiner (1994), as well as for what Gardner (1983) has called 'self inquiry', and Bion (1963) calls 'a meditative review of analytic work'. Now, writing this paper, I see my hopelessness when faced by Leon's defended, split state, and feeling of just having to endure it, as very likely coming from my sense of failure as an analyst with Leon – so limited my therapeutic result.

In recent years much attention has rightly been paid to the strain of bearing the state of not knowing, and the analyst's impulse to clutch at certainty out of the anxiety of not knowing. Here I put the emphasis the other way – on the anxiety of *knowing* with its inbuilt risk of being wrong. I wish to emphasise how interpretations may be delayed or vaguely framed by the analyst as a defence against the exposure of his fallibility. Our ego's old wish for omnipotence, the omnipotence with which our patients also endow us, the severe demands of our superego, our concern for our patients for whom we carry clinical responsibility, all of these make us reluctant to expose ourselves to public view, when just as we think we know the clinical facts we may turn out to be wrong. Such anxiety, which starts with our patient, continues before our colleagues when we give clinical presentations, and involves, I think, anxiety both about the standard of our work and about our theoretical orientation. We may not have seen what a more gifted or experienced colleague may see, and we may not have seen what a colleague with a better theory might see. The question is always lurking: could I be analysing my patient better from a different theoretical perspective?

Such reflections on our fallibility and our limitations bring again the unease, which I referred to at the start of the paper, over claiming there are clinical facts. When so many individual and theoretical views are possible, may not the psychoanalytic field be more subjective than factual? 'Subjectivity' is a word with many meanings. For a start, psychoanalysis studies psychic reality, which, in one sense, is subjective reality. And then, all human studies depend more on the knowing mind than the study of physical nature; in a psychoanalysis the analyst's mind is *the* instrument investigating the mind of the patient. This raises the alarming idea of psychoanalysis being doubly subjective, from the analyst's as well as the patient's side. The further fact that analysts are not standardized, that analysts have 'an individual idiom' as Bollas (1987) calls it, plays into the common presumption that the psychoanalytic enterprise is subjective in the pejorative sense of lacking all objectivity. However, the presumption of 'no objectivity' needs investigation (for an extensive inquiry see Nagel, 1986). In our age the objective achievements of machines dazzle us and can make us see them as everywhere superior − even in questionable areas. Some philosophers are writing as though, without question, it would be fortunate for us all were the mind to be reduced to the brain, and the brain to be equated with 'artificial intelligence'. In the same vein, a tape-recording is presumed to be a more objective record of a session than an analyst's written and mental notes. However, there are other views in contemporary thinking about the mind, brain and machines, in which the mind is not the loser, among them those of the philosophers McGinn (1991), Nagel (1986) and Searle (1992), and for an exploration of consciousness as nature's 'empowerment' to know objective reality, see Brian O'Shaughnessy (1991).

That said, we must now return to the topic of subjectivity − taken in the pejorative sense of 'lacking objectivity'. We are not all the ablest, nor are we always or with every patient at our individual best. Among analysts of all schools there are variations in the capacity to know the clinical facts of an analytic hour. In this sense one person may be more subjective, or less objective, than another, or than himself at another time. Leon illustrates this when in the first session he cannot see the analyst objectively at all after the carton collapses as he drinks. In great distress, he is then anxious about the analyst's condition. He looks at me to see how I am, but his vision is so clouded by his inner state at that moment that he cannot see how the external analyst is. This small example of the impairment of objectivity comes from a large area, to which psychoanalysis itself has contributed not a little understanding, by showing how out of flooding phantasy, as in the case of Leon, or anxiety, pain, narcissism, envy, etc., the mind may block perceptions or the sense organs become psychogenetically impaired. Psychoanalysis has shown also how projective identifications distort reality, how one mind may be invaded and controlled by another and unable to think freely and objectively, etc. In despair over these troubling problems of subjectivity in the practice of psychoanalysis we may be tempted to clutch at 'objectivity' through methods such as tape-recordings, or the 'pronoun counting' advised by Spence (1994): methods which I believe to be misguided. Better, in my opinion, to struggle with these problems by analysis for the analyst, and by supervision and discussions with colleagues; remembering that because there are impediments to attaining objectivity, this does not mean we have none: it means it is hard to attain.

In sum, I have tried to show that facts are not stark: they are bound up with the species we are, with the language in which they are couched, the method of their investigation, and the theories we hold about them – all of which implies that a fact may be described in many different ways. Plurality and science are compatible, though it must be admitted that there are too many theories in the psychoanalytic field. Any claim of clinical fact is, in my view, a truth claim; but, as with any empirical enterprise, not a unique or an infallible claim. An analyst may be wrong about the clinical facts because of the insufficiencies of his theory, or because of his personal limitations – including impairments to his objectivity.

The clinical facts again

In the first session we can see some distinctive features of the facts discovered in the analytic hour. The ending of Leon's analysis drew forth from his unconscious inner world his early object relations. In plain view are his primary object, represented by the Ribena carton collapsing from his drinking, and himself, looking and feeling like a terrified unsatisfied baby. We see how psychic reality is formed from a blending of internal and outer reality: his inner world is the source of the subjective meaning of the external event of ending analysis in 15 days. To Leon in this session (there were other meanings in subsequent sessions) it means weaning after a feeding that leaves him desperate and unsatisfied and his object grotesque and ruined in his mind.

The past is in the present in the way that is familiar to psychoanalysts, which yet is still so very striking. And how individual the relation to the past is! Another patient might experience the infant in himself without being overwhelmed, might wonder about his early history, or be able to discriminate the analyst's condition from that of his archaic internal object, but Leon cannot. His ego collapses under the psychic weight of contact with his unconscious internalised early past, and it terrifies him, all the more because his primary object is also collapsed, useless for modifying the situation. The coming out of these unconscious phantasies in concrete form so dominates Leon that he cannot relate to the analyst as a figure in the present different from his archaic object, and inner and outer reality persecute him. In an attempt to escape he hurls away the empty misshapen carton, but he does not succeed in freeing himself of his damaged and useless object; instead somatisation takes place (how should we understand this clinical fact?) and he wheezes painfully with feelings of collapsing lungs. At this point Leon projects into the analyst overwhelming feelings of anxiety and pain, and for respite he resorts to sleep.

It can be seen that Leon's unconscious inner world came into impressive prominence during the analytic hour; and that there was an interaction between inner and outer reality as an entire constellation of object relations, anxieties, needs and feelings, emerged into view. Leon could also project into the analyst and so communicate unbearable feelings of pain and anxiety. That is to say, under the unusual conditions of an analytic hour an analyst gains privileged access to a patient's *interiority*. Inner life emerges with a detail and depth not elsewhere accessible.

These facts of Leon's mental life, his personality, the internalised history of his object relations, have, at the same time another aspect: they are also clinical facts, living instances of the facts; that is, they are the clinical relations between patient and analyst, part of a therapeutic or not therapeutic process. In the first session this process brought a welling-up of infantile feelings. The following day was different. The extremity of Leon's state had impelled him to use massive defences and split off the infantile object relations threatening to overwhelm his ego. In the second session he is a schoolboy again, without emotional depth, with surface feelings and, above all, with a functioning ego once more. This, in fact, was an achievement of his analysis. He began treatment in a state of inertia, absorbed in secret psychotic preoccupations.

This second session seems to me to show the difference between a fact and a clinical fact. I mentioned earlier how I mistakenly interpreted that Leon needed to project the helpless baby into me. This was a fact; but it was not a clinical fact, not the immediate emotional reality of the session. When I mistook the emotional reality, the clinical facts of Leon's relations to me changed for the worse. I think he experienced me as very dangerous, as trying to undo his security and to force the overwhelming baby back into him. I drove him to a renewed splitting of himself (as shown by his tearing his name in half) and to louder defensive school talk. When I recognised Leon's anxiety that I would undo his defences, and interpreted his terror that I would cause him to lose his schoolboy self, his fears diminished and another change, this time for the better, occurred between us in the session.

At that moment I think I found what Bion has singled out as 'the selected fact', i.e., that fact which gives coherence and meaning to facts already known, namely, Leon's recovery of his schoolboy self, his loud reading of bits from schoolbooks to block out the analyst and to stop his chest from wheezing, his increased anxiety and defensiveness at the mention of a helpless baby. When the 'selected fact' was interpreted the interpretation is mutative and new possibilities then exist for patient and analyst. Leon became communicative and was able to show me, by moving into view and then hiding again behind his box, his need to be half in contact and half out of touch; and then I remembered what he had told me in the first months of the analysis when, very unusually (he mostly sat passive and silent), he was eager to speak. Intensely, he told me there had been a biology lesson at school about evolution and Darwin. 'There could be new species', he said, 'like', he added, 'half humans, half birds'. When I spoke to him in these images, they were alive in the session. I am no longer a figure watching him and threatening to breach his defences, but a figure who knows him and accepts how he is, and by the end of the session his defences, box and emotional, come down.

171

It is clear, I think, that my clinical facts are selected on the following basis: they are the lived facts of the shifting object relations between myself and my patient – as I saw them. In every session observations would have been made and not been included because, though they were facts, I did not see them as clinical facts. Moreover, it is evident that as analyst I both observe and, through fallibility or understanding, contribute to making the clinical facts what they are. It is a further clinical fact that a selected fact, the ground of a mutative interpretation, is highly time-sensitive: it must come from the immediate emotional reality between patient and analyst. And lastly, it can be seen that not all sessions are therapeutic. Leon's first session was an acutely painful emergence, a repetition in the presence of the analyst, without therapeutic benefit. By contrast, in the second session some working through took place between patient and analyst, as it did in the third session.

In the third session Leon continued to communicate. He openly showed me that he is making a mocking caricature as he draws his watch, measuring everything exaggeratedly 'exactly'. Unlike the previous session, when the external analyst was experienced as a threat to his security, in this session he was showing me an inner danger to his security. His own destructiveness was stripping the internalised image of his analyst of the very quality most important to him the day before, namely, being seen in a way that does not measure him but accepts his being 'different', his feeling of being half-bird, half-human. When Leon began analysis he was paralysed by a superego that watched and measured him cruelly against father, brother, or other ideals. When I interpreted the caricature he was making of his internalised analyst, Leon responded and himself took a decision to stop it. By the end of the hour he could acknowledge his gratitude for an analyst who both saw his destructive mockery, and comprehended also his need for emotional distance – as expressed by his lips going near to, yet not quite, kissing his hand.

These clinical facts are not 'stark' facts. Items are not sorted and labelled 'observed data', 'inference', 'psychoanalytic context', 'analyst's emotional experiences', 'analyst's memory of patient', 'hypothesis or theory invoked', etc. Mostly, the clinical facts are an amalgam of some of these items, some being simpler than others, e.g., the way Leon looks. In the first session he arrives with his Ribena carton, looking tense and fearful; in the second he comes looking like a much-defended schoolboy; in the third he looks nasty and hard when he arrives, and warmly tender by the end. There are also his actions: he makes the box barrier, he drinks, he reads loudly from schoolbooks, he draws, and there are his words and my own. (I have not included the details of how I spoke to him, since 'formulations to the patient' is a topic for other papers in the present series.)

However, even such apparently simple data are often complex. Consider descriptions of his appearance, such as 'He looks like a much-defended schoolboy'; or, in Session 1, as he sucks the juice from the Ribena carton, my record has it that he 'Looks no more a schoolboy but every bit a baby.' Or, even more complex, consider my perception of Leon drawing his watch in the third session. As he draws, measuring everything in an exaggerated way with the ruler, I see him in the context of the analytic process to be destroying the analyst internalised from the day before, who did not criticize or measure him, but accepted his being 'half-bird, half-human'. I see him as undoing the analytic work and reverting to an old identification with a superego who used to paralyse him by always watching him and measuring him unfavourably against father, brother, or other ideal: a cruel figure dominating hours of analytic endeavour. That is, my perception of Leon's action is informed by the history of the analysis, and by my knowledge of the patient's internal figures. Moreover, my perception is also infused with a particular psychoanalytic hypothesis, first stated by Melanie Klein in an early paper on tics (Klein 1925b), that unconscious object relations and identifications will be found to underlie all mental and somatic phenomena; and with her general theory (1940 onwards) that in the mind are continual unconscious phantasies of an inner world of objects which, by identification, projection and introjection, are constantly interacting with outer reality. My clinical observations were not made by observing 'basic data' and then making inferences or invoking an hypothesis or a theory, but by experiencing phenomena in a certain way. It is an individual way of seeing, hindered by my limitations, using what capacities I have, infused with theory, or with knowledge of my patient, or with memories of our psychoanalytic endeavours, sometimes devoid of theory or even contrary to theory, and so on: it is very much – and considerably more so than in the case of other scientific methods – 'my view from somewhere'.

The gap between clinical fact and relevant theory is not, in my opinion, in the consulting room. It is to be found elsewhere: in the imaginative extrapolation, the scientific leap from the clinical facts from one or more pairs of patients and analysts to hypotheses about the psyche, its structure, its development, its treatment by analysis, and so on, which form part of a psychoanalytic theory of mind. At work with my patient, when aspects of theory are relevant they seem 'experience-near'; sometimes, however, by contrast, the clinical facts may upset a theory – a different and important possibility for the analyst.

So far, rather than defining the essence of a clinical fact, I have been trying to gather from the three sessions some distinctive features (others might be chosen – see Caper 1994, 'What is a clinical fact?') of what psychoanalysis discovers. Given that the method of discovery is in the seclusion of an analytic hour, unrepeatable by another analyst, how then is an alternate view possible? In his paper 'What is a clinical fact', given at West Point earlier this year, Spence says: 'We need to find a mode of presentation that will honour the clinical fact ... [and give] ... the opportunity to take an alternate stand' (Spence 1994). With facts like clinical facts, this looks, and is, not easy to do. Yet I think it is not impossible.

Several things help. First of all, though I have an individual style and a Kleinian orientation, these are of less moment than the vast area of training, practice and theory, which is common to all psychoanalysts and which underlies my work, e.g., the analytic attitude and setting, the recognition of an unconscious, of psychic reality, of the ego's need for defences against intense anxieties, the assumption of a repetition of the past in the transference situation with the analyst, symbolism, etc. In Kuhn's (1962) terminology, these form the 'shared paradigm' of psychoanalysts, the common ground from which all analysts can assess my work. And we should note that the clinical record itself may communicate to colleagues more than I consciously know, both about the patient and my relations with him, and about my awareness and objectivity or lack thereof. Moreover, colleagues may make enquiries of me, for a fuller clinical record, for further facts which, if they are taking a different view, they suspect might be there. As I see it, an alternate view is not so much the building of a different understanding on the grounds of the same clinical facts – though it can be that – but is more often akin to a shift of perspective that brings about a change of perception, which in turn re-describes and re-orders the facts. Naturally, a new view of the clinical facts must, like the first one, be subject to validation, as being a truth about the immediate emotional reality between patient and analyst.

Whichever our school of psychoanalysis, clinical facts have increased the understanding of the human mind enormously. Until Freud invented the unusual conditions of the analytic hour, the mind's interiority was waiting for the light of a scientific day – even one such as ours, which yields clinical facts with some unusually troublesome problems.

Acknowledgements

A previous edition of this chapter was presented at the IJPA 75th Anniversary Celebration Conference, London, 14–16 October 1994. It was first published in the *International Journal of Psychoanalysis*, 1994, 75: 939–947.

── 13 ──

RELATING TO THE SUPEREGO

The author aims to demonstrate the disjunction and antagonism between normal and abnormal forms of superego through an enquiry into clinical material from two patients who manifest abnormal forms of the superego as recognised by Freud, Abraham and Klein, later termed by Bion 'the ego-destructive superego'. The abnormal superego usurps the status and authority of a normal superego and entices the ego to turn away from life, to dissociate itself from its objects and ultimately to destroy itself. While the normal superego originates from the emotional relations of childhood, by contrast, the abnormal superego stems from dissociations that have been inflicted and suffered in childhood. In clinical work the abnormal superego manifests itself in a transference situation where patient and analyst relate as abnormal superego to abnormal superego. No working through can take place, only an impoverishment and deterioration of relations, with an escalation of hatred and anxiety that results in psychotic panic or despair. In this dangerous situation, the significant event for the patient is to be enabled to move away from his abnormal superego, return to his object, and so experience the analyst as an object with a normal superego.

In Freud's writings over the years we find diverse types of superego. In the *New Introductory Lectures*, for instance, he says: 'The superego is the representative for us of every moral restriction, the advocate of a striving towards perfection ... of what is described as the higher side of human life' (Freud 1933b: 66). Earlier, however, Freud had observed a quite different type of superego in the afflictions of obsessional neurosis and melancholia where the superego develops an 'extraordinary harshness and severity towards the ego' (Freud 1923: 53). In obsessional neurosis it inflicts 'interminable self-torment' and 'and a systematic torturing of the object'. It is even more dangerous

176

in melancholia, where it is 'a pure culture of the death instinct ... [which] often enough succeeds in driving the ego into death'. This superego is 'the representative of the internal world, of the id' (Freud 1923: 36). Such stark divergences suggest that a unitary conception of the superego may not encompass the varied phenomena met with in our patients: in some the superego, even when primitive and strict, is a guiding force, but in others an abnormal form of the superego is a destroyer of the self, its relations and its objects.

As is well known the concept of the superego had a long evolution in Freud's thinking. It started under the name of 'a self-critical faculty' that induced a sense of guilt, and later was called also 'a special agency' that watched and measured the ego by the ego–ideal, and then in *The Ego and the Id* Freud, as part of his new three-fold division of the mind, called it the 'superego' and saw it as 'a differentiating grade in the ego' (Freud 1921: 129), apart from and over the ego, its genesis through the internalisation of the prohibitions and ideals of the child's earliest objects on the dissolution of the Oedipus complex, a further distinct source of anxiety for the ego, adding to the dangers in the external world and the dangers from the id. As is also well known, in her early writings Klein (1932) described fears of punishment and feelings of remorse in small children arising from a primitive pre-Oedipal superego. What has been taken less notice of is that she came to think (Klein 1958) that there was another early superego, formed in a defusion of the instincts, a superego that stood apart and was unmodified by the normal processes of growth. When Rosenfeld (1952) described how in an acute schizophrenic patient 'the super-ego is responsible for ego-splitting' and Bion later described what he called 'the ego-destructive super-ego' (Bion 1959: 314) I think they were referring to the same abnormal superego that Freud and Abraham studied in melancholia and obsessional neurosis, which in turn is Melanie Klein's deeply split-off superego. I shall describe two patients who lose their links to objects with normal superego aspects and relate almost totally to an abnormal superego. I shall enquire into the nature of this abnormal superego domain and the ensuing transference situation where patient and analyst relate as abnormal superego to abnormal superego.

Mrs A is the first patient. In the waiting room she is anxious and eager to speak. On the couch she is changed. Mrs A is silent, hating what she calls 'my set-up' where I expect her to speak first 'because she is the patient'. I fear that if I let her silence continue too long she will feel I have judged her as useless to work with and her anxiety will escalate, and yet if I speak she almost certainly will condemn what I say. I might try remarking that when she first saw me she seemed to want to speak to me, but now on the couch felt I was wrong and could not. Mrs A, covering her anxiety, would start to sneer, 'O God, I've heard that stuff of yours before' at once in communion with, and under the protection of, an 'O God', criticising and refusing my 'stuff'. If I speak of her suspicion of what I say or her anxiety that I reject or criticise her, or her hatred of me as the analyst, I might get back, 'I hate you telling me my feelings.' And if in the tangled skein of hatred, fear, defensive aggression, sense of failure, evacuation, envy, I also experience, and talk to her about, her wish for me to know what she is suffering by giving me again and again these experiences of criticism and rejection, she responds tartly and falsely, 'I'm not aware of that', so negating the possibility of a recognition of the projection into myself of the distressed child in her.

I am unable to help her. She gets no relief and gains no insight. Our relations deteriorate as she becomes more of an 'O God', reducing any effort on her or my part to nothing, intent only on proving her superiority.

In a session in which she evoked much sympathy, I spoke about how underneath her dismissals she felt desperate, afraid and disappointed with me. She replied accusingly: 'What I extract from what you say is – you're critical and pointing at me that I can't do it.' Mrs A extracts my sympathy and attempt to understand, and knows me only as a pointer at her failure, even as she too is a pointer at my extraction of her initial willingness and my failure to make her better. Mrs A believes I hostilely extract her worth, and more, she feels I judge her with the verdict: 'unable to do it'. For Mrs A both of us are a pointer and extractor, who confront one another as abnormal superego to abnormal superego.

Of such a superego Bion writes:

> It is a super-ego that has hardly any of the characteristics of the super-ego as understood in psychoanalysis: it is 'super' ego. It is an envious assertion of moral superiority without any morals. In short it is the resultant of an envious stripping or denudation of all good and is itself destined to continue the process of stripping ... till [there is] ... hardly more than an empty superiority-inferiority that in turn degenerates to nullity.
>
> (Bion 1962a: 97)

Bion's hypothesis is that this pathological superego arises during failures of communication between mother and infant, failures that are experienced as attacks on linking by either the mother who refuses ingress to her infant's communications, and/or from the infant who withholds or denudes communication with hate and envy. In these ways a 'super' ego that destroys links is formed and internalised. It can be seen that Freud, Abraham, Klein and Bion converge on the same dissociative area in regard to the abnormal superego: Bion's idea of attacks on linking fits with Freud's description (Freud 1930: 118) of the 'instinct of death' 'seeking to dissolve units', which coincides with Klein's idea of an 'extremely bad figure' formed when 'defusion seems to be in the ascendant' (Klein 1958: 241). Briefly, I would say that the normal superego is formed from the earliest relations, while by contrast, the abnormal superego arises from the earliest dissociations, and its dangerous aim is to dissociate the patient, to attack the link with the object, the feature both Freud and Abraham emphasised as crucial, since it is upon the link with the object that the safety of the ego depends.

In the case of Mrs A, I think there was evidence of yet another psychic condition leading to the formation of an internal figure like her extractor of worth and pointer at failure: an abnormal state of mind in the mother condemning the baby for not matching her anticipated ideal. Mrs A believes she failed to measure up to the maternal ideal, as now, in analysis, she believes I am dissatisfied with her as my patient. She is thus in distressing double competition: enviously with me, and also, with my 'ideal' patient, and she accuses me, as she experiences it, of censuring instead of accepting her, the repetition in the analysis of her infantile distress with her object for not accepting her states of mind, and instead accusing her of being 'unable to do it'.

In the session reported Mrs A was by turns terrified by and identified with an abnormal superego that attacks links so omnipotently that all we see are the consequences for analyst and patient – she and I stand as abnormal superego to abnormal superego in a narrow line of confrontation, condemnation and denudation where neither of us is 'able to do it', i.e., no psychic work, let alone working through, can take place. I shall explore this situation with a second patient in whom there is a more fluctuating transference situation.

Mr B came for analysis in a depressed – almost melancholic – state, on the point of resigning his job, feeling unable to carry on with his life. Married, with a family, he had spoken to no one of his inner state. Once the analysis began I saw how deprived he was of communication. Feeling unlikeable, agitated, anxious, he was without links in himself and between himself and others. He almost could not project. I was often without any emotional link to him and could do no more than make descriptive commentaries. He tried to find respite in an idealised soft closeness with a lap-woman, represented by the couch and the pillow, escaping internally into drowsiness, sometimes sleeping, waking ashamed for spending his session so.

Our lack of contact was one focus of the initial phase of the analysis. At first Mr B's presumptions were that I was critical of him for not being how I expected a patient to be, that I withdrew from him, and he spoke in a void. But as time went on Mr B was less certain who was at fault. He saw that our contact was also stopped because he suddenly withdrew, or had an obscene daydream, or, and Mr B was astounded and disbelieving when I first drew his attention to it, because he made a sudden $h^\wedge e - h^\wedge e - h^\wedge e$ sound, a clearing of the throat, which when one listened, was a mocking hyena laugh at the futility of our attempts to talk.

Mr B had a recurring memory. His parents arranged a special treat for him – a theatre performance, unusual in their local town. They bought three tickets, prepared a box of sandwiches for him for his tea. He was to take the bus after school to meet them at the theatre. He forgot. He walked home on the common as usual, wanting to tell his mother about school, how he'd lost his cap, and that he might be in the choir. When nearly home he saw his parents coming towards him, worried he hadn't arrived at the theatre. His father was extremely angry, Mr B couldn't understand why, since he just forgot. But he often remembers this incident and feels guilty, he doesn't know why since he just forgot, wanting to go home as usual.

This is a screen memory rich in childhood meanings, its central theme clear. Mr B 'forgets' the special performance his father and mother wish to show him and tries to return to an unpartnered mother to talk to her about himself. Here is his developmental impasse: he knows but forgets about a feeding mother (the sandwiches for his tea) and an Oedipal scene (the three tickets for the theatre) and tries to construct a narcissistic sufficiency with an erotised Oedipal illusion (Britton 1989) to serve as a psychic retreat (Steiner 1993). He fails because a normally worried parental couple reappears and, in addition, an extremely angry father – an abnormal superego – arrives.

In analysis this configuration emerged in many ways, such as his liking for the lap-woman, his retreat into erotised fantasies, and his frequent way of taking interpretations. He listened, was silent; then he spoke, a little pedantically, about the interpretation. When I asked him what he did in the silences he said he 'studied' the interpretation. What I think happened in these little silences was that Mr B 'forgot' my performance, 'studied' the interpretation unlinked to me, and then narcissistically told me about it. Later, he would grow anxious, feel he was being watched for doing things the wrong way, and at this point the hyena laugh, the $h^\wedge e - h^\wedge e - h^\wedge e$ of the abnormal superego father, often sounded.

I move now to 3 years later when Mr B was communicating more and stayed in contact for longer and in more depth. He now dreamt sometimes. He had held on to his job in which he thought he was more successful than before. However, he was ambivalent about the analysis. Though aware of feeling better he doubted whether analysis was helping him.

Looming over Mr B at this time was the ending of a contract at work with no new prospect in sight. For many sessions he chatted inconsequentially, stayed silent, fell asleep. As the ending of his contract drew nearer, his isolation and his hostile and anxious silence about it were ever more central. Then a few days before his last day of work he talked about a homeless woman whom he had seen in the street. He had watched her. She was preoccupied, rummaging in her boxes. He saw she was dirty and lame. He was walking off when she lifted her skirts, pulled down her knickers and peed. Mr B ended saying: 'I'm a bit critical of my attitudes to the homeless, but I don't like dirty unpredictable people.' The homeless woman on the street is Mr B's ideograph for his analyst. He has been watching me, a lame analyst, homeless both from the projection of his homelessness into me (he is losing his job and in the analysis he has had no home with me) but much more, I am homeless from his refusal to give me a place in his troubles for so many sessions. I think he expressed the immediate transference situation when he said he didn't like dirty unpredictable people – and it was this that I first interpreted. I said he feels by his long non-communication about losing his job that he has pushed me to the brink of getting out of control; he hates me and fears I might suddenly pour a urine-like stream of words on him. Mr B replied: 'Just that'. After a silence he said: 'Yes, yes', and came emotionally alive. He spoke in some detail about his situation at work. His feelings there, and about the analysis, could be explored, including his self-criticism from his normal superego for his long retention of material and cruel watching of me as he did it – you will remember how he'd said 'I'm a bit critical of my attitudes to the homeless.' During these quite alive exchanges, though he sometimes disconnected momentarily for a silent study, there was real contact between us.

Our good contact continued the next day, the last before the weekend. However, as the end of the hour neared, Mr B deserted our interchange. Obscene ideas swept into him. He said he'd just thought of a bright idea from *Playboy* magazine – a pass key that would let you into the house where the girls were! He was having all sorts of fantasies! 'I just thought of you with all your clothes off – I've never done it so completely before!' His excited smirking tone was jarring and unreal. I tried to call his attention to how he had panicked as he neared the time to leave for the weekend, and disconnected from our talk, and now had unstoppable fantasies smashing me as his analyst and taking him off into a different erotised world. He bypassed these words and left very excited. On Monday Mr B returned looking depressed and persecuted. He said he had had a dream. It was only a dream, he added anxiously, and he thought it was disappearing. He fell silent. Then he rallied and related the dream.

> I was looking at a book with the title 'Sceptic of the Renaissance'. It had a place on a shelf. It was by a woman author. There was a lull. The room got darker. Then the room closed down.

I asked for associations. He said bleakly he had none. In the silence that followed the session became like his dream: we were in a lull, the room seemed dark. I spoke to him about this atmosphere, and how we were closing down and could not talk today. After a silence, he said, sounding suffused with disappointment, 'Nothing has come of one or two new possibilities of work I'd hoped for. I'm leaving the office this Wednesday. I just want it over.' After another silence he said: 'It was all right, now it's all wrong.' I said, 'Yes, there was a renaissance in the analysis last week when it was all right, and you could talk to me and let me be an alive analyst. Today you're afraid I look on you with scepticism.' Mr B grew extremely agitated. 'Scepticism. Why do you say that?' he asked. He was astonished when I reminded him that he had told me a dream about a Sceptic of the Renaissance. He referred agitatedly to his father who always was, and still is, aloof and sceptical. I spoke to him about his belief that I in this session was sceptical of him and his words after his undressing fantasies destroyed our work at the end of last week. His agitation and despair left him and he regained contact with me as someone with whom there were possibilities of communication until near the end of the hour when he started talking about masturbating watching erotic Indian films on TV.

The next day (the last I report) Mr B began as he had ended the previous day – consciously fantasising. Thinly chirpy, he said he had Batman fantasies and sexy slave fantasies going through his head, and a theme from Bach, ideas from theoretical physics that he elaborated, etc., etc. What I think was intended as a rich brew became more irritating and childish. He suddenly interrupted himself to say vehemently, 'I'm leaving the office tomorrow. I just want it over, now.' Surreptitiously looking at his watch he continued fantasising. I said he was trying to evade the distress of leaving the office tomorrow and to evade also his inner feeling of being a poor child – poor and guilty because he keeps losing our analytic work, and he wants a punishing interpretation to get his guilt and depression over with now by a verbal blow from me. Mr B began to cry, saying with unusual full conviction: 'Well, yes. It is so ... I know I've been doing this all my life.' With a sense of release and recognition he wept quietly till the end of the session. To Mr B's surprise his last day at work ended with a farewell lunch, speeches and so on, and with no disastrous acting out on his part.

To review this clinical sequence. It starts with attacks on his link to the analyst as Mr B withholds all talk about the ending of his contract. This is his envious, and also anxious, refusal. The homeless woman, the mother he keeps out, though she has the projections of his rejection of her, is seen by Mr B as herself preoccupied, rummaging in her boxes, and becoming unpredictably impatient and critical.

When I interpret his anxiety that I, the homeless woman, will pour a stream of urine-like words on him, he replies, 'Just that' and then says, 'Yes, yes', and comes emotionally alive. We then communicate fairly freely. However, as the end of the session nears he becomes frantic and deserts his object, evading the impending separation with pornographic fantasies of entering me as a 'girlie' house.

Next in the sequence comes Mr B's abnormal superego, which emerges in his dream as a Sceptic of the Renaissance. The dream is lived in a long silence in the session. (*The room got darker. Then the room closed down.*) As the possibility of communication with me closes down, we see how Mr B has lost his link to the object. In Money-Kyrle's (1968) sense he has become disoriented, lost in the domain of a terrifying superego. This terrifying superego is the reverse of an internal object that modifies anxiety – it magnifies anxiety. Mr B's Sceptic has total scepticism about the renaissance of Mr B's communications, about all of his and my talking in the analysis. The mocking hyena sound mentioned earlier was the Sceptic's laugh.

During the session Mr B cannot bear the psychic reality of this Sceptic who arouses limitless anxiety. Mr B says it is only a dream and is disappearing, and when he tells me his dream, the telling becomes his way of shedding the dream. He is greatly agitated when I then speak of the Sceptic of the Renaissance – I make the Sceptic real again, and am possibly myself the Sceptic. However, when I interpret the destructiveness of his undressing of me, a named crime replaces the nameless dread aroused by this ego-destructive superego and with great relief Mr B regains his orientation to an object with a normal superego i.e., an analyst who can call things by their proper names. By so doing, I make finite his erotised destructiveness. Then as the session nears its close Mr B again escapes into erotised fantasies, though this time he himself knows he is using a masturbation fantasy about a film.

The next day, you will remember, he produces a rich brew of ideas and fantasies – clever, erotised, childish – a manic defence against inner guilt and emptiness that became increasingly irritating to me. When I interpret that he is trying to evade the distress of leaving his office without other work, and to evade also his inner feelings of being a poor, guilty child because he keeps losing our analytic work and who wants to get his guilt over with by punishment from me, he says, 'Well, yes. It is so. I've been doing that all my life.' He then is in touch with his vast underlying depression that comes from a lifetime's attack on his links to his inner objects and to external reality.

In this sequence Mr B makes a small yet important movement of growth. He leaves the domain of his abnormal superego, regains his orientation to an analyst with a normal superego, and even though such an analyst might be felt as strict, it is a huge relief for Mr B that his own ego can function again and he and I can do a little ordinary psychoanalytic work: first he is manic and tries to provoke me to punish him; but after I interpret his manic and masochistic defences against guilt and emptiness, Mr B is able to experience his underlying depression.

I shall relate a final clinical incident that opens to fuller view Mr B's abnormal superego and its sinister aim – in which it succeeds in this next sequence – of detaching and alienating Mr B from his objects. It is from later in the analysis when Mr B was no longer habitually evading impending absence with erotised fantasies, and when his whole problematic constellation, internal and external, especially as it arose at moments of separation, was dynamic and accessible.

Mr B failed to arrive for the last session before a Bank Holiday Monday on which I would not be working. During his hour he telephoned, saying, 'I have a bad cold. I won't be coming. See you Tuesday.' His voice was cold, his manner casually dismissive. He arrived on the Tuesday and started by saying he had had two dreams that he had written down so he wouldn't forget them:

1. He was in a cold town, trying to fix a cable for a radio or something electrical. A small short man with a black moustache who was supposed to be helping him walked out.

2. It was uphill. He was a street-sweeper. He was sweeping leaves in the gutter in an ever-increasing pile. (He raised his arm as he spoke, making repeated sweeping movements that were also beating movements.) A big spar got in the way of his sweeping. Then a friendly man came and said it must be nice to wear casual clothes for work like he did, being a street-sweeper. In the dream Mr B told him he was a ... (he gave his profession) and that he wears a suit to work.

Mr B's first association was that his dreams were strange because he wasn't being himself, and yet there was also a lot of him in the dreams. His second association was that the place in the dream where he was sweeping (again he raised his arm to sweep and beat) was like a small town in a TV programme on Alaska – cold and bleak.

As it was most unusual for Mr B to write down his dreams to keep them, and thinking also of how the first dream begins with his trying to fix a cable, I started by remarking that he had made sure of keeping his dreams to repair his connection with me. In a cold, superior voice he said: 'No. You are wrong. I wasn't repairing. In the dream I was installing a cable.' I said that indeed we were in cold territory after

I walked out on him on Monday. He doesn't stay himself, he gets like his image of me, and sweeps me aside now, in the same way he dismissed me on the telephone. Mr B replied aloofly and unpleasantly that he could actually have come to that session when he rang – he had no temperature.

And indeed I felt this was true for most of the current session: he could have worked with me, but he was choosing not to. At one point I referred to the uphill (his second dream had begun: 'It was uphill'). Very superior, he said: 'No. You are wrong. In the dream I began uphill, but then I turned left, and it was downhill when I was sweeping the leaves.' I felt nastily reproved and tricked. After again interpreting his projective identification with an analyst whom he felt had tricked him by leaving him, I suggested that at the same time he had a different view of my leaving him in which I was not so cold and treacherous but remained someone to return to and talk to – which he was refusing to do. I thought Mr B inwardly understood me but out of unrelenting revenge and envious hatred would not acknowledge it. I was again in the position of the homeless woman, perceived here in a distorted way.

There was no working through of his dreams or the events in the session. In his first dream when the falsely 'friendly' man tries to cajole him into believing that the casual dismissal of his analyst was good by suggesting it is nice to wear casual clothes and be a street-sweeper, Mr B protests that he has a profession and wears a suit to work; however, when he is with me, retaliation for my leaving him on the Monday overrides self-preservation and he deserts his self that has a link to me, and as time goes on he turns more towards his cold abnormal superego and identifies himself increasingly with it. I felt pushed into degenerating into rebuking him, and so to say, lifting my skirts and peeing on him as he spoke unpleasantly of unsophisticated persons he and his wife didn't want to be friends with – I was supposed, of course, to see myself as one of the unsophisticated persons, while he paired with a superior being that cut its links with such as me. I found myself getting very depressed and pressurised to condemn him in a way that would draw me into his cruel terrain, to become, that is, sceptical of any renaissance with him and beat him for his cold destruction of human attachments. By the end he was disoriented, non-listening, superior, in total identification with a pathological superego.

Here we gain a clear view of Mr B's abnormal superego and how its nature is not constituted even by an exaggeration of the traits of a normal superego – critical self-observation and normal ego–ideals have disappeared. Usurping their place is immorality and unreason, which in Mr B's dream appear in the guise of a friendly man who says: isn't it nice to wear casual clothes, i.e., casually dismiss your analyst, go mentally downhill, become a street-sweeper? You may recall that when Mr B sought analysis he was on the point of giving up his job and putting himself at risk of really landing in the gutter. His pathological superego is a culture of the death instinct; we see its chilling tricks and its installing of repeated cycles of cruelty and punishment and how it aims to detach Mr B from object relations, personal development, his life and his life instinct.

Mr B's alienation starts with a cold, deliberate turning away from the object and the self that relates to the object – as Mr B himself says 'I could have come.' This means that early in the session Mr B still has the possibility of listening and understanding, although he chooses to misunderstand and retaliate on the basis of misunderstanding, a cruel treachery to the analyst that enormously increases his guilt. Driven on by vengeance and an escalating fear of guilt, he attacks all his links to the analyst and orients himself instead to his ego-destructive superego. By the end of the session his ego is stripped, his guilt is shed, and he is in a superior domain, identified with a 'Super' ego that is not moral, but immoral. Mr B will not hold to the cold, superior line he takes with me in this session; on the morrow, anxiety and persecutory guilt will return, hugely magnified, and he will be beating himself mercilessly, sweeping himself downhill.

We see here the full adversity of Mr B's psychic predicament. He has at best only a doubtfully good object with whom he identifies intermittently; his instinctual conflict between making or breaking contact remains undecided. Internally, his ego does not cohere around a good object; on the contrary, his orientations are fickle – he is susceptible, as we have seen, to perverse fantasising as a way of evading the distress of separation anxiety, persecution and guilt, and most important of all, he is vulnerable to alienation from his more normal self and object relations, and becoming instead in thrall to and identified with his abnormal superego.

To conclude with some general remarks, I think, though not everyone does, that we are ethical primates. Midgley (1994) gives good philosophical support for this view. I think therefore that a superego is part of the very form of what a self-conscious consciousness is and must be a constituent of whatever psychoanalytic theory of mind we hold. Money-Kyrle (1944), for instance, writes of a 'primary morality' that arises naturally because of awareness of our profound conflicts of love and hate towards our objects. I also think that a unitary conception of the superego is inadequate and this paper aims to illustrate the disjunction and the antagonism between normal and pathological forms of superego. On the many unresolved problems about the superego, in addition to those already referred to, there are a vast number of important writings from analysts of all schools. See recently in particular Schafer (1960), Rosenfeld (1962), Stolar and Fromm (1974), Joseph (1978), Garza-Guerrero (1981), Brenman (1985), Hoffman (1994), Kernberg (1992), Malcolm (1999).

As it observes the ego and its relations to its internal and external objects, the normal superego is a compound of 'super' and 'ego': 'super' in that it is over the ego, i.e., self-reflective; 'ego' in its 'trying to know' in a blend of reason and feeling through distinctive moral categories which include aspirations and ideals. There is the possibility that the patient's profound conflicts of love and hate, as well as his conscious and unconscious fears, his remorse and reparation will emerge in the analysis and be repeatedly worked through so that the severity and primitiveness of this superego will be modified.

The pathological superego also watches the ego from a 'higher' place, but it is dissociated from ego functions like attention, enquiry, remembering, understanding. Mrs A's 'O God', for example, is not trying to know; it is denuding and condemning me, and with violent projective identifications establishes a transference situation where she and I are relating as abnormal superego to abnormal superego – both extractors of worth and pointers at failure. Nor does Mr B's Sceptic of the Renaissance remember that a living development, a 'renaissance' between patient and analyst occurred in the analysis, or enquire how it was that this renaissance came to be destroyed by a rush of erotised fantasies. It is full of hate and prejudice, sceptical of all renaissance; its aim is to destroy links within the self and between the self and its objects. It generates enormous anxiety in the patient, being the manifestation of the Death Instinct within, an immoral sweeper downhill to destruction, and a punishing incessant beater.

Analyst and patient both suffer difficulties peculiar to this situation. Mrs A, you will remember, while anxious was eager when she arrived, yet the session was a deterioration I was helpless to prevent. This induced in me what Bion calls a 'peculiar' guilt, something I think Mrs A also felt. Looming over both of us was an ideal; not, however,

188

an ideal to which either of us could aspire; it was also 'peculiar' in being an ideal that manifestly we both were not. She felt bad simply for being who she was, and I felt bad for being who I was, and I had to disentangle guilt over possible poor analytic work and work less good than that of a more able colleague from my 'peculiar' guilt for making her not 'better' but 'worse' in the session. Of such guilt Bion writes: 'the guilt is meaningless … [and] contrasts therefore with conscience in that it does not lend itself to constructive activity' (Bion 1962a: 98). Furthermore, Mrs A had to have courage to persist again and again with an analyst she believed to be wrong and I had to bear many sessions where I was experienced as harmful by Mrs A, or misrepresented as a sadist by Mr B, without becoming defensive, or reassuring, or so despairing as to be denuded of an analytic stance and actually extract all worth from the interchange between my patient and myself.

Mr B, however, is more able than Mrs A to pull away from his abnormal superego. He did so, for instance, in the session with his dream of the Sceptic of the Renaissance; though in despair and near to panic, he was able to hear me interpret that he believed I was Sceptical about him after his undressing fantasies destroyed our analytic work. When I named his actual crime his terror and despair left him, and instead of being a Sceptic I became a normal superego who called things by their proper names – a normal superego, but one with an analytic attitude. This means not giving verdicts (guilty, not guilty, etc.) or pronouncing sentence (on probation, condemned to … etc.) on the patient, but recognising things for what they are in the ethical domain. Mr B then knows a named crime for which he himself may (if he is able to) feel guilt instead of near-psychotic panic. In my view, because of the antagonism between the pathological superego and the operation of normal ethics, escaping its clutches and regaining contact with an object with normal superego aspects are among the more significant analytic events in clinical work with patients like Mrs A and Mr B.

Acknowledgements

A previous edition of this chapter was published in the *International Journal of Psychoanalysis*, 1999, 80(5): 861–870.

14

DREAMING AND NOT DREAMING

Freud's great work *The Interpretation of Dreams* (Freud 1900), combined with the findings of a hundred years, constitutes what Sara Flanders (1993) calls *The Dream Discourse Today*. Today we know that dreams are of different kinds, and that not dreaming has diverse origins, and that during analysis the evolution of the transference and the course of dream life are connected. About the patient I shall present here, it would be hard to say which is more important – her dreaming, or her particular way of not dreaming.

Mrs A, in her mid-forties, holds an administrative post and her husband is in finance. She admires him and she is also afraid of and for him. She speaks of his making nasty deals and his disturbing influence on family life, and how it is always she who must do what needs to be done (e.g., for their now grown-up son and daughter). Mrs A sees her parents and her two brothers as disturbed, unlikeable people and herself as the one in her family her mother turned to.

At the time she dreamt the dream, Mrs A had been in analysis for some while. At the beginning she was very anxious, did not like me, and withdrew, suspicious that after she disclosed that she wished she had gone to a different analyst I had turned hostile. As these feelings and anxieties were analysed over some months she became pleased to be my patient, which I think she genuinely was, at the same time as being unconsciously excited by a belief that she was my favourite who, unlike my other patients, was free of disturbance and had a special intimacy with me, just as she had felt she was, and is, the sanest in a disturbed family into which I think her disturbances were, and are, projected and hidden. Over a period, and with much difficulty, this phantasy seemed to give way and Mrs A and I settled into an analysis with more real contact. Relations with her husband and colleagues improved markedly, and she gained a senior post, though she is currently disappointed at not being offered a promotion she expected, even though, and this is important, she had not contended for it.

However, I have been troubled that at a deeper level my patient has not changed. Though the analysis is on-going it seems so only within certain limits; that is, it has become what I think of as an enclave (O'Shaughnessy 1992) in which the full potential of our work is never quite realised. Mrs A remains something of an observer who is not fully participant, which leads to my prompting her or even saying things that are really hers to say. She apparently now dislikes nothing about me, has no strong feelings of envy or jealousy, or feelings of love or hatred toward me or anyone else. If I try to draw Mrs A's attention to any of these features we get nowhere. In sum, though Mrs A has improved it is within some 'not get-able' structure – the psychic structure which came into view in her dream.

The session

The session with the dream was on a Monday. On the previous Friday, Mrs A had been very agitated about a lump she had detected while examining her breasts the evening before. Mrs A started the Monday session by talking in a lively way about her dreams. She said she had had two dreams. Now there was one. She had dreamt: She was in a beautiful place. The queen, Queen Elizabeth, was there. Mrs A laughed and commented, 'I'm laughing at myself for dreaming about the queen. I don't like her.' She continued:

But in the dream. There the queen was, just like an ordinary person. The palace was beautiful, with many pictures and antiques, and there were lots of people there. The queen came over to me and spoke to me. She said she would show me round the palace herself. She was friendly and intimate. The queen took me about and pointed out things.

Mrs A then said, 'In the dream of my dream, I mean'—she corrected her slip of the tongue – 'in the palace of my dream I did like her.'

'The queen took me and showed me where she lived in a little cottage outside. I told the queen I was amazed that she was living

191

there, but the queen explained it. She said, "What's the use of living in a palace? The Americans would come and bomb it."' After telling her dream Mrs A fell silent. I waited for a moment, and then asked if she had associations. She answered, 'No!' as if I had asked a wrong and irritating question. A long silence followed. I found myself remembering the lump in her breast which had worried her on the Friday, and thinking that what had happened about the lump, or indeed anything else on the weekend, was absent, and by contrast, how bright and present Mrs A's dream palace was. I also thought how meaningful her dream was and how it seemed to illuminate many troubling features of the analysis.

Mrs A suddenly broke the silence to speak resentfully about her friend from Paris, Regine. She pointed out that 'Regine' too means 'queen'. She said how annoyed she is with the way Regine lives in London – Regine's always visiting them, just arriving, and her (Mrs A's) husband doesn't like Regine's husband, yet if they both come he understands he has to be there. Mrs A concluded, 'We feel really *put upon* by them. I can't just say, "She's my friend, I'll see her whenever I like." I can't go there because my husband has nothing in common with Regine's husband.' I remarked that she also could not see me whenever she liked and I wondered whether with her worry about the breast lump on Friday this might have been especially hard for her on the weekend.

Mrs A ignored the content of what I said and talked about Regine and how annoyed she was that Regine keeps visiting them. She fell silent again. After a while, speaking as if remote from her session (i.e., with no glimmer that her thoughts might hold also some immediate meaning related to her or me), she said that yesterday she had heard her husband make a telephone call about a sum of money. She could hear him behaving very badly on the phone, though he didn't have as much money as people thought.

Mrs A stopped and stayed silent. I felt all the work of thinking about what was happening was being lodged in me (e.g., that she'd felt put upon by my visiting her like an annoying Regine, first asking for associations and then making uninvited remarks about her breast lump, and having to wait for me on the weekend, and then feeling even more resentful, she had behaved badly and ignored me). Furthermore, it was I who had to worry that what with her resentment and our long silences, time was going by, and the potential of her insightful dream was at risk of being lost.

Suddenly, from the street outside voices and then a child crying could be heard. Mrs A remained silent after these intrusions, still passively waiting for me to speak. I remembered her slip of the tongue when she related her dream; how instead of saying, 'in the palace of my dream' she had said 'in the dream of my dream', and I thought she was dreaming her dream in the session, and wanted me, instead of being the psychoanalyst who annoys her, to act like the queen of her dream who points things out to her personally and intimately.

So I spoke about how it disturbed her when she did not like me and was annoyed when I asked for associations, or mentioned the breast lump, or that she couldn't come to me on the weekend. I said she was trying to lose her resentful feelings by dreaming her dream here with me. Suddenly, Mrs A was attentive. She nodded her head. I continued saying that if I stop functioning like an analyst and become part of her dream, become a queen who shows her around like an ordinary friendly person (e.g., mention the voices and the crying child we'd just heard), then she feels we are both in her dream and she likes me.

I was sure Mrs A was listening but she stayed silent, waiting for more from me. It was unclear now who was the queen, she or I. I commented that during the session she herself seemed to have become more and more like the image she has of me, a queen waiting to be served. And indeed Mrs A went on waiting.

Eventually I spoke about how though she and I might seem to be here together in a beautiful dream palace, each of us is really being diminished. Her picture of me is that I, supposedly her analyst, admit to abandoning my real place (the queen doesn't stay in her palace but lives in a cottage to escape bombs). That is, I conceal my status to avoid rousing her hostility. She loses her active mind and what she really feels, and passively persuades herself she likes me as this queen, though enduring condescension and a false intimacy form me. I concluded by saying something about how with her dream she had been able to recognise a painful truth – that this bright dream palace is a false sort of place. Mrs A responded with conviction: 'Yes. I get your point,' she said.

It was almost the end of the session. In its last moments, sarcastic and disparaging, Mrs A almost shouted, 'But are you not going to say anything at all about the *actual* events and people I mentioned?' This sudden eruption of antagonism and attack on the analytic enterprise was a bomb falling on the bit of analytic work we had done.

193

Discussion

In the course of this session some marked, and I think interrelated, changes took place – in the mode of the dream, in the relations between Mrs A and myself, and in the balance of Mrs A's instincts.

The dream itself occurred in two forms in the session. There was the dream Mrs A dreamt in her sleep, which she remembered and reported, and there was also what she called 'the dream of my dream' which was not a dream but an enactment. When the session began, Mrs A was awake and active. As she reported her dream she was able to comment on and laugh at herself. There was a glimpse of a lively self-reflective ego. She said, 'I'm laughing at myself for dreaming about the queen. I don't like her,' and a little later, 'in the palace of my dream I did like her.' At that moment she was herself very near to the insight that her dream palace was her defence against her dislike of her object. All seemed set for productive work between patient and analyst – until I asked for associations. As soon as I tried to work with her, her feelings changed. She was irritated. Her irritation and refusal to associate were important. They were part of not wanting us to stay patient and analyst, of wanting us instead to 'dream her dream' together: I should be like the queen who, although, as in the dream, there were many people present, singled her out especially to show things to, so that together we could look at her dream, which I think would then become in the session like a picture in her dream palace.

When I waited, instead of starting to enact her dream with her, Mrs A was annoyed. She spoke of feeling 'put upon' by an annoying little Regine who visited her whenever she chose and whom she can't visit when she wants to. When I took this annoying little Regine to represent myself, and spoke of my unavailability on a weekend when she may have been worried about the breast lump, she felt even more resentful and I think was alarmed by the rising violence of her feelings. She withdrew from contact with me and projected her guilt at ignoring what I said instantly into the husband (it is he she heard behaving badly on the telephone the day before).

An overall change then ensued. She no longer wanted to think about her dream or talk to me. She grew silent and passive. Her silence and passivity, soundlessly aggressive and intrusive, altered our relations. Mrs A lost her initial lively contact within herself and with me through the projection of her active ego into me. She and I lost

194

our distinctive identities and we began to fuse: We were queen and Regine (a name she pointed out also means *queen*) and she as much as I became a waiting queen. We were now in a setting where deeds were more important than words. I was in the dilemma of enacting her dream if I started interpreting its valuable content to Mrs A, or neglecting its worth if I said nothing about it and then still enacted her dream, though less obviously, by being a queen with no real interest in her subjects.

I decided to do neither of these and to do something different. I addressed the overall change in our relations and the altered function of her dream, which was now not for analysing but for enacting. I spoke to her about how she wished to make the session be the dream of her dream so she could lose the disturbing feelings of resentment she had toward me as her analyst and instead feel she liked me as the queen in her dream with whom she had especially intimate relations. In my view this was the key interpretation of the session. It reached her and she became attentive, and even though she was still half in her dream, she was also enough out of it to listen and to understand what I, still the active one, said. For her I too was half and half: half defined by her dream as the queen pointing things out to her, and also half her analyst interpreting to her.

And just as during the session her dream existed in two forms with a corresponding shift in our relationship, so there was a corresponding shift in the balance of Mrs A's instincts. The striking discrepancy between my patient's capacity to dream a dream rich in meaning, with valuable antique pictures of childhood feelings and primary relations that had lasted to the present day, and her refusal to work with the analyst about it, reflected an unresolved conflict between her impulses to work with and her impulses to escape from psychic reality. When she dreamt her dream in the night and when she first spoke to me and told her dream, life instincts were in the ascendant. But as soon as I wanted to work with her, the balance tipped the other way, dislike of reality started to be in the ascendant and she wanted to cut off from and to depart from mental life.

The session went silent and the dream's potential for creative use between analyst and patient began to die. Mrs A enacted her dream with me in the way she enacted it in her life, and there was the same loss of potential in analysis as in her life. I mentioned earlier that for some months she waited like a queen to be offered a promotion at work – without actively contending for it – and she was currently very resentful, though she took care not to show it, that another colleague whom she felt was less able and less hardworking than she (and I believe her) had obtained the higher post. In such ways she ended up identified with the unconscious image she had internalised of her analyst, undervalued and overworking. During the session, insofar as she enacted her dream, what took place was akin to what Ignês Sodré, describing the fate of Emma Bovary in Flaubert's novel, called *death by daydreaming*. Sodré wrote in her paper:

> in his exploration of the restrictive impoverishing quality of Emma's inner world, Flaubert offers a clear differentiation between the creative use of imagination which enriches life and its perversion into addictive daydreaming used to replace awareness of life, and so destroy real meaning.
>
> (Sodré 1999: 49)

Emma Bovary was driven to suicide by the terrible enactments of her conscious daydreams. Mrs A was not so extreme. When she enacted her night dream, she did not kill herself, but denuded herself and her objects, and contrived an inauthentic and somewhat deadened life in an attempt to escape the anxieties and pains of psychic reality. However, there were some 'nasty deals' inherent in this situation which was a declining one of increased persecution and guilt, all of which was split off and kept projected in the husband.

I will now leave my patient when awake and describe her when she sleeps. Mrs A only rarely dreamt a dream like her queen's palace dream, the kind of dream Freud's classic theory is about. Mostly her dreams were static, images presented without associations, whose meaning and reference were left to me to determine. Until her dream of the queen's palace with its antiques and pictures revealed that these image dreams were pictures that were part of a wider underlying defensive phantasy, I had not even arrived at so clear a description of their nature as I have just given. Mrs A reported also a third type of experience at night in addition to the few dreams like her palace dream and her many picture dreams. She was disturbed during sleep; she said it was not a nightmare, she was not dreaming, but she muttered and called out and was unable to wake, and her husband had to wake her.

Bertram Lewin (1946) conceived of a *dream screen* as the surface on which a dream appears to be projected. He linked the dream screen to the internalised maternal breast and connected the sleeper's relation to the dream screen with the waking transference relation to the analyst. In her valuable introduction to the *The Dream Discourse Today* (1993), Flanders[1] located the dream screen in the history of analytic inquiry into dreaming. Especially consonant with my Kleinian approach was Gammill (1980) who related Lewin's dream screen to Esther Bick's (1968) work on the skin and, most significantly, to Bion's (1962a) work on the container, which converts a screen with its connotation of being projected into a space that can be projected into, a space which I understand to be the inner world of the object.

I would suppose that when Mrs A kept in contact with her internalised object it gave her when asleep a space to dream in. Then she could dream dreams like her palace dream. When her dreams were merely pictures, she was beginning to intrude into her internal object with a consequent flattening of the dream space and a loss of her ego's dream function. This accords with Segal's (1980) account of the significant effects on dreaming of increasing degrees of projective identification with its concomitant loss of symbolisation. On those disturbed nights when she muttered and had to be woken out of a distressed sleep, I think Mrs A's projective identification into her internalised object had increased to the extent that she felt concretely inside her object and she had lost entirely both a dream space and the capacity to dream.

Analogous variations occur, we may recall, when Mrs A was awake in the session. At first she had a lively ego, remembered her dream and related it to the analyst, then she cut contact with herself and her analyst, began to project her lively self into the analyst and half lost her dream as a dream by enacting it. Furthermore, Mrs A grew increasingly passive, trapped in a state of projective identification in a phantasy world that for her was being concretely realised and she then needed the analyst to reach her to help her at least partially out of it. Harold Stewart noted about a patient not unlike Mrs A how 'the intrapsychic and interpersonal changes that had occurred in the transference were mirrored by the changes in her experience of her dreams' (Stewart 1973: 124). Awake or asleep, Mrs A's experience shifted uncertainly: She could have a dream about an unconscious phantasy and she could enact it and not dream it.

Gammill said about not dreaming: 'This phenomenon can be found in a wide clinical range (characterological, rather than neurotic or psychotic), extending from the schizoid personality to the apparently normal individual ...' (Gammill 1980: 127). Leaving aside the incapacity to dream of the psychotic patient who hallucinates rather than dreams (Bion 1963), where should we place Mrs A in the range of not dreaming? Mrs A is unlike those patients whose world is static, a museum in which movement and psychic work are at a standstill, who never dream. I think Mrs A is on the long continuum between enactment and dreaming, neither at the one end of enacting unconscious phantasies there is no dreaming of, nor at the other end of dreaming without enactment, but midway. Mrs A could know her dream was a dream and she also enacted her dream as 'a counter-belief' — as Britton (1998: 16) calls it — to psychic reality. She kept a precarious division between, on the one hand, emotional truth and object relations with contact, and on the other, deadening, falsifying forms of projective identification.

What kind of dream then is Mrs A's queen's palace dream she told at the beginning of the session? I quote two authors: Hanna Segal writes in her book *Dream Phantasy and Art*: 'a dream is a way of expressing and elaborating an unconscious phantasy. ... It provides a phantasy expression of unconscious conflict and seeks a phantasy solution — wish-fulfilment. ... It provides also an intrapsychic communication between the unconscious and the conscious ...' (Segal 1991: 64). Jean-Michel Quinodoz described a special class of such dreams as 'dreams that turn over a page'. He wrote of their 'clarity and coherence' and how 'such dreams often reveal more clearly than others the structure of the unconscious intrapsychic conflicts' (Quinodoz 1999: 232). He called them 'integration dreams'. Mrs A's dream is, in Segal's sense, an intrapsychic communication between her unconscious and her conscious. Its clarity and coherence make it potentially an 'integration dream' in Quinodoz's sense. Yet as the session unfolded we saw that Mrs A was not able to integrate her dream, that is, to work with the analyst and work through and keep the insight she was so near to at the beginning of the session, into her need to disavow those aspects of psychic reality that aroused her hostility. She said no to my request for associations, irritated and I think also alarmed that psychic work with her analyst would link the dream to the transference. Indeed the hatred she defended against finally erupted at my last interpretation about the painful truth that her queen's palace was a false and damaging place to both of us. Mrs A was still unable to integrate either her violent envy, or, what is different, her dislike of me as an analyst who came and went, who waited to be served, plus as yet unspecified unlikeable qualities, or her guilt about the 'nasty deals' in the queen's palace way of being, which I think is the most disturbing of all to her. At this stage, Mrs A could not keep contact with day residues from session to session: Just as she never referred again to her breast lump, so she never referred again to her palace dream. Even as she had a dream about her queen's palace, she could not yet relinquish the actualisation of it.

If Mrs A's palace dream was not an integration dream that 'turns over a page,' what kind of dream was it? Money-Kyrle (1968) distinguished three stages of representation: concrete representation in Segal's sense of symbolic equation; true symbolism; and between these, a stage of what he termed ideographic representation. I think Mrs A's dream is best conceived of as an ideograph, an ideograph that can go either way, become more concrete or more truly symbolic, depending on what analyst and patient do with it. Not only the dreams of patients like Mrs A, but also their other clinical communications, are often ideographs poised between concreteness and meaning, which pose for the analyst characteristic problems of technique (Joseph 1989). The analyst has to try to interpret in such a way as to reduce inescapable enactments to a minimum. Moreover, since much of the patient's personality is often lost in the analyst, the analyst has to contain, and retain in herself, much that is obvious at times when it cannot be emotionally experienced by the patient. In Mrs A's session, I struggled all the way with these problems, not entirely successfully, but not I think failing altogether either.

I end with the old question: Is the dream the royal road? At the beginning of the paper I described my concern that Mrs A's analysis had become an enclave in which, though she was better, she had not changed at depth. Until her dream came I could specify what was wrong only obscurely. Mrs A's dream of the queen and herself in the beautiful palace revealed her unconscious phantasy *in her own individual iconography*. What I had recognised only partially and in general terms, that Mrs A was not fully participant, that strong feelings were absent, that many of her dreams were images she passively listened to me talking about, all this was given coherent meaning by her dream which revealed the whole of a deep defensive phantasy. I can now understand that her image dreams were part of a dream palace, in which when we discussed them we become a couple of queens. Her dream also confirmed my suspicion (though this is one of its several aspects that we did not get to in the session) that though she had overtly relinquished her sense of being mother's, and the analyst's, favourite, at depth she still existed in what was really a homosexual dyad that disavowed a dislikeable and dysfunctional Oedipal family of parents and contending siblings whose true state was still blurred by her projections.

To have a patient's dream in a session is like having a Rosetta stone in the session. When a dream is present along with the other languages of the analysis – the patient's actions, verbal and nonverbal communications, the analyst's interpretations, countertransferences, and actions – it is the dream that enables the deciphering of the patient's unconscious depths. I think the dream is the royal road though a slow one with those patients who are like Mrs A.

Acknowledgements

A previous edition of this chapter was published in M. Lansky (ed.) (2004), *The Dream after a Century*, Madison: International Universities Press.

Note

1   See also the section Flanders calls 'The Dream-space' in which she has assembled papers by Stewart (1973), Khan (1974), Pontalis (1974), Segal (1980), Gammill (1980) and Anzieu (1989).

15

A PROJECTIVE IDENTIFICATION
WITH FRANKENSTEIN: SOME
QUESTIONS ABOUT PSYCHIC LIMITS

I am looking back at an analysis of some 40 years ago. A 12-year-old boy came mentally broken down and left at his urgent insistence after 3 years, able to resume his life and his education, while maintaining a projective identification with Frankenstein.

I present this as a case study in order to ask questions about psychic limits. What was the nature of my patient's recovery? What impelled his identification with Frankenstein? Were there inherent limits in his psyche requiring some such outcome? And my limitations? Would a different or better analysis have enabled a different type of outcome?

Clinical material

As told by his parents, Hugh was their youngest child, born when his mother was stressed by having to run a too-large house. At 6 weeks their housekeeper thought Hugh screamed because he needed a bottle to supplement breast feeding, but Hugh still screamed. Later, Hugh disliked and did little and poor work in a succession of schools and his education finally ceased when Father brought him home weeping and panic-stricken from a weekly boarding school. From then on Hugh stayed at home, unable to be alone, go out, or let his parents be out together. They told me he ruled the household. He had what they called 'habits', his chief one being collecting and keeping rubbish. His parents also told me that an elder son had been born with a physical disability and that, in regard to Hugh, they were desperate that he obtain a good education. They were angry with Hugh (especially Mother) and frightened, as well as concerned and worried that they demanded too much of him.

Father brought Hugh to the first session. I saw a beautiful boy with a nice smile, rigid and sad, clinging to father. In the playroom Hugh was terrified and clung to a small chair. He gazed out of the window to empty his mind or looked, not at me or the furniture, but at the spaces between.

From his hovering gaze I could tell that these spaces seemed to him to be full of particles. He also showed feelings of curiosity about the open drawer of playthings, of contempt and expectation of my contempt that he was interested. Unspontaneously – he needed the prompt of a question from me – he spoke a few words, while rubbing finger and thumb together. I spoke to him about all he had let me observe.

On the second day Hugh came with two books and a newspaper (the start of a characteristic way of communicating). On the cover of *More about Paddington* was a picture of a small bear on a cushion, which I took as offering a picture of himself and his new analysis. Hugh stared anxiously at the wall, minutely rubbing his belt, eventually telling me he was watching a hand pointing a finger. He moved the book aside to reveal headlines on the newspaper: 'BOY FRIEND, EXTRA'. I interpreted that he felt frightened and pointed at, accused of masturbation, and he wanted me to know that his penis was like an extra, a boyfriend to hold on to in a frightening world.

Hugh felt himself to be in a space of small particles and over-sized looming things, another of which was a watching eye on the latch of the window. The little chair he held onto, like his penis, father, and later myself, signified the real world that stopped him from succumbing to a psychotic panic in a menacing space of fragments and bizarre objects (Bion 1957). Though terrified and placatory, he was grateful and gained relief from having his terror and the nature of his threatening world recognised. He often made an affirmatory 'Mmmm'. He communicated through morsels of sometimes confused speech, body movements, pictures and headlines in newspapers. When he was able to sit down, he played a little with toys and paper. Mostly he made vivid drawings for which he had a gift.

He began to carry everywhere a transparent bag with a book in it called *A Creepy World*. I understood this as his ideograph (Money-Kyrle 1965) for his belief that, like the book inside the bag, he was with his creepy world inside the analysis. Some days he lost his capacity to distinguish the real world from his psychotic world, which was always there. Then, with finger movements, or the flicker of an eye muscle, or the grinding of a top tooth on a bottom tooth, he launched attacks on enemies in order to survive. Pulverising persecutors made him fear a return attack from small things; any slight noise or movement made him rigid with fear. He drew bits, pieces and vague trailing shapes, and I came to know what he already knew, that he felt in danger of bits from his self and his objects seeping out in his breath and speech or his hands as he drew and getting confused with me and the room. To staunch and to recoup his losses he had to be sparing of movement and words, take his drawings home, and whenever he saw a piece of fluff or speck of dirt he put it in his pocket: 'One of my habits', he told me tonelessly.

In a needed omnipotent phantasy, Hugh felt me as continuously with and around him until I told him about the Easter break. He swung round and stared at me, his face wide in a shock of disbelief. The next day he came bearing a drawing of misaligned concentric circles with a sunken gap. He said accusingly, 'England and France were once joined. Then a volcano came and they got separated. The middle bit got sunk and now they are like this', pointing to the mismatching, the sunken bit and the gap. I said he was showing me what I had done to him. He no longer felt as he had before, that, whether we were near or far, we were joined and I was around him. My holiday words had pushed into him and sunk him in his middle. Hugh drew a moon with four (he had four sessions) rockets round it which he said dropped darts of air onto the moon and then there would be enough air to live. He made smell after smell, frantic when he could not stop. He drew an earth and a distant moon with craters which the four rockets were leaving. In sum, Hugh responded to the first separation with elemental intensity, a characteristic of psychotic children described by many authors (e.g., Winnicott 1945; Mahler 1961; Tustin 1972). The shock of my withdrawal left Hugh sunk and angry, his orifices open and incontinent; he accused me of failing to match his unlimited need of me to be always round him and to breathe life into him. He is left like a dead moon, marked by craters of my and his violence.

After this first break Hugh's beauty vanished. He returned with sores and pimples round his mouth, a cut on his thumb, dirty and dim looking, like a too-long-neglected infant. With trembling hands he took from his drawer a paint box he had not touched before. He drew it from its wrappings and grew calm as he gazed at the colours. I spoke to him about his feeling in the holiday that he and I were dead and how seeing the colours meant there still was life here. But life had changed.

Instead of his *Creepy World* book in the transparent bag, Hugh brought a flicker booklet. By flickering its pages he made a 'film' of a figure jumping up from the end of a seesaw so that the figure on the other end was shot into space and the two figures changed places in the air and landed on the opposite end of the seesaw. Hugh often anxiously halted the film with a figure stranded in the air to picture his chronic anxiety that at any moment I could get up and go, and hurtle him into space. He could, and did, reverse our places and make me know and endure his position by keeping me stranded in silent horrific dead hours. Hugh brought a cloth cap with a 'popper' on its 'flap' and pressed the popper in and out, to show me his repeated attempts to pop into objects, who keep pushing him out, to escape his flap, i.e., his anxiety. Rosenfeld (1965) emphasises that this is central to psychotic object relations. In this battling hostile world, very much also the situation with his parents who were trying to get him out and moving, he showed me his subtle methods of entry and control. He made paper squirrels and frogs with extending tails and tongues, and drew eyes on stalks. Specific omnipotent phantasies emerged about how the flatus from his tail, or his spittle, or his tongue, indeed any organ or body product, could dart out to bridge the gap between himself and an object, enter it and control it. In consequence, his world is threatening and eerie: invisible threads and wires connect him to objects.

He also brought two boomerangs, which he threw repeatedly towards the wall, saying despondently, 'They never go anywhere, they just come back to me', which I understood as his showing me how his signals were not received. He conveyed intense despair, still feeling in himself a neglected baby, now a youth, whose parents (as I could currently observe for myself) did not comprehend the enormity of his mental handicap, distress and anxiety. He represented them by circles with swastikas, and as devils with horns. These they were not; these were Hugh's distortions. Hugh was excited by, and admiring of, his 'opposite of the ordinary' ways, as he called them, his omnipotent masturbation phantasies (such as his secret methods of entry and control) that, for him, were concretely realised. Indeed, his contemptuous refusal at home even to try 'ordinary' ways was one of the many sources of his parents' resentment.

With analysis Hugh's bizarre world and psychotic anxieties receded. He perceived again, in his fashion, the ordinary world and took from it the minimal necessary for survival by a process I thought of as accretion; e.g., when he saw me he squeezed the muscles round one eye so it flickered like a camera eye and 'took' me. In this way he accumulated picture slices. I think all his senses were impaired and had become mechanical collectors of sights, noises, words, etc., acquiring not vital introjects but concrete bits and pieces.

At home he became able to stay by himself, at first for brief periods. Then he made expeditions on his own to his local town. In my notes of that time, I record that he was much less anxious and more alive. Hugh started lessons again with a private tutor. His parents were enormously relieved. They soon insisted, in my view prematurely, that he make the journey to his sessions, by country bus, train and London underground, alone. Except for one or two days when they yielded to his entreaties to be brought by car, Hugh came on his own, sometimes suffering horrendous levels of fear, which his parents, recognising that he needed to be pushed out, and persecuted by their bondage to him, could not allow themselves to know.

Hugh had been in analysis for a year. He made a declaration: 'I can now see two-way traffic; last term in the road there was only one-way traffic. But now there are some road-works at the top of the hill.' It was his acknowledgement of a two-way interchange of work between him and me. That evening his mother telephoned to complain she was unbearably depressed, Hugh was impossible and she could not stand it, and the next day Hugh cancelled his appreciation of the day before, saying, 'Why do I have to come? I don't find you do anything', after which he collapsed into worrying about 'bits of dirt shining in the sun', the rubble of our two-way work. Here was a first glimpse of how the recognition of helpful object relations precipitates an unbearable depression which he at once projects, after which he destroys the self and object that are helpfully linked (cf. Segal's (1957) account of depression in the schizophrenic).

Nevertheless, a new era had begun. Over the next months, though short-lived, there were sequences of acknowledged two-way endeavours between him and me, the most intense occurring when his parents went away for two weeks on their first holiday in years. Alone, Hugh made the long journeys to and from his sessions.

205

He felt his parents had been torn out of him, leaving a hole from which more and more of him was lost daily. He stood at the window watching leaves being blown by the wind and told me in a voice choked with fear that there was a tree without any leaves on it. This was his ultimate dread: he would fall to pieces, be dispersed like leaves in the wind and cease to exist. By the end of the fortnight he had dwindled to a standstill.

His crisis in his parents' absence repeats his traumatised reaction to the first analytic break, but with a difference: he now had an object to come to. Afterwards he was movingly grateful. During the next weeks our relations were more alive, and full of contradictions. Hugh felt needy, grateful, resentful of his dependence, and hated all these feelings. He made a puppet of paper and string, explaining that the strings went into the puppet and held its bits together and that the strings pulled the puppet along and made it walk. The puppet expressed the truth of his invaded and controlled world of omnipotent psychotic phantasy, but, as a model, it negated all the human side of our link that was also present.

In the next analytic break Hugh's experiences again had more human elements. On the Monday of his return he spoke of a Morse code buzzer with a missing part, of its needing to be picked up and wanting to send messages, and of being recharged when the two parts were fitted together. But by Thursday Hugh had turned sullen. He saw me as a 'Snow-white' who made him one of her inferior dwarves. He had brought with him 'a green man tied by strings to a parachute' and he dropped the green man repeatedly onto the table so that it pulled the parachute down. Concentrated and thoughtful, he said, 'The green man is too big for the parachute.' On the Friday, Hugh came for the first time with his Frankenstein mask, and a newspaper.

He placed the mask of papier mâché on the newspaper saying, 'It's a mask I made of Frankenstein; it's Frankenstein's monster, but I call it Frankenstein.' He made a speech. 'Frankenstein is human, not a robot. There' and he indicated the wound with stitches he had drawn on the forehead – 'he got hit with a chair when he went mad and broke the wires that held him. There should be a bolt' – he meant the bolt at the monster's neck – 'but I did not put it in.' He rubbed the back of the mask where there was an opening, saying, 'I cut it down the back.' Then he moved the mask aside to reveal an advertisement in the newspaper: 'LONDON PRIDE – BEAUTY

IN BLOUSES', after which he completely ignored me and gave all his attention to Frankenstein. I said he had turned away from me whom he today saw as full of pride in tying him to the analysis like a bottle puppet, so that he missed it in the holidays and wanted it like a breast, the beauty in blouses. I said he was wanting me to understand he had human feelings: like the green man he felt too big to be tied to me. Later Hugh said: 'The monster is grey-green, hard and not soft, and the professor made him from old things dug up from graves.' I spoke about how he was losing his new worrying mixed feelings about me by breaking his ties and digging up old things and being like Frankenstein. As the session neared its close Hugh grew dead-looking. I said that hardening and escaping from being what he calls 'a bottle puppet' deadened his feeling of being alive and there being colour.

From then on Hugh always brought the mask. He remodelled it or sat with his head in it. He related over and over Frankenstein's story as if it were his story. Hugh knew the story not from Mary Shelley's book *Frankenstein, or The Modern Prometheus* (1818) but from James Whale's 1931 film in which Boris Karloff plays the monster. In the film, Frankenstein the scientist transgresses the limits of nature and makes a living creature who is a monster whom he then rejects. The appeal to Hugh of this story was very great. It expressed his deep sense of rejection by his objects and his painful feeling of being different from others, and because Frankenstein is monstrous only from rejection and being misunderstood, it freed him from the anxiety and depression of being 'a green man', whose narcissism and envy pull his objects down. With each element of the tale Hugh claimed an affinity. He would tell me how Frankenstein was not born but built bigger than normal by science from old things dug up from graves, pointing out that he had made his papier-mâché monster from bits of old newspaper and glue. He was describing a Promethean act of self-creation, a transmuting of dead bits and pieces into a being whose birth and care was not owed to parents and whose current better state was not owed to analysis. On the mask he often restitched the wound 'where Frankenstein got hit with a chair' to close the wounds of separation through which he disintegrates. By making an ever-present artefact which he could get into and get out of, one that was a victim of rejection and maltreatment, Hugh, in his omnipotent phantasies, freed himself from dependence on, confusion with, and fear, guilt and envy of, his ambiguous objects.

207

Hugh put his Frankenstein mask in a suitcase and carried it everywhere. He made a drawing of 'a framed picture of Frankenstein'. Frankenstein occupied the entire picture. Outside the frame was a small pudgy face, about which Hugh said contemptuously: 'It is ordinary, it has a low forehead, it is not intelligent.' He continued: 'The monster has a high brow and is intelligent, and there is more of him.' This mental state, in which Hugh projected himself into and identified with Frankenstein, was never, except fleetingly, undone in the analysis.

For reasons of space I omit the details of the period in which I struggled with a patient mostly little available. Sometimes Hugh played or acted being Frankenstein, sometimes Frankenstein was a mask behind and in which he could hide. Often Hugh felt changed; he was Frankenstein. There were cycles when his contempt for me and his excitement escalated and he grew alarmingly mad and manic, followed after a while by a collapse when, with pain and despair, he would say something like, 'Shadows are real' and be, in his way, more in contact for a few sessions. Nevertheless, Hugh did not wish to relinquish his Frankenstein; his aim, it emerged, was to learn how to avoid madness, mania or despair and he secretly listened to what I said for this purpose.

Though his 'habits' continued, e.g., his collecting bits of rubbish, which for Hugh was the retrieval of lost fragments of self and objects, at home and school there was ongoing improvement. In analysis Hugh became more split and projected into me all opposition to his Frankenstein state of mind. He brought a gadget with a skinny hand that shot out to snatch away money and maintained this was what I was: a robber stealing money from his parents, and more immediately, aiming to steal his Frankenstein away. For the first time since the start of treatment he began to nag his parents to stop. He found them willing allies. Enthusiastic about his improvement (he was now attending a crammer and coping with larger groups of children and several teachers) they felt all energies should be directed to placing him in a good school.

Very occasionally his lost self returned in horror. He would say, 'Frankenstein is not real' or 'Frankenstein is a kind of dead thing.' Even if relieved for a while, despair, anxiety and suspicion of me drove him back to idealising Frankenstein who brought him another sort of relief by shedding anxiety and despair, gaining a feeling of all problems solved, plus excitement and energy at his triumph over me with his 'opposite of the ordinary' solution by means of the monster.

Hugh was in earnest to hunt the analysis down. He took a Judo course and did menacing karate cuts in the session, saying he could smash the table in half. He met interpretations with hostile silence or a loud, 'Stupid!', 'No!', 'Wrong!' At home he insisted he wanted no educational arrangements that would allow him to continue coming for analysis. His parents entered him at a public school for the following academic year, at which point Hugh spoke of Judo tricks and a film in which a ruler was setting himself up as a god and that it was a bit mad to do that. This was his moment of fear that his parents and I were being ruled by his mad tricks into ending his analysis. His parents came to see me. I told them my opinion that Hugh needed to continue his analysis. They acknowledged there was 'some very odd behaviour indeed', but could not let themselves see more than that and so we agreed a date for termination.

The end was approaching. Hugh said one day that he had been thrown in Judo and had hurt his foot. He then talked of an old programme, *Top Cat*, the one where the alley cat saw an abandoned baby in a park. I said he saw the ending of the analysis as his parents and myself abandoning a baby. He said he was tired and had been working at his history last night. He rubbed his fingers backwards and forwards saying, 'Crooked, not straight', and spoke about vampires, werewolves, and then, with an arch intonation, Poe's *Tales of Mystery and Imagination*. I thought he was pointing out that while he had his stories, the grown-ups had Poe, which he thought had a rude meaning, so the grown-ups too had their unreal lavatory phantasies and were not really straight. I said he was in despair about his analysis stopping. It seemed to prove I was crooked: how else could I abandon him?

Hugh could feel despair for a moment only. To his last session he brought two books and laid them on the table. One was his Judo book with the cover of the Judo expert pulling his opponent down. The other was called *Frankenstein's Revenge*. These were the high and powerfully controlling images through which we were both meant to see the ending.

I was left pulled down, anxious about my patient and anxious about my work.

I had two later communications from Hugh: a letter telling me he had passed his school exams, and a few years after that, a coloured postcard of a peacock fanning its tail, on the other side of which Hugh wrote to say he had finished his course of study and obtained his diploma.

Discussion

Hugh's identification with Frankenstein, as an outcome of a psychoanalysis, is perturbing. Yet, he started broken down and when he left his analysis he could function. How shall we understand this?

As I see it, because I recognised he was broken down and struggling with psychotic panics in a bizarre universe that was his mental world outside of him, Hugh could expose more of his condition to me and feel it was known. And because I spoke in an analytic way, he felt I was not submerged by his psychosis and so he could hold on to me, even though, as we have seen, he tied himself to me in an intrusive and abnormal way. Our 'two-way traffic', the analytic work, enabled Hugh to recover.

This recovery put him in a predicament, which he saw as 'too big', i.e., beyond the limits of himself and his objects to resolve. You will recall Hugh's recognition of being helped, of need, of feeling more alive when with the analyst, but dwarfed and humiliated, believing the analyst to be full of pride, purifying herself to Snow-white, disavowing both her own deficiencies in understanding him, and also, that although he was better, his vulnerability to disintegration on separation and the envious 'green man' in him who deadens and fragments were still uncured.

Fearing breakdown again, he sees it as 'more intelligent' to break his ties and project himself into a new identity, the hard impervious Frankenstein monster, a second skin as described by Bick (1968), an identificate as described by Sohn (1985). Monstrous, with a justified black and distorted vision, ingratitude and unreality, and carrying dangers of madness and mania, Frankenstein, even so, rendered Hugh many services: he appeared to integrate Hugh's fragmented mind into a coherent identity, he was not humiliated but bigger than normal, and he disposed of fear and guilt. Moreover, he is always there and so closes the wounds of separation through which Hugh disintegrates.

Very near the end, using again the phrase 'too big', Hugh said, 'The rest is too big', and a few days later he related the first and only dreams of the analysis: 'I had three dreams. In the first dream I was emptying bits from my pockets and my mother was crying. I went up to her to put my arms around her'. He started laughing.

Oh, and my mother turned round and said, 'Don't worry; I am going to kill you'. I interrupted to remark that he was laughing because his dream is frightening. He said dismissively, 'It was scaring in the night' and continued telling his first dream: 'I woke up and I must have turned round because I went to sleep with my blanket round me and my arm under it, and when I woke up' – his voice was throttled by anxiety – 'I was round the other way and my arm was out. I got out and ran away.' I asked if he knew why he went to his mother in the dream. He answered, 'Because I was sorry'. I then spoke to him about his deep unhappiness; he was sorry his habits upset his mother and he wanted her to know he was sorry. Yet he was terrified of turning round and reaching towards her, because, as he saw her in his dream, she would not accept his sorry – the mother in his mind is murderously revengeful.

There was a long pause. Then Hugh said bleakly: 'In the second dream you pursued me to my home and whichever way I ran, you caught me.' I spoke to him about how he was appealing to me to understand that he felt it was impossible for him to stay in analysis or to admit being sorry about ending it, because, as he sees me, I pursue him to rob him of the home and blanket around him that Frankenstein is for him. After a pause he said: 'In the third dream there was a great hunt and I was with the great hunter. I was looking at a picture where guns were hidden.' This third dream is Hugh's tragic answer to the monsters in his inner world: they are deadened into being merely pictures and he joins the hunters, his murderous superego and pursuing analyst, and becomes himself the hunter Frankenstein.

We can now see more fully Hugh's plight and his limits. He has monstrous objects, cruelly unaccepting and vengeful, which in external reality to some extent they are, though it is by no means all they are; these monsters are full of his deadly projections. Hugh functions with a preponderance of death instincts and registers few benign experiences, e.g., he deadens even the small event of an analyst recognising he laughs from terror when he tells his dream of the murderous mother. His narcissism is at variance with his unlimited dependence, and his intolerance of frustration is at variance with reality. In omnipotent phantasies he intrudes into his objects and hates and fears return invasions from anything alive, and he fragments and deadens experience (see Feldman 2000). Hugh knows he does this and he is sorry that he does.

But working through, the binding and modifying of conflicts and feelings, is beyond the limits of the ties that exist between him and his objects. Indeed, any further evolution of their relations, Hugh believes, will threaten him with paranoid and/or depressive breakdown. In despair, he breaks away from his objects, and like a modern Prometheus aims to construct an artefact, and by intrusion into it to gain a new existence and identity. It is important to mention that near the end, as Hugh remodelled the mask, in some sessions it more and more took on the look of his mother. For Hugh these were moments of horror, when he recognised he had not after all made a transcendental escape, but that his 'new' identity was an old maternal monster.

Hugh is limited, on the one side, by objects with whom there can be little working through and who threaten deterioration, and on the other, by the limits to his belief in his artefact: total belief will make him mad and manic, but if he does not believe enough, he will know it for a fraud, or feel that after all he has not escaped but is imprisoned inside his old monstrous object. Hugh has to maintain a position between psychotic breakdown at the one end and madness at the other. He must aim for a mental state with a projective identification with a 'new' object that serves as his container and a protective hard mask, while hedging – often by means of jokiness – his knowledge of what is real and what is unreal, as cycles of deadening, fragmenting and ejecting continue, along with some live, though aberrant, mental activity. In some such way Hugh can ward off both breakdown and madness, and can manage to function.

Is it right though to try to describe Hugh's psychic limits without bringing in my limits as his analyst? Is not such a one–sided approach even outrageous? My work certainly had its limitations. There are things I would now do differently. To mention only two. There is the question of language. Especially at first, I used too much part-object body language. This language was also mistaken in another and more seriously misunderstanding way. Hugh's parts, like his wholes, were not natural kinds like breast or penis or person; they were bizarre bits and entities. I conflated my world and his world, and Hugh did not forget or forgive this error: remember how on the day he first brought the Frankenstein mask, he brought also the newspaper advertisement: 'LONDON PRIDE – BEAUTY IN BLOUSES'. I also worry that later in the analysis I was too much controlled into fitting in with his Hugh–Frankenstein world.

I do not wish to say Hugh could not have had a different or a better analysis. Even so, I submit, for consideration, the contention that with any analyst Hugh will have some such limited and quasi-delusional outcome. Freud expressed it thus about Schreber: '*The delusional formation, which we take to be the pathological product, is in reality an attempt at recovery, a process of reconstruction*' (Freud 1911b: 71, Freud's italics).

Had Hugh stayed longer, what might one hope for? Not for normal progress, the integration of split and projected parts of the self, mourning or Oedipal resolutions (see Steiner 1996). Psychoanalysis is no modern Prometheus. As Bion (1957) observed, the psychotic personality does not become non-psychotic, but has its own aberrant evolution. I would hope Hugh might have been able to find a less bizarre object as his identificate. I would also hope, when I think of the world of monsters which he briefly let come alive in his three dreams, that more analysis would lessen his horrific anxieties about a murderous superego and a relentless analyst. However, it may not have been possible, given our problems with two-way traffic, and the confusion and anxiety that follows upon any good development, for Hugh to acknowledge that I could come to know his and my limits and not demand he be other than he is, without his being precipitated into a deep, even suicidal depression.

The questions I ask in this chapter about limits are the questions I ask myself when I look back and try to understand my disturbance and anxiety. What were Hugh's psychic limits? What were the limitations of my work then? And my limitations when compared with other colleagues? What might be the limits now, when there have been advances in psychoanalytic understanding and I am more experienced? What are the limits of any psychoanalysis? And finally, when I think of the urgency of his insistence that the analysis end, I think that perhaps Hugh knew his limits and stopped while the going was good.

Acknowledgements

A previous edition of this chapter was published in E. Hargreaves and A. Varchevker (eds.), *In Pursuit of Psychic Change: the Betty Joseph Workshop*, London: Routledge, pp. 168–180.

The author is grateful to Dr Ron Britton for insightful comments on an earlier paper about this patient given to the British Psychoanalytical Society, and for his encouragement to explore again its Promethean theme.

Note

Hugh's Frankenstein has affinities, which reflect the overlap and the difference between psychosis and autism, with Tustin's (1986) autistic objects in that it is self-generated, idiosyncratic, hard and serves some of the same psychic functions, e.g., protects from separateness, but it is unlike them in not being a sensation object. For Hugh, Frankenstein was mainly an object of omnipotent thought and phantasy. Anxious about destabilising him, I did not find a way of really addressing, in addition to its defensive services against multiple anxieties, either the distortion and deadening of which this dominating vision was the concrete end result, or his attachment to me which was also 'somewhere' unavailably there. And colleagues will surely have criticisms of my understanding and work with this case and suggestions to make.

16

WHOSE BION?

I thank the Editors, Glen Gabbard and Paul Williams, for inviting me to be one of three contributors to a series about one of the most gifted analysts of our time: W. R. Bion (1897–1979). His work continues to attract and influence analysts of different orientations in whose books and papers will be found widely different readings of his writings. It is these 'different readings' of Bion that I shall enquire into – the books and papers themselves being beyond the scope of this short piece.

First of all, there is the reading of Bion's opus itself. What I regard as his powerful and original contribution to psychoanalysis begins with his first papers on groups in the 1940s and continues through the two subsequent decades. During this time, Bion (1948–51, 1950, 1952, 1954, 1955, 1956, 1957, 1958a, 1958b, 1959, 1961, 1962a, 1962b, 1963, 1965, 1966, 1967a, 1967b, 1970a, 1970b, 1970c) wrote on an astonishing range of subjects – groups; schizophrenic thought and language; the mind and world of psychosis in contrast to neurosis; a theory of thinking; psychic transformations; arrogance; hallucination; learning from experience; the elements and the practice of psychoanalysis.

After a study group lasting 8 years, Leon Grinberg, Dario Sor and Elizabeth Tabak Bianchedi published in 1975 the first exposition of these ideas. In the preface to their slim and valuable volume, the authors remark on 'the particular impact of the experience of immersing ourselves in Bion's thought in all its depth and of finding it surprisingly *coherent* ...' (Grinberg *et al.* 1975: 9) (my italics). I think the key to this coherence is Bion's ever present concern with the instinct to know – the K link, as he calls it, and I think this is also the main reason why Bion's writings are of such notable psychoanalytic significance. From the start, K was – and so it has remained – at the very centre of psychoanalysis. Freud wrote in 1919, for instance, 'we have formulated our tasks as physicians thus: to bring to the patient's knowledge the unconscious, repressed impulses existing in him, and, for that purpose, to uncover the resistances that oppose *this extension of his knowledge about himself* (Freud 1919: 159, my italics). Bion's wide-ranging work advanced our understanding of K in clinical practice, and furthermore brought about an overall shift in psychoanalytic theory by placing K in a new position where it has the same pre-eminence as the instincts of love and hate, so that instead of a duality there is posited a trio of interacting human instincts: love, hate and trying to know – L, H and K.

That there are different readings of Bion's work is a tribute to its originality and richness; even re-readings reveal, as they do with any classic work, new things previously missed. However, I think different readings are also encouraged by qualities intrinsic to Bion's style. He has vivid titles: 'Attacks on linking' (Bion 1959), 'Opacity of memory and desire' (Bion 1970c: 41–54); memorable sentences:

'The choice that matters to the psychoanalyst is one that lies between *procedures designed to evade frustration and those designed to modify it. That is the critical decision*' (Bion 1962b: 29); and striking descriptions: container–contained. He invents tools: the grid, types of transformations; and coins new terms when he needs (as he explains) no penumbra of previous associations, e.g., α and β-elements, α-function. And he offers a new symbolic armoury. Bion desires to disturb the reader's complacency and to be what he calls 'pro- and e-vocative' by means of a language that is designedly new and unsaturated so as to leave room for the reader's thoughts and meanings. These striking qualities of language, in combination with Bion's vigorous disciplined thought, give his brilliant texts of the 1940s, 1950s and 1960s a high tension, which, with the newness of a terminology that takes them away from old psychoanalytic controversies, has enabled them to leap the barriers of our plurality.

After these main writings, however, in my view, Bion's thinking becomes less disciplined, and his language then begins to suffer the defects of its qualities. By 'less disciplined', I mean mixing and blurring categories of discourse, embracing contradictions, and sliding between ideas rather than linking them. These features are apparent, indeed intentional, in *A Memoir of the Future* (Bion 1975, 1977, 1979); they are part of the spirit in which Bion offers his autobiographical trilogy. They are present, too, in his later psychoanalytic papers and in the seminar records.

Consider one small example of what increasingly becomes an overall style: Bion writes, 'I shall use the sign O to denote that which is the ultimate reality represented by terms such as ultimate reality, absolute truth, the godhead, the infinite, the thing–in–itself' (Bion 1970c: 26). This statement mixes the psychoanalytic idea for which the sign O was originally introduced with the vast 'penumbra of associations' of an assortment of philosophical ideas. Earlier, in *Learning from Experience* (Bion 1962b), O, as part of his exploration of K, denotes the process and experience of getting to know – in opposition to the static state of possessing knowledge. Later, as O mingles with 'ultimate reality, absolute truth, the godhead, the infinite, the thing–in–itself', Bion's earlier work rather than being developed, in my opinion, is confused. Moreover, how shall a reader align O if it is to denote, among other ultimates, 'the godhead', with Bion's observation about the meaning of symbols for the psychotic patient? In 'The mystic and the group', Bion states, 'When the psychotic symbol is met with in practice … it indicates that the patient is in private rapport with a deity or demon' (Bion 1970c: 65) – a statement that instantly resonates with clinical experience of psychosis in psychoanalysis. How then shall we read Bion? Is being in rapport with God and the Godhead to do with O or to do with psychosis? Or both? If both, then, if we follow through the two lines of thought, a contradiction is being embraced – with pleasures and perils for the text.

In 'Dreams and occultism', Freud observed how 'when life takes us under its strict discipline, a resistance stirs within us against the relentlessness and monotony of the laws of thought and against the demands of reality testing. Reason becomes the enemy' (Freud 1933a: 33). Contradictions have their appeal: breaking the laws of thought and reason brings a quantum of verbal fun. Yet, in scientific writings, such transgressions lead us to anything and everything we fancy – because, as is readily logically demonstrable, from a contradiction any proposition follows. Texts with contradictions risk an unending proliferation of meanings.

Thus, my reading of Bion's opus is that the arresting qualities of language in his main writings free the reader's thinking, but that, as his late thinking becomes less boundaried, the defects of these very qualities make the texts too open, too pro and e-vocative, and weakened by riddling meanings. Some, for example Bléandonu (1994), take something of a similar view. Others read Bion's opus oppositely and see his later writings not as less disciplined and proliferating of meanings, but as freely transcending caesuras in a way that brings the author's thinking to a culmination, especially about clinical practice. For such a reading, see, for example, Grotstein, 1981. And, between these extremes, there are various shades of opinion.

No one could doubt that Bion has illuminated the relations between patient and analyst. As I see it, he showed how projective identification, used as a defence in the way described by Melanie Klein, and also more directly, as discovered by him and others, as a means of communication, enters into transference and counter-transference. Furthermore, he offered a cluster of new ideas about the relation he named 'container-contained', the 'transformations' of experience, and the role of K and −K between analyst and patient. He saw movements in the session as oscillations between Klein's two positions (PS ↔ D), and had his own perspective on Freud's evenly suspended attention: the analytic state of mind is based on the eschewing of memory and desire. All of this taken together illuminates the nature of clinical practice, and many analysts (well known and too many to cite) in Britain and elsewhere have found in Bion's writings fertile ideas and clinical inspiration − though in different ways.

There are many analysts who would disagree that Bion's conception of clinical practice is closely related to the Kleinian development of Freud (I discuss this dispute below) and who use Bion's formulations to underpin different conceptions of the interaction between patient and analyst. Among important examples are Ogden (1982) with his idea of an 'analytic third' constructed by patient and analyst, and Ferro (1992 [1999]) with his distinctive conception of analysis as a 'bi-personal field' formed by the projections of patient and analyst. In her introduction to Ferro's book, Elizabeth Spillius has an excellent discussion of the particular way in which Ferro understands and uses Bion. Others choose and use Bion's later writings on clinical practice, especially what he says about the mystic and faith. A simple, literal reading of Bion can be found in Eigen's 1998 book in which therapy (among other things) is seen as a form of prayer. In a complex and detailed exposition, Symington and Symington (1996) read Bion as claiming that the aim of a psychoanalysis is to come as close as possible to a mystical experience. Interestingly, in a review of their book, Caper offers an opposite reading:

My own reading of Bion suggests that his idea of the mystic and the group is an abstraction from psychoanalytic experience—specifically, the experience of a new idea or state of mind being resisted. A 'mystic' in this reading is a new idea or something that conveys a new idea (this may be an interpretation, for example, or a projection of some state of mind, for another). ... Bion is providing a model of mysticism abstracted from his psychoanalytic experience of the interplay of interpretation, projection, containment and resistance. But this is a psychoanalytic model of mysticism, not a mystical model of psychoanalysis.

(Caper 1998: 420)

An enduring quest in Bion's work, one that accords with Bishop Butler's maxim that 'Everything is what it is and not another thing', was a search for the unique elements of psychoanalysis, to be used in clinical work and in a tool like the grid. Bion had the further hope that psychoanalytic elements might be shared by all psychoanalysts, so that these multiply diverse readings of his writings, though arising from his texts, are also something of an irony. In my opinion, however, it is too soon to seek a universal language for psychoanalysis; our subject is young, still in the state of an over-exuberant plurality like 19th century chemistry, which, in part, accounts for our diverse approaches and terminologies.

I come now to a large and contentious issue: How shall we view Bion's highly original work? As a development of what was there before? Or as a radical discontinuity? Roy Schafer (1997) contends that 'there is bound to be continuity within change'. He writes 'Change is best approached as a matter of transformation. Consequently, we should think of ourselves as engaged in the study of transformations in theory and practice rather than radical discontinuities' (Schafer 1997: x). I follow Schafer and read Bion's opus as a *transformation* of the work of his predecessors, especially Freud and Klein, and as also being interdependent with the work of contemporary colleagues, especially Rosenfeld (1952) who in the early 1950s broadened projective identification into a whole mode of relating to an object that could help the analyst to understand the transference situation. Bion's work is also inter-related with Segal's (1957) differentiation of symbolic equations and symbols. I place it too alongside Winnicott's contributions. For sustained readings of Bion's opus as a transformation within psychoanalysis, see e.g.,

Bléandonu (1994) and Meltzer (1978). All this is to say that I do not see Bion as a revolutionary thinker who makes a new Bionian world that breaks with what was there before in the way Einstein's General Theory of Relativity is discontinuous with Newtonian physics. But others – even though Bion himself never tired of acknowledging his debt to Freud and Klein – read Bion exactly so. 'Psychoanalysis seen through Bion's eyes is a radical departure from all conceptualisations which preceded him', write Symington and Symington (1996: xii). I think it is sometimes difficult to see what is new and at the same time not be blind to what is old though said in new terms. And because Bion's language is so different from other psychoanalytic writings, a reader can easily unshackle his formulations from their source in the history of psychoanalysis, or free them from their connections with his contemporaries or even from their evolution in his own writings. Some analysts have seen a radical divide between Bion and Klein; some see more than a divide, they see an antagonism, and accept Bion and reject Klein, connecting Bion instead with Winnicott, e.g., the Symingtons and also André Green. Our contrary readings of Bion arise from complex sources; they are not merely a matter of a choice of emphasis – on, say, transformation as opposed to discontinuity, nor simply a reflection of past animosities, or of our plural psychoanalytic perspectives – though all these may enter into why one reading rather than another is preferred.

Do different readings of an author like Bion, whose writings are designedly so open textured, matter? Yes, surely, if they are misreadings. Foucault (1977) asks 'What is an author?' He writes, 'We are accustomed ... to saying that the author is the genial creator of a work in which he deposits, with infinite wealth and generosity, an inexhaustible world of significations. ... The truth is quite the contrary' (Foucault 1977: 119). The truth, says Foucault, is 'The author is the principle of thrift in the proliferation of meaning'. What this means for us is that as widely different readings of Bion multiply, we need to return attentively to his texts and read them as a thrift barrier to the proliferation of any meaning we might just fancy.

There is a further question: What is the nature of the text? Foucault reminds us that texts are of different kinds. There are, for instance, sacred texts, and fiction, and also scientific and studious discourses. Sacred texts can have only exegesis, whereas fiction and scientific writings are subject to commentary and criticism. Furthermore, scientific writings have, in Foucault's words, 'a membership of a systematic ensemble' that needs to be taken into account. Bion's writings are not sacred texts. They are open to criticism and his psychoanalytic writings belong *not to any one of us* but to the 'systematic ensemble' that is psychoanalysis. Given the magnanimity of Bion's spirit, he would of course like us to exclude any false directions in his thought and to save and develop the truths – truths which, as he himself might say, since they belong to the assemblage of investigations which constitutes psychoanalysis, do not – in the end – require a thinker or even an author.

Acknowledgements

A previous edition of this chapter was published in the *International Journal of Psychoanalysis*, 2005, 86: 1523–1528.

17

MENTAL CONNECTEDNESS

Richard Wollheim was, most notably, among those philosophers who contributed to psychoanalysis as a philosopher, and conversely, who found psychoanalytic theories and findings relevant to their work in the philosophy of mind. My plan today is to illustrate this beneficial interdisciplinary connection by means of a discussion of Wollheim's paper 'On persons and their lives' (Wollheim 1980), while keeping in mind, also, some questions about the nature of inter-disciplinary relations. Wollheim read his paper in 1977 in New York; the revised version which is the one I am quoting from appeared in 1980 in a collection of papers called *Explaining Emotions*, edited by Amélie Rorty.

Wollheim begins the paper with this sentence: 'Every person has a life of his own, his one and only life, and that life he leads' (Wollheim 1980: 299). His aim is the philosophical exploration of personal identity. He asks: what is it that tells us that 'a boy who once stole apples from a particular orchard and some general who, years later, won renown on a famous battlefield would be one and the same person ...'? (Wollheim 1980: 300). As well as this question about 'being the same person', identity in that sense, Wollheim asks another, about the personal identity that is constituted by the

> varying degrees to which people, persons, manage to give to their lives a pattern, an overallness, or the different measure of success that they have in making their lives of a piece .... [We] recognize in such integration of a life, in the life of wholeness, something that, in many ages, for many cultures, has been in the nature of an ideal.
>
> (Wollheim 1980: 299)

He is asking: how does the inner unity of persons, an ideal which is realised in varying degrees, relate to the continuity of persons over time? That is to say, how shall we understand personal identity?

Wollheim reminds us that historically philosophers seeking for a criterion of personal identity have been divided into two about where to look. Some have looked in the domain of the physical and found the identity of a person to be in the continuity of the body. Others, historically notably Locke (1690), have looked in the domain of the mental, especially at memory as being constitutive of personal identity.

Wollheim rejects the dichotomy, the either/or of physical or mental, and thinks personal identity must rest on both. Brian O'Shaughnessy has put it thus: 'We are embodied psychological objects.' While keeping the physical, Wollheim's emphasis is on the mental. He writes: 'I contend that somewhere at the core of personal identity … is a … property called mental connectedness' (Wollheim 1980: 303). This thesis, that mental connectedness is at the centre of personal identity is not new. Wollheim himself notes that it has often been put forward by philosophers, but he thinks that hitherto philosophers have misconceived the nature of mental connectedness, and his paper 'On persons and their lives' develops his particular philosophical understanding of what mental connectedness is.

The mental connectedness at the core of personal identity is a relation that holds between two from a wide range of mental events: experiences, thoughts, emotions, anxiety, shame, guilt, sensations, acts of will, intentions – and others. Where there is mental connectedness, the earlier of the two mental events will cause the later, and furthermore (and here is Wollheim's distinctive perspective) 'the later mental event is caused by the earlier mental event in such a way that it … passes on to the whole person the causal influence of the earlier mental event' (Wollheim 1980: 304). When we hear Wollheim beginning his philosophical analysis of mental connectedness by bringing in the engagement of the whole person I think we may legitimately wonder – and of course in Wollheim's case, we know so – if his philosophical conception of persons and their mental connectedness has been influenced by psychoanalysis. In fact, this is the very aspect of his thinking that runs counter to most other philosophers on this topic. Wollheim says: '… it is this second occurrence of causality, the onward transmission of a causal influence once generated, that is simultaneously the key feature of mental connectedness as far as personal identity is concerned and that feature which its [philosophical] advocates have failed to recognise ...'. He concludes with a strong statement: 'Mental connectedness is not simply indicative of personal identity, it is creative of it' (Wollheim 1980: 305).

He begins to unfold his thesis as follows:

> Mental connectedness is creative of personal identity because, on each occasion of its instantiation, it brings the person somewhat under the influence of his past: A mental event is assigned to a person because of its relation with some earlier event in his life: and, when this happens, the relation ensures that the later event is a carrier of the influence of this earlier event, an influence that then pervades the person so that his biography is bound together even as it unfolds. The present is tied to the past, a new past is thus constructed under whose influence the future may then be brought, and so the diachronic expansion of the person, his life, gets its unity.
>
> (Wollheim 1980: 305)

Wollheim then describes the type of memory that is involved in mental connectedness which he calls 'experiential memory' (Wollheim 1980: 306). Experiential memory is such that if a person experientially remembers an event, the point of view from which he remembers it is *from the inside* with some particular affective tone, in contrast, for example, to family stories he might have been told. For instance, X who suffers from vertigo, had many times been told how as a boy he had become stranded in a state of frozen terror on a roof and his father had to come and lift him down. Such a story is recollected hearsay and not X's own experiential memory. Wollheim thinks that philosophy has hitherto neglected the essential features of the special type of remembering in mental connectedness that is distinctive of human beings: it occurs within a bodily continuity that is essential though secondary and it is remembering from within with an affective tone; it is twice causal – on the surface in the present, and also with the depths of the whole person and so brings in the past, and in this way, 'a new past is thus constructed under whose influence the future may then be brought, and so the diachronic expansion of the person, his life, gets its unity' (Wollheim 1980: 305). These are the features that create personal identity and distinguish persons from other creatures.

As one would expect from Wollheim, this is a highly crafted thesis and a philosophically condensed one. Much has been written by contemporary philosophers on the subject of persons and personal identity with orientations quite different from Wollheim's. As well, there is Sebastian Gardner, of a similar outlook to Wollheim, who devotes a large part of his book *Irrationality and the Philosophy of Psychoanalysis* (Gardner 1993) to the illumination of the conceptual issues in what he calls 'Dividing persons'. Now, dividing, though not the same, is not far from disconnecting, and I hope we may hear philosophically from him, and from other philosophers about Wollheim's thesis. I, lacking such competence, shall leave philosophical assessment to them and reflect on Wollheim's views in other ways.

Though his understanding has been influenced by psychoanalysis, as philosophy, it goes beyond psychoanalysis, just as psychoanalysis in its own field goes beyond philosophy. Each field enlightens the other and the value of a convergence is given to both. I would like to understand better the nature of such enlightenment and convergence. What are the relations between the two fields? Does psychoanalysis change the very concept of mind or does it change only our conception of the mind? And how does this affect philosophy? After all, some philosophers look, for example, to cognitive psychology and not to psychoanalysis; and some – while they do not shed the relevance of 'folk' psychology, and of course cannot since the meaning of 'mind' comes from common usage – think all 'psychologies', in other words theories of mind, are irrelevant to the philosophy of mind.

Just as the findings of psychoanalysis opened up for Wollheim a fresh perspective on the philosophical problems of personal identity, so I think does his philosophising increase a psychoanalyst's understanding of all that may fall under the notions of mental connectedness and experiential memory. Indeed, it is my opinion that we psychoanalysts, and others who are interested in psychoanalysis, have need of philosophers. We have need of philosophers of mind generally about the perplexities of mental concepts, and more specifically we need also epistemologists and philosophers of science to clarify for us and our critics – in relation to our clinical method of enquiry – the perplexities of how there can be objectivity where there is also subjectivity; the nature of clinical facts; the problems of evidence and verification; along with the meaning of that big stick 'evidence-based', which is wielded about to intimidate us.

I think Wollheim's thesis that mental connectedness creates the identity of persons offers to psychoanalysts a way of looking at psychoanalysis. We could begin by noting that where there can be connectedness, there can also be disconnectedness. And we could go on to think about how one long thread in the history of psychoanalysis – a *fil rouge* – is the evolution of psychoanalytic understanding of mental connectedness and disconnectedness. Mental connectedness and disconnectdness were crucial to psychoanalysis at its beginnings in Breuer and Freud's thinking about hysteria, and both remained so in Freud's own thinking until the last, and indeed have continued to be centrally significant in later developments of psychoanalysis. Breuer and Freud started with the idea of an hysterical patient being in a hypnoid state in which she (it was almost always 'she') is unable to connect with herself and her history. As is well known, Freud then conceived of defence hysteria characterised by defences that disconnect the subject from unpleasant emotional ideas. He soon dropped the notion of a hypnoid state supposedly analogous to a state produced in hypnosis, as he discovered that defences play a part in every type of hysteria, and indeed his clinical findings were that defences are present in all neurosis and psychosis. There are, of course, many sorts of defences, but I think some form of disconnection is involved in them all – be it overt, as in splitting off instincts or feelings, or concealed, as (say) in avoiding contact by compliance. There is a long evolution of the notion of splitting in Freud's thinking which I cannot trace here other than to remind us that in his last late phase in relation to fetishism and the psychoses he explored the 'Splitting of the ego in the process of defence' (Freud 1940 [1938]); and that his final version of the duality of the instincts made connection and disconnection the over-riding duality in our lives. In *Civilisation and its Discontents* Freud writes: 'besides the instinct to preserve living substance and join it into ever larger units, there … exist[s] another, contrary instinct seeking to dissolve those units …' (Freud 1930: 118). All of this is in accord with, and is a psychoanalytic laying out in detail of, Wollheim's thesis that mental connectedness – and disconnectedness – is central in persons and is that which creates the identity of a person.

Following Freud's work on the splitting of the ego, Melanie Klein described the splitting of the object in a new developmental theory of the paranoid-schizoid and depressive positions that places the disconnection i.e., splitting, and the connection i.e., integration, of impulses, object relations, anxieties and defences at its very centre. Later she brought in the notion of splitting and projective identification: all this, and the development of it by Klein herself and others I also take as known, and remind us only that Rosenfeld (see for example Rosenfeld 1965) studied the intrusive forms of connection and disconnection, while Bion (in *Learning from Experience* (Bion 1962a)) looked at how connections are made – and how connections are destroyed or lost (in 'Attacks on linking', Bion 1959). I also think Bion endorses, in his own terminology, Freud's over-arching duality between our 'instinct to preserve living substance and to join it into ever larger units, ...[as opposed to] another, contrary instinct seeking to dissolve those units' (Freud 1930: 118) when he (Bion) writes: 'The choice that matters to the psycho-analyst is one that lies between *procedures designed to evade frustration and those designed to modify it. That is the critical decision*' (Bion 1962a: 29, Bion's italics). And indeed it is!

Here I must break off to mention an omission: identification. Laplanche and Pontalis note the centrality of identification. They write: 'In Freud's work the concept of identification comes little by little to have the central importance which makes it, not simply one psychical mechanism among others, but the operation itself whereby the human subject is constituted' (Laplanche and Pontalis 1967 [1973: 206]). In the Kleinian strand (which is the one that influenced Wollheim) of the development of Freud, Hanna Segal identified and named the strange and concrete identifications formed by symbolic equations, and Betty Joseph explored clinically the function for the person of a whole range of introjective and projective identifications. Wollheim himself notes his omission of identification from the short paper I am discussing and in his later writings he gives to it a due place.

To return to where I interrupted myself. When Wollheim philosophises about several concepts that figure centrally in the psychoanalytic theory I have so sketchily adumbrated, I think he crystallises them and clarifies them for psychoanalysts, and they are all concepts that analysts need often to reflect about, with their own kind of reflection. Philosophy is conceptual and general, while psychoanalysis is theoretical and clinical, and the clinical is, foremost, individual. It is the old problem of universals and particulars, but the peculiar particularity of persons means that analysts have peculiar problems about generalising from an individual analysis – *this* individual analyst with *that* individual patient. Another problem, I think, for the philosopher of science.

As clinicians, we have to be open to the anxieties underlying the individual ways in which there are links, or a lack of links, on the surface of, or with the depths of, a patient's communications, and we need to attend to whether the patient is telling us what Wollheim calls, in his apt and helpful description 'experiential memories', or whether it is stories the patient has been told – by his family, or, another psychic situation, stories told by internal figures that revise his experience. We need to notice whether the process of analysis itself is experiential, or tending to become a situation of 'hearsay', in which the patient hears the analyst saying interpretations but is not learning from his inner experience of them. An analyst must also reflect on mental connectedness in regard to himself: to consider where and how he connects with his patient, and where and how he fails.

And then there is time. What Wollheim says about time and time's relation to mental connectedness, is for me, most thought-provoking of all. It so happens that psychoanalysts have also lately been thinking about time: in the British Society there has been Andrea Sabbadini (1989) on 'Boundaries of timelessness'; Cathy Bronstein on 'Borges, immortality and the circular ruins'; Dana Birksted-Breen (2003) on 'Time and the *après-coup*', with discussions from Gregorio Kohon, Ron Britton and Rosine Perelberg; Roger Kennedy (2007) on 'Restoring history to psychoanalysis'; David Taylor (2005) on 'Interpretation and Anticipation'; Michael Feldman (2007) on 'The illumination of history'; and there are others. In these papers there is new thinking and also the resurfacing of old controversies. Some of these unsettled controversies are clinical and concern analytic technique, e.g., whether, and how, interpretations in the 'here and now' do or don't connect with the patient's history and the compulsion to repeat. Also lodged in these clinical issues are philosophical questions about the concept of time: how can the past and the future be in the human present? And here Wollheim's philosophical analysis is illuminating:

> Mental connectedness is creative of personal identity because … it brings the person somewhat under the influence of his past: A mental event is assigned to a person because of its relation with some earlier event in his life: and, when this happens, the relation ensures that the later event is a carrier of the influence of this earlier event, an influence that then pervades the person so that his biography is bound together even as it unfolds. The present is tied

228

to the past, a new past is thus constructed under whose influence the future may then be brought, and so the diachronic expansion of the person, his life, gets its unity.

(Wollheim 1980: 305)

I think every clinician needs to reflect on how time occurs, or is absent from, an analysis. Do the patient; the analyst and the analysis have a past, a present, and a future? Or has the whole enterprise become repetitive, with that peculiar atmosphere of *timelessness* that a stuck analysis gets? Wollheim expresses this beautifully as being under the undue influence of, or having an undue pre-occupation with, the past – '*undue*' is in contrast to '*somewhat*' (as in the quotation above) – an important distinction this, which Wollheim discusses very interestingly towards the end of his paper. But I have to leave time and timelessness, because, before I stop, I want to discuss another idea, one that Wollheim brings in right at the beginning of his paper.

You will remember how he begins his paper with the sentence 'Every person has a life of his own, his one and only life, and that life he leads. But some more so than others.' (Wollheim 1980: 299) A little later he continues: '[there are] varying degrees to which people, persons, manage to give their lives a pattern, an overallness, ... [there are] different measure of success that they have in making their lives of a piece ... such integration of a life ... in many ages, for many cultures, has been in the nature of an ideal' (Wollheim 1980: 299). Wollheim calls this integration of a life 'the ideal unity' (Wollheim 1980: 299) of persons. That persons realise this ideal unity only to varying degrees is of the first importance and connects with the way Freud altered our view of what a person is – as great an achievement as the way in which Freud altered our view of the mind.

Freud changed our conception of mental illness and its treatment, and also our conception of mental health. As early as 1895, as though speaking to a patient, he makes this well-known statement: 'much will be gained if we succeed in transforming your hysterical misery into common unhappiness. With a mental life that has been restored to health you will be better armed against that unhappiness' (Freud 1895b: 305). His work showed that in so far as we are unhappy, in addition to external causes, common unhappiness comes from conflicts between our desires and reality, our needs and narcissism, love and hate, our criminal tendencies and our wish for civilisation, and that our ego will deal better with these conflicts, if – to express it in broad terms – rather than disconnecting (which in one way or another brings the misery of illness) the ego can bear more connections with the pain and guilt of its conflicts. At the end of his life in 1937 in 'Analysis terminable and interminable' Freud wrote again of the aims of psychoanalysis:

> Our aim will not be to rub off every peculiarity of human character for the sake of a schematic 'normality', nor yet to demand that the person who has been 'thoroughly analysed' shall feel no passions and develop no internal conflicts. The business of analysis is to secure the best possible conditions for the functions of the ego; with that it has discharged its task.
>
> (Freud 1937: 250)

On these issues Melanie Klein's work is continuous with Freud's. Development from the splitting of the P/S position to the integration of the DP is not once and for all – the journey from persecution and disconnection to a more depressive integration has to be gone through again and again. Moreover, the ideal unity of complete integration is a destination never reached – because of the conflicts in persons and the limits set by their natures and their primary object relations.

The common unhappiness of which Freud spoke is common in the sense of being an aspect of ordinary lives, and common also in the sense of being common to us all, though our tendency to disown and project unwanted aspects of ourselves constructs divisions, between an 'us' and a 'them' that would deny the connection between the well and the ill, the sane and the psychotic, the law-abiding and the criminal (we all are guilty e.g., of inner crimes like parricide). It is a fundamental understanding that mental connectedness is an ideal achieved in different degrees by different persons, and never totally by anyone, and that it is in the very nature of persons that in Wollheim's words there will be 'different measure[s] of success that they have in making their lives of a piece' (Wollheim 1980: 299). In this way of thinking, the atypical being, the mentally ill, the disordered, the perverse, the criminal, are not dehumanised; they remain persons who are different, difficult, psychotic, borderline, perverse, criminal. Such a conception has broad consequences for their rights, their treatment, our connections with them, our interest in and concern for them, the function of prisons, hospitals, etc. It bears on the debates about abortion. When does being a person begin and end? Necessary though physical continuity is, if it is mental connectedness that is creative of personal identity, what then of the tragic state of being in a coma?

You will remember that Freud subsumed the ego ideal under the broader concept of the super-ego. There it remains, perhaps a little neglected. Persons have an epistemophilic instinct to know themselves and others (including knowing their tendencies not to know) and in the distinctively human type of consciousness, a self-conscious consciousness, a person knows (or disconnects from knowing) about ideals his failure to achieve ideals. In some psychoanalyses, the 'ideal unity' may turn into a therapeutic ideal that the patient experiences as a super-ego demand emanating from the analyst for a mental connectedness that he cannot achieve. Meanwhile, the analyst has his own super-ego to contend with, as well as his professional ideals about connecting psychoanalytically with his patient – ideals he too will achieve only in varying degrees. In regard to his patients, as Freud said, an analyst does not aim for some 'schematic normality', but works towards enabling each patient to become not what he *should be* – fulfil some set of demands, but instead, what he *could be*. As Wollheim writes: 'Every person has a life of his own, his one and only life, and *that* life he leads' (Wollheim 1980: 299, my italics).

Wollheim's philosophical understanding of persons, their varying degrees of mental connectedness, the distinctive nature of memory and time in persons – all of which he much expanded in his later book *The Thread of Life* – has been of great value to psychoanalysis. I am profoundly grateful for it. As I have been for many years to Richard and his work.

Acknowledgements

This chapter was written in 2007.

18

INTRUSIONS

In the first paper in his book *Psychotic States*, Rosenfeld writes of a patient that her 'central anxiety was a fantasy of the persecuting analyst forcing himself into her to control her and rob her, not only of her inner possessions, for instance, her babies and her feelings, but her very self' (Rosenfeld 1947: 22). Persecutory anxieties about an invading analyst, following on the patient's phantasies of intrusion, is a theme that runs through Rosenfeld's pioneering papers of the forties, fifties and sixties. He describes the whole syndrome: the infantile anxiety and greed that impels the intrusion, the new identity the patient obtains by this type of projective identification, which carries with it fears of ego-disintegration in addition to anxieties of being trapped in and confused with the object, and how, in order to keep the analyst out, the patient does not speak about events that might arouse interest, withdraws and negates interpretations. If these things are now not new, it is because Rosenfeld, foremost among others, made them familiar.

At the time Rosenfeld was writing these papers Melanie Klein was still alive. 'Notes on some schizoid mechanisms', where she named projective identification, appeared in 1946 (Klein 1946), and *Envy and Gratitude* in 1957 (Klein 1957). These works greatly influenced Rosenfeld, as they did all who followed Klein's new thinking. It was a time of fertile Kleinian development. Rosenfeld was investigating psychoanalysis as a treatment for schizophrenic and severe borderline patients, as were others, notably Bion and Segal. Bion proposed new hypotheses about the psychotic personality and Segal made the important differentiation between symbols and symbolic equations – both areas in which Rosenfeld also made contributions. He focused on the impairment of the psychotic ego, not from Bion's angle of the fragmentation and projection of the ego to form bizarre objects, but from the perspective of the impairment of the ego that results from an intrusion into the object, also the angle from which he approached the loss of symbolic functioning. He writes for instance

> whenever verbal contact was disturbed, through the patient's difficulty in understanding words as symbols, I observed that his phantasies of going into me and being inside me had become intensified .... For it is the quantity of the self involved in the process of projective identification that determines whether the real object and its symbolic representation can be differentiated.
>
> (Rosenfeld 1952: 77)

Rosenfeld is here making an important clinical point: there are degrees of intrusion into the object; intrusion is not always 'all the way'.

As we know, Herbert Rosenfeld has had a huge influence. John Steiner's (1989) essay records the wealth of observations and measured assessments and the original conceptualisations that are to be found in Rosenfeld's papers. Rosenfeld was not afraid of mental illness and he eschewed what a patient of his called 'the bluff' – the bluff of transference peace. He had an extraordinary capacity to be where ill patients were, in schizoid, manic and depressed places, to understand their compressed utterances and interpret in strong plain words, often making what he called an 'integrative interpretation' of their total situation.

Rosenfeld's work on intrusions into the object, i.e., invasive projective identification, is invaluable when trying to work with patients like Mr B, who omnipotently take themselves into the analyst, mostly not going all the way, so that they are in, and at the same time out of, the analyst.

Mr B came for analysis in a desperate state. He was depressed and anxious and complained he had no memories of his parents, both dead, and that he was insecure about his gender. From the start he was in a double world. He tried to talk and to listen, and at the same time was anxious he was in a void and just as anxious that I might communicate with him dangerously so that he quickly withdrew, sometimes into sleep. What he managed to hear he was cautious about, often detaching it from me, so gaining 'pieces of knowledge'. Our verbal contact was anyway thin and experiences of communicating to me and being understood were weakly internalised. To protect himself from his huge anxiety Mr B gave most of his attention to sensations: of snuggling into a soft place, of feeling himself to be a girl with breasts, or feeling remote like a superior phallus. Sometimes his sensation world collapsed into being only a lavatory world of urine and faeces.

These sensations were based on projective identifications consequent on omnipotent phantasies of intrusion that began before his session. Mr B arrived early in my vicinity, concretely for him the psychoanalysis area; he went into the Heath for a walk to the pond, and then came out of the Heath to walk to my house for his session, where, in another mode, he repeated his two journeys. On first seeing me, unable to wait or stay separate, he went omnipotently inside me with his eyes, and then on the couch some of him came back with anxiety to the reality of being outside. The phantasies of being inside were idealised as offering a pleasurable 'other reality' that was meant to free him from unwelcome knowledge and all anxiety. However, they never quite succeeded in freeing him from anxieties of entrapment, weakness of self, of being watched and disparaged by a pathological super-ego and, in addition, of a pervasive guilt about withdrawing and keeping me out.

Thus, objects entered Mr B's mind in an imbalanced way: incorporations that followed upon his projective identifications predominated over identifications that were a sequel to introjections, with the result that Mr B enacted identities, acting out and 'in', far more than he was mentally active. Segal (1991) has examined the opposition – so significant for clinical work – between acting out and mental action.

Freud (1911a: 219) describes the 'momentous step' of the setting up of the reality principle as requiring a heightened awareness of attention and memory, a system of notation, and a passing of judgement to decide whether a notion is true or false. All these ego functions were interfered with – I think from a young age – by Mr B's divided way of being which distorted his relation to reality. His attention is largely engrossed with a sexualised watching of his objects' insides, so that his notation is predominantly from a sex and bottom world that he 'sees' in his voyeuristic phantasies. Feeding might be noted as shitting, talking misconceived as sex, and so on, and he makes no assessment of the truth or falsity of these confabulations. John Steiner describes how 'in most retreats reality is neither fully accepted nor completely disavowed' (Steiner 1993: 88), which was exactly so with my patient. Steiner's theory of psychic retreats (Steiner 1993) which is based on Rosenfeld's theory of narcissistic organisations has been of much help in trying to understand Mr B.

It was difficult to make contact with Mr B. I had to take account of the variations in his capacity for symbolic thinking and not miss his meagre attempts at communication which came almost unaccompanied by emotional projections, all the while being provoked and pressured by Mr B to involve myself with the details of his erotised sensations and phantasies. Had I done this last, it would have been, in Rosenfeld's phrase, to 'lose my very self'. Despite Mr B's annoyed protests that I kept ignoring his gender problems, I focused not on their details but on their invasiveness and function.

At first my main focus was on their defensive function, against the anxiety of waiting, separateness, or being with a narcissistic and self-preoccupied analyst who was not attending to him, or was trying to force her way into him. Later the hatred that drove his intrusions was more prominent – the degradation of the imagos he forced on and into me as being my identity, though he knew, if dimly, since he was not in a total state of projective identification, that these images were false perceptions.

Of course all this was interpreted piecemeal as it emerged. With time and analysis Mr B revealed unambiguously that the target of his hatred was knowing. He tilted himself backwards, stealthily bent his knees up, swayed his bottom over the couch, and consciously fantasised about undressing girls with his eyes, or feeling his 'breasts' on his chest, or awaiting a homosexual overture from a male friend known 20 years ago with whom he had never had sexual relations. He was perversely playing with troubling themes familiar to him from his analysis with contempt for an analyst who did not prohibit his excesses of erotised distortion on the couch. We began to realise that Mr B, in the mode Betty Joseph (1982) describes, was not so much playing as addicted to these phantasies. The realisation that he was enslaved to conscious fantasising that turned analytic thought into rubbish was very distressing to Mr B, but then his initially painful insight was turned into 'sexy slave phantasies' in which he was a slave forever rowing an ancient vessel, and, in due course, 'sexy slave phantasies' were continually intruding into his mind and plagued him.

The accessibility of such a cycle was part of a significant change taking place in Mr B. With the resolution of some of his anxieties, where previously he had split and dispersed some of the elements of his psychic life he was now tending to gather and assemble them. Mr B was more present and mentally active and some days I was astonished by his liveliness and capacity for thought. Some significant memories of family life returned. His earlier mental configuration in which to the fore were erotised dyads of soft girls, brute phalli, and bottoms, while in a recessive area were remote parents far apart with so little life or character they were almost spectral, was changing.

I come now to the period I present in detail. Mr B had left for the summer holiday in good spirits, notably freer from his usual anxieties and erotised preoccupations. In the new term he obtained a new contract which he told me about saying 'I got that job by the way. I explained to them I couldn't start early on some mornings.' His evident pleasure in his success, and his direct manner with me and with his new employers, were in good contrast to how he would previously have been very anxious about a clash of times between analysis and work, feel I was invading his career, try to exploit my guilt and act out to alienate his employers – once losing a prospective job in this way. There was a sense of separateness and difference.

Yet, along with his new directness the old destructive intrusive acting out continued. An on-going example was a philosophy course he had begun that year. In several sessions just before those I report he came with his head full of books he was reading: Aristotle's *Ethics*, Boethius etc., etc. told in a way so that I wondered (as I often had) if he knew I had been a philosopher once, and/or that my husband was a philosopher still, teaching at the very university he was attending. I felt he knows, is watching me, 'reading me' from inside, and yet, of course, it could be a co-incidence. I felt invaded, and made impotent in analytic function. When I drew his attention to how he felt his eyes were inside me watching me not knowing what to do, he became again direct, and moreover was distressed by the inconstancy of the way he sees me.

Monday

Mr B started quickly, as though to pre-empt me coming in about my weekend, saying he had had a busy weekend. The chief event was that he had gone to a theatre to see a play with a group of people. After the theatre they had all gone to a restaurant. There were nine of them. It was late and he was hungry. The man who organised it, who should have ordered the main course right away, did not. Instead he ordered drinks. And after that, he ordered starters. It got very late so that by the time they left the restaurant it was after 1.30 a.m.

During his lively telling, Mr B made me curious – I wondered: How does one find a restaurant in London these days that stays open so late? There had been pauses in Mr B's account, yet each time I wanted to come in, he said 'No', and talked on, giving me a taste of how it is to be a child refused entry to, and made curious about, night-time goings on, which eventually, when he let me, I interpreted. All so far had been straightforward.

Then Mr B repeated what he had said about the restaurant and the man who organised it and made the main course so late, going over it all, talking for a long time. I noticed how there were no names of the people, the theatre or the restaurant they had been to. There was a silence. Then Mr B said, 'There is something very annoying. I don't know what to do. Somebody is wanting a reference.' He stopped. I thought: Yes, I want a reference. I don't know what this is about or what is annoying. He broke the silence with more of the same about his weekend and then said, 'There was a review in a Sunday paper about …?' (he left his sentence incomplete). 'By Kathy …?' (he left the name incomplete). I did not complete his sentences or supply what most likely was the missing information – it so happened there had been an article that weekend in a Sunday paper in which some analysts, among them myself, were mentioned. Even this was tricky – it was an article not a review, and the writer's first name was not Kathy, though there has been a Kathy O'Shaughnessy writing reviews in Sunday papers, but not for a while now. Mr B waited, mentally inside my mind, I thought, watching to see how he had organised me. When I stayed quiet, he talked again about his weekend, sounding angry and isolated. His legs came up and he swayed his bottom in his usual way for a brief spell as he said he thought he might do some more philosophy even though there was no course he really liked and the group he'd organised had collapsed.

During these prevarications, which so evidently were prevarications, the atmosphere had quite changed. At the beginning of the session we had been straightforwardly engaged about issues of curiosity and exclusion on the weekend. Now, in place of curiosity there was an intrusive voyeurism aimed at preventing a continuation of a straightforward 'main course' to the session, although even as he

237

persisted in trying to organise me into opening myself to his invasions he knew and was angry that he wasn't succeeding.

I eventually made a rather long interpretation. I hope it was of the kind Rosenfeld might call 'integrative'. I spoke about how he had let me see his two selves: one straightforward about the difficulty of feeling excluded and curious on the weekend, the other trying to organise us with a way of talking – telling, not telling, misleading – into seeming not separate but inside each other, watching in a knowing way. This self hates me to be potent with him and aims to delay and disable me so that I cannot continue to give him whatever should be the main course of the session that his other self is hungry for. I finished by saying he knows his attempted organising of us is failing, and he admits he doesn't even really like it, yet he is tempted to keep on doing it. There was a long silence. I added something. I said that I thought that when he'd been talking before he'd also recognised that it was the same disabling way in which for a long time in analysis he has been talking about philosophy. There was another long silence. Then Mr B responded in a straightforward and strong voice saying: 'I like what you said. Because it is accurate.'

As he left the session he turned and looked at me with respect.

Tuesday

I was shutting the door of the consulting room as Mr B was going to the couch when he turned and took a few steps back to the door. He stood there, looking afraid and depressed, and said 'I need to get my handkerchief'. I opened the door for him, he went out, came back and lay down.

Making a broad gesture with his hand at the room, me and himself, he pronounced: 'There's no reality to any of this.' There was a long silence. When he spoke again his talk took him away, to a miscellany of things in his home and office. I said that I thought he felt trapped here and was now talking himself away and out, like before he had physically to get out of the room. Very hostile and negating, Mr B said 'No. I wanted my handkerchief. That's all,' crushing out meaning.

He began to talk about his handkerchief. 'What comes to mind is boarding school and masturbation. It's disgusting really' he said as he pulled out of his pocket an orange handkerchief with dots. He went on to say that when he goes to his old university town he buys these handkerchiefs from a special shop. One can also buy them in London in Jermyn Street, dotted like mine. Near the men's clubs, you know. My wife's first boyfriend has the same handkerchief! I often find it amusing he turned out to be homosexual. He's lived with his partner for 35 years. In fact they're the longest surviving couple among our friends. We all have the same handkerchiefs.

Mr B went on like this, trying to construct an exciting club atmosphere of masturbating men who hate women, along the way referring to and explicitly fouling some recent analytic work which had led to realisations of his own about his adolescence and couples and thirds. He ended talking to me as though he were chatting amusingly to a female companion at a dinner party. 'I've got two views about women: the public one – tolerant, feminist – of course they're equal! And also the old-fashioned one: a woman should revolve around the man – have his meal ready on the table, look after his clothes.' During all this he rubbed his forearm from time to time – everything short of actually masturbating his penis and ejaculating into his handkerchief had gone on. It felt excessive, a misuse of a session, as though a setting for analysis had been subverted into a room for sexual 'personal services' such as a brothel supplies. Even so, Mr B remained anxious and depressed, unable quite to sustain his belief in having me as a voyeur in a high world of homosexual males nor in his amusing me as a 'lady' companion, and I think it was disgusting to him to be driven to so destructive a masturbation phantasy.

I tried to make a link with the previous day's session, saying that yesterday he felt the self that intruded and disabled me felt caught and exposed, and now feared my hostility. I said I thought he was also frightened of his hatred, which feels so huge it's dotty, mad. I also pointed out how in yesterday's session he had hated me but also respected me, which makes him feel so bad he can't bear it, and so that he has to de-realise it and make a phantasy world to get away into. I saw however that words – I was unable to find any interpretation that was of help – were unbearable and provoked further excesses. I stopped talking. I became a spectator, full with his evacuated depression and the acute pain of seeing my patient driven by fear, depression and hatred to enacting what he himself thinks is disgusting really.

Wednesday

At first Mr B affected a thin cheeriness underneath which I could hear in him something so worn-down it was almost expiring. Then, snide and challenging, he gave a warped version of the previous session saying among other things that I had accused him of being a homosexual and a woman hater. I said I thought he wanted to provoke an argument to test whether I had enough life left in me to know a distorted version when I heard it. To this he replied 'Well. Yes.' and was briefly a little hopeful but then fell again into despair. I spoke about his despair that within himself he felt a world was almost dying after yesterday's session. He could not bear to hear me. He got sleepy, struggled against it, succumbed. An atmosphere of ruin, hatred, despair was palpable.

He woke when I said it was time to stop. He left saying it was the worst session ever.

Thursday

In the waiting room Mr B looked lost. He lay low down on the couch in acute distress. He said he was cold. He said the central heating had broken down in his house all week and it had got very cold. (The weather in fact was very cold.) I said he was telling me he felt something central to do with warmth had broken down: he felt out in the cold, and within himself he also felt cold – he had no love left and he feared he was himself unloved.

He made some attempt to negate this painful psychic reality by means of unreal fantasising to raise a spark of warmth in himself or me. It was weak, confused and did not work; such constructions had been exposed as masturbation phantasies and had lost their power. Interpretations I tried were dead and useless.

Communication between us had broken down. At the end of the session which was the last of the week (he comes four times) Mr B left in acute distress.

It was now 6 weeks before the Christmas break. Mr B was gripped by wrenching anxieties. Both systems of central heating had broken down: enactment and erotisation on the one hand, and true warmth for and from his objects, on the other. He believed I did not like him because, as he put it, he had 'crossed a line', 'gone too far'. He feared his inner world was beyond repair, and felt trapped with fear, hatred and persecuting guilt towards his analyst.

He became doubtful about psychoanalysis. He said he knew when he came to me he needed something. He knew his life wasn't right. But was my method right for him? He presumed I thought it was, which was important to him. For several sessions he was tormented by doubts. Then he seized on the idea of escaping his torments by stopping analysis – after Christmas he would not return.

For a few days this plan relieved him, then he doubted it. He said feelingly 'I am tempted to stop and not return, but when I think of that I feel most unhappy', and he regained some inner freedom to think. He told me he recognised his present predicament and his impulse to give up analysis as a return of the terrible time he'd had a collapse at work, when his chief appointed someone who was his junior over him, and he gave up his job with a resulting hiatus in his career.

For a few sessions he was enormously relieved to be still with me and in analysis. A memory returned to him of standing on the edge of a steep valley in Jerusalem. Birds were flying in the fresh air, and he could see the dome of a church below. Mr B spoke so vividly he seemed there again, on his own, out in the fresh air, using his eyes not to intrude but to observe what's there. It could have been kitsch, or a setup for me. I did not think it was. I stayed quiet. Suddenly he produced some violating psychoanalese about this memory. His spoiling self had intruded and his liveliness vanished; he gave up and surrendered to sleepiness.

After this, his torments about what to do returned. There was an atmosphere of last chance and danger. I thought I might really lose my patient. Stopping analysis was multiply determined, but what was foremost was Mr B's fear of invasion by, and enslavement to, irreparably damaged objects. Typically, he was at this time reading a book about the abolition of slavery.

In the last fortnight Mr B made what he called a 'decision'. He would return after Christmas, but he would not come on Tuesdays. He was enormously relieved to have found a way to come back. He tried to force me to be overtly friendly about giving up Tuesdays, 'proving' to me that it made him feel better. He was again anxious, sleeping poorly, had diarrhoea, etc.

Not wanting to push him into a position which might make it impossible for him to return, I said nothing about what I would, or would not, do about his 'decision', except wondering out loud if he was unsure whether I was going to be able to stand up to him. He responded with sudden goodwill – 'Well, are you?'

He was still reading his book about slavery. He told me he always reads something while he eats his breakfast. He was 'reading me',

241

excited that I was now 'enslaved' by his decision to return but not come on Tuesdays, but also anxious and guilty. In one of the last sessions he was more accessible and I spoke about his fear of his intrusive hatred that continues even while, so to say, he has his breakfast with me, and his fears that I will force into him a state of anxiety and guilt from which he will never escape and which will make it impossible for him ever to leave me, and how in this regard not coming on Tuesdays proves he can get out. To all of this he responded with a straightforward, appreciative, 'Exactly right'. In one of his last sessions Mr B told me, 'I'm still sticking to my decision about Tuesdays, though I know it's wrong'.

In his very last session he was rampant in a state of total phallic projectification, enacting equivalents of taking his trousers down and defecating on the couch and refusing to listen as I tried to speak about his being an image of an analyst shitting on him on this last day, an image he knew to be distorted to evade the pain of parting. Then, at the door as he left, he said pertly, 'Have a good break', watching me, waiting to see me return his good wishes as I customarily do. This time I could not. I was suddenly too angry and just managed to say 'Good-bye'. Mr B had found my limits. He had provoked in me an anger that lasted for hours.

After Christmas Mr B returned, but not on Tuesdays.

Discussion

In the Monday session after the weekend we see Mr B's two selves. One communicates in a straightforward way about going to a theatre and a restaurant, by projecting into me feelings of exclusion and curiosity such as a child might feel about night-life. Mr B's other self speaks in a different mode – half-telling, stimulating, misleading – with the aim of intruding into my mind and watching voyeuristically as he tries to delay and disable me from giving him what should be the main course of the session for which he is hungry. Mr B himself has seen what 'the man who organised it' is doing in the restaurant, and when I interpret how it is happening in the session Mr B likes it – as he says 'because it is accurate'.

At that moment Mr B has preferred an accurate analyst to his prevaricating self. In a way that is most disturbing for Mr B this upsets his more usual internal balance in which his prevaricating self, a narcissistic structure (I have left aside Mr B's narcissism – waiting to hear Dr Britton on the subject), feels superior, both to the analyst and his other self, both of whom it regards as his juniors. Indeed, later Mr B himself recognised that this analytic crisis was a repeat of a life crisis of some years before when a junior was appointed over him, making his place of work so intolerable that he gave up his job with a consequent hiatus in his career.

On the next day, Tuesday, his intrusive self, its idealised cover blown, feels trapped, frightened and depressed. He hates and fears the analyst who has become very threatening. Mr B tries to de-realise this situation, and with his dotted orange handkerchief to re-project himself into the identity of a popular misogynistic phallus in a world of split, inferior and seducible objects. However, he finds no sustainable power over me or himself and only reveals yet more clearly that these are aggressive masturbation phantasies whose purpose is to evade and destroy psychic reality. It was a horrible session. I could find no useful interpretation and was reduced to being a pained and depressed watcher of my patient.

On the next day, the one Mr B said 'was the worst session ever', he has internalised an analyst reduced to impotence. His despair about his hatred and the ruin of the analysis, which for him is concrete, overwhelms him and seeps out and envelops everything. By the end of the week Mr B's systems of central heating have broken down – both the excitement of intrusion and erotisation, and love for and from his objects. He is in an acute state of distress, tormented about what to do. Should he end his analysis? Or should he return after Christmas?

To give up his analysis was seen by Mr B as an escape from an analysis believed to be forcing into him unendurable pain and anxiety about himself and a damaged, irreparable world. Rosenfeld, in a discussion of this type of crisis (Rosenfeld 1964), draws attention to another feeling impelling the patient to give up at a time like this: unconsciously it is a self-sacrifice to appease the super-ego who, as Rosenfeld puts it, accuses the patient of building up his life at the analyst's expense. You will remember Mr B saying 'I knew when I came for a psychoanalysis that I needed something; I knew my life wasn't right'. I think Rosenfeld is right; stopping analysis would have meant to Mr B ending his hopes of a better life in order to appease his enormous sense of guilt.

Yet, to return after Christmas meant a return to a painful and uncertain prospect. He faced a struggle to renounce his orientation to and identification with his invasive self and to reorient himself to objects which arouse huge anxiety and distress. Any withdrawal from his substantial state of invasive projective identification painfully exposes his unmodified infantile self; terrified, greedy, envious, whose intolerance of real relations will continue to handicap him. Moreover, the way his objects have entered his mind means the analyst as a good figure on whom he can rely is peripheral, while more central is a persecuting analyst whom he fears will invade him with more than he can stand.

Can Mr B bear it? After all, he has his limits, and I have mine. It was difficult to discriminate when he was available for thinking from when he had projected himself all the way into his object and lost his capacity for verbal thought – which needed a different interpretive approach. At times I could not find any way to talk to him, especially when Mr B, in a state of projective identification with an omnipotent phallus, grossly enacted a masturbation phantasy.

Consider the last complex session, the one in which I was left full of anger. Mr B was intruding violently, venting his hatred of an analyst who takes a break from him and who persists in trying to understand him; he was misunderstanding the ending as his being forcibly ejected like shit, while refusing to listen to my saying that this might be his defence against parting, and misunderstanding too any quietness on the analyst's part as indifference – hence his excesses to penetrate. Mr B knows he 'goes too far', 'crosses a line', and I think he was trying to elicit the hatred of him he believes must be there inside me. This complex condensation of communication and evacuation, intrusion and distortion, plus his final provocation off the couch aroused an anger in me I could not hold.

In the event, as I reported, Mr B neither stopped nor returned fully. He came back, but not on Tuesdays. This made it possible for him to continue, yet it was also an acting out that attacked the framework of the analysis. Mr B was doing what Michael Feldman (2008: 747) describes as 'a deal' with himself and with the analyst. In 1964 Rosenfeld warns the analyst to expect pressure from the patient for 'overtly friendly acting out' in such situations, and his view then was that the analyst should not act out with the patient in an 'overtly friendly' way but interpret the patient's underlying fear of the analyst as a persecuting figure. However, in his later book *Impasse and Interpretation* in the course of exploring factors in the patient and the analyst that either augment or resolve an impasse, his emphasis was different. He thought it a better technique not to disturb the patient's idealisations too quickly – as is well-known, a controversial change of Rosenfeld's views. I have followed Rosenfeld's earlier understanding. I think Mr B is hungry for accuracy and something new from me, and it was important – while I accepted it to work with – not to collude with his deal, or prevaricate about his hostility, or his fear of me as a disturbing and invading figure. At that point it was still uncertain whether the crisis would become an impasse or whether my patient and I, in some way, would resolve it.

In summary

After briefly describing prior stages of the analysis, the paper presents in detail the period when the analysis turned into a crisis. I am deeply indebted to Rosenfeld's understanding of the phenomenon of intrusive projective identification – so central in Mr B, and which I think always, even when less present in the personality, exerts a disproportionately large and pathological affect.

Acknowledgements

A previous edition of this chapter was published in J. Steiner (ed.), *Rosenfeld in Retrospect*, London: Karnac Books, 2008, pp. 3–14.

19

ON GRATITUDE

Envy and Gratitude, published in 1957, is one of Melanie Klein's last writings before she died in 1960. She begins the Preface to this marvellous short work by saying: 'I have for many years been interested in the earliest sources of two attitudes that have always been familiar – envy and gratitude' (Klein 1957: 176). The work is a distillation of reflections from her working life-time, and her reflections, in their turn, concern a whole life-time. She continues:

> I arrived at the conclusion that envy is a most potent factor in undermining feelings of love and gratitude at their root, since it affects the earliest relation of all, that to the mother. The fundamental importance of this relation for the individual's whole emotional life has been substantiated.
>
> (Klein 1957: 176)

In her work she examines the role of envy more fully than gratitude, though this does not mean she thinks envy is more important than gratitude. Like Atlas carrying on his shoulders a whole world, envy and gratitude both bear a terrible weight: envy 'interferes with the building up of a secure relation to the good external and internal object' (Klein 1957: 239), and gratitude 'is essential in building up the relation to the good object and underlies also the appreciation of goodness in others and in oneself' (Klein 1957: 187).

In this chapter, about Klein's ideas on gratitude, I explore, in the circumstances of a psychoanalysis, some forms of the emergence of gratitude and also some of its problems. First, I would like just to note that there is no rule that envy must manifest itself before gratitude. Sometimes, in relation to the analyst, gratitude emerges before envy.

Leon

After his very first session, an 11-year-old boy left the playroom and went away. I was still in the room, putting away his box of toys, when I became aware he had returned and was standing at the door. I turned round to him, and he said with great seriousness 'Thanks. Thanks. Thank you', and went away. What was he thanking me for?

When his parents had come to see me about an analysis for their child, they were distressed and at cross-purposes with each other. Father was in a panic that Leon (as I shall call him), nervous of all new prospects, would not be able to move to his new school in a few months, and for him it was urgent that Leon have an analysis. Mother was humbly dubious about this, insisting that Leon was just an ordinary boy, not academic, no trouble at all – but she was over-ridden by her husband.

As they had made no mention of depression, I was not expecting the very depressed child who arrived for a first session: a crushed, lumpy boy who sat himself down in front of me on a small bench, apparently not anxious about being with an unknown person for a strange purpose called 'psychoanalysis'. Indeed, he wore a conspicuous, incongruous air of 'This is ordinary'. When I spoke about how he needed to make everything ordinary to keep his fears away, Leon nodded assent. Then his face clouded and reddened, and he was weeping. After a while I asked him if it was that he did not know why he was crying, or was he crying for some reason he knew. He replied 'The first one' – meaning he didn't know why he was crying – and I said he was letting me know there is a deep sadness in him and that he doesn't know what it is about.

He looked very depressed, and at the same time, his crying which continued, took on another quality: it was meant to make me feel sorry for him. So I spoke about how he also wanted me to see that, sent to me by his parents, he is suffering – he wants us all to feel sorry for him, and wrong for offering him analysis. He nodded again in assent. All the while his feet were moving out towards me and then retreating back under the bench; and at times he looked round the room, at the sink and the taps, and the box of drawing materials and toys with interest. I went on to say he had opposite wishes: he wanted to go away and he also wanted this new chance – though the wanting must be secret, from me and – I suspect – from his parents and brother at home. He nodded again. At the end of the hour his face puckered and his hands got shaky. Fear had flooded into him: for an instant he looked like a small baby. I said I thought that he, a big boy, felt he had a small child in him who was very afraid of me and unsure what this was all about. To this he nodded vigorously. He left, and then, as I described above, he came back, and said 'Thanks. Thanks. Thank you' and went away.

I imagine we all have known patients who say a grateful 'Thank you', not during the session, but after it. As split-off envy affects an analysis by its underlying negation, so split-off gratitude supports an analysis by an affirmation that is, for some reason, kept outside the session. Leon's gratitude showed itself at once; it was only later, when what turned out to be his watcher of events came into the sessions, that we discovered that this watcher could have other emotions, like contempt and envious gratification. In this connection, Hanna Segal (1979: 148) draws attention to a disagreement between Freud and Klein. As a consequence of his hypothesis of primary narcissism, Freud believed hatred of the object to be older than the love of it; Klein sees love and hate as present from the beginning.

What was Leon thanking me for? I think it was for addressing his psychic reality, for attention and interpretation, and for withholding from, as we say, 'acting in' (Joseph 1989) with him. He was grateful too that in this new circumstance of a psychoanalytic session, when he let me see his depression, fear, pleas to be softly pitied, I could – without denial or getting over-anxious or over-solicitous (i.e., without repeating his enmeshed object relations) – know his feelings and speak plainly about them. That is to say, I think he was grateful to me for doing my job. It also had for him the significance of his father giving to him something that he, father, who was himself in analysis, valued, and I think Leon was grateful for that too.

Melanie Klein writes of gratitude in infancy: 'A full gratification at the breast means that the infant feels he has received from his loved object a unique gift which he wants to keep. This is the basis of gratitude' (Klein 1957: 118). She refers to Abraham, mentioning that 'Abraham did not speak of gratitude but he described generosity as an oral feature' (Klein 1957: 176). Abraham describes generosity in a paper on manic character formation. He writes: 'Generosity is frequently found as an oral character-trait. In this the orally gratified person is identifying himself with the bounteous mother' (Abraham 1924: 403).

I think there is a continuum of psychic giving to which bounteousness belongs, a continuum that ranges from meanness and withholding at one end, to generous giving at the other. The bounteous mother with whom the generous person identifies is the bestowing loved object to whom gratitude can be felt. Of course 'bounteousness' will have particular features in each instance. I shall give a sketch of a manic patient (known in supervision) whose objects had contrary, conditional elements in their bounteousness, as did also Mr M's generosity, which, even so, I think contained gratitude.

Mr M

Mr M's work is to furnish interiors for affluent people and join them in social excitements with a blurring of boundaries and roles – a situation continuous with his early history. There was no father in the home, and he seems to have needed to excite his mother's 'interior', and then, in mutual excitement, he and his mother had a sort of false high-living, which, he knew, had an underside where he was unaccepted, forgotten, and neglected. Currently, Mr M has a domestically neglectful partner; it is he who tends to the children, shops, cooks his 'haute cuisine' for the family.

He had been on the verge of financial bankruptcy when he began analysis, and his analyst reduced her fee to what he could manage – a fact that he was aware of. In the first months Mr M might arrive too early, ring the bell too much, bring presents. He bounded into sessions, talked fast, went from one subject to another, made jokes, moved about on the couch – on his side, propped up on an elbow, onto his stomach to stare at his analyst, or sitting up in various places on the couch. Only for moments – and such moments had significance – could he lie on the couch in the ordinary way. His analyst had to struggle to maintain an analytic framework – both externally (e.g., find ways to deal with his times of arrival, or a gift), and also internally within herself. Mr M is used to designing 'interiors', and with his speedy, profuse talk was adept at using warmth, cleverness, and jokiness to target and intrude into his analyst's mind. In Abraham's terminology, Mr M is a patient with a constitutionally high oral erotism. His speed and excitement made him difficult to contact, and his analyst had to struggle not to get excited or collapse with laughter – be almost forced into the patient's mania. At times Mr M, too, felt pulled to the place of analysis or into the analyst herself, his excitement almost uncontrollable, with a confused, anxious belief that excitement and mutual transgression was what the analyst really wanted, along with the knowledge – at times dangerously near to being lost – that there was a different reality of sessions with an analyst struggling with a needy patient excitedly defending himself from fears of an icy, vertiginous drop.

During this first year Mr M gradually became less excited and exciting in his way of communicating. He began to keep the boundaries of session times, and bell-ringing and gifts stopped. In his work life he was notably more able to stand his ground with clients, and his money affairs were put into better order by a financial manager. As the first year drew to its end, he expressed his gratitude on two occasions. His analyst had called attention to his withholding payment of her bill; it turned out that he had the cheque in his pocket, but had not handed it over. Mr M then said

> The thing is, I feel pathetically grateful to you. I'm embarrassed at how grateful I am, because I know I couldn't function without coming here. And I'm very grateful for the discount that you give me, and if someone did to me what I do to you, I'd be very pissed off … but I don't understand it, because I am so grateful, and I really hope you don't take it personally, because you know, more than anyone, it's a problem I have with everyone. [Consciously he meant his tendency not to settle bills.] I'm pathetically grateful for all of this.

And again, on the last session before the Christmas holiday, after speaking about his anxieties about travelling and his dissatisfactions with his partner, he said how different it felt to have his finances in order before going away: how his current account was actually in credit, and all his suppliers had been paid; and he mentioned possible profitable business projects for the next year. With a jokey cover, he said to his analyst: 'We're not doing Christmas presents this year, are we? I don't think I could cope with the talking about it for sessions on end anyway.' And then seriously: 'But I want you to know that you have something that only my children have, which is my deepest gratitude. Ninety-five percent of this is down to you and my sessions. I am very clear about that. And maybe in the New Year we can talk about increasing my fees, because I am aware of the huge discount you give me, and I think I will be able to afford a little more.' His analyst told me she was moved and thought Mr M was not – as so often – designing her interior, but expressing his gratitude.

Is Mr M's gratitude authentic? Or are the analyst, and the supervisor, too, deceived? When Mr M says 'I want you to know that you have something that only my children have, which is my deepest gratitude. 95% of this is down to you and my sessions', is this sincere, in every particular, including that his gratitude is '*down* to you' – that is, he knows he is still high? Such questions are among the uncomfortable issues that recur in working with Mr M. As with all patients who are 'bi-polar', Mr M's communications often have a dual aspect. Could Mr M, even as he expresses his gratitude, also be supplying it as the type of Christmas present he thinks the analyst wants, so interfering with and spoiling his gift of gratitude? Or is he, as the analyst took it, genuinely expressing his gratitude?

Taking it as she took it, I think Mr M's gratitude was foremost for her emotional struggle with, and containment of, the wild forces of his erotised excitement. I think he keeps his eye on her, watches and tests her, wants to see whether her acceptance of him is conditional on his doing what she wants or whether she can accept him as he is, whether she is sceptical and prejudiced against him or is able to discriminate and know when to trust him and when not to. In this analytic sense, has she the 'bounteousness' for all?

Not unexpectedly, when the following year's work started, Mr M had a manic episode only just containable in the treatment. Several strands became clearer: the stimulation of the sequestered analytic situation; his mad hatred of its frustrations (e.g., that the analyst withholds from touching him or being touched); the nature of his destructive sexualised excitement, which, while it defends him from persecution by the analyst on whom he depends, also has a psychotic lure for him. Along with all of this, what he calls his 'pathetic gratitude' continues.

The analyst

I shall now shift the focus from the patient to the analyst. Not all patients concentrate on the analyst's internal world to the degree that Mr M does. I think, though, that most patients scrutinise us and target our minds (Brenman Pick 1985) to find out how we attend and listen, whether we join in or withhold from acting 'in', what we neglect and select for interpretation, and in what manner we bestow our interpretations. Under the patient's scrutiny will come our capacity and our incapacity to do analytic work, our narcissism, coldness, undue warmth, rectitude, whether we speak with or without conviction, from on high to a patient down below, and so on. The nature of the patient's internal objects, his love and hate, affect these perceptions of the analyst, and the scrutiny itself is anxious, concerning as it does the very nature of the analyst with the fear that the analyst may not tolerate the patient perceiving psychic things about him – especially the analyst's 'no-go' areas.

'No-go' comes from a patient's dream reported during a supervision. An analyst whom I thought serious and hard-working, yet with a coldness about him, reported a patient's dream of a *frozen, snow-bound landscape in which there was a single small house. Near the house was a signpost saying 'No-go'*. The analyst interpreted the dream not as his patient's perception of him, but as a representation of the patient's coldness and isolation. His patient made no objection to the interpretation, so accommodating the analyst. Easy, of course, to see such a 'no-go' area of coldness, or narcissism, or whatever, in others; not easy, though, to see the no-go areas in oneself (Money-Kyrle 1956: 361).

If the analyst is cold, say, or narcissistic, a patient feels warmth to be withheld from him – in the case of narcissism, because the analyst bestows too much of his attention on himself. If these remain no-go areas, they interfere with gratitude. If it is possible for them to be talked about by patient and analyst, it can to an extent repair the situation; it can't, of course, take away the analyst's coldness or narcissism, but the patient may be grateful to have an analyst with the capacity to allow him the expression of such thoughts and feelings.

What, then, are our patients grateful to us for? There are some uncomfortable issues for the analyst here. Is it for the bounteousness of our invitation to bring all to us? Is it for the unique gifts we bestow upon them with our interpretations? If we start to think we are the bounteous bestowers of unique gifts, then we are, of course – as Freud warned – forgetting the phenomenon of transference. It is a dangerous area that can recruit our narcissism, seductiveness, tendencies to couple in spurious idealisations, our capacity for self-deception, or our mania – as is a danger with Mr M. And, as Gabbard (2000) notes, there also are the stresses for the analyst of the ungrateful patient. I think our patients perceive, and we communicate, such things about ourselves, which make it difficult for a patient to feel grateful – we are not bounteous enough; consider, in this regard, Mr M's expression of gratitude as a response to the contrarieties of his object. Moreover, our own fear of these things may cause us to shy away from gratitude when it is expressed.

Yet it is true, in a way that needs making clear, that a psychoanalysis offers a patient something unique. It is true simply in the sense that a psychoanalysis is the unique thing it is. 'Everything is what it is and not another thing', said Bishop Butler. The circumstances for a patient to feel gratitude to a psychoanalyst, though not unconnected with the circumstances of gratitude in family, social, and working life, are different: they relate to conscious and unconscious meanings in a patient's external and inner life – that is, to psychic reality, and, as well, to the analyst as foremost a psychological object, and to the enterprise that psychoanalysis is, which has its own categories, which Bion called the 'elements' of psychoanalysis. All this is a wide subject, and I leave it, as I also leave untouched the related question of the analyst's gratitude to the patient. I turn now to another patient, Dr Y, to inquire into a different area: the keeping, losing, and the internal regaining of gratitude, and all that comes with this.

Dr Y

Dr Y is a psychiatrist. Near the end of a long analysis, she told me the following dream:

> In my dream I was looking for the text of Shakespeare's *Hamlet*. I knew there were some small volumes of the play, but I couldn't find one, and I was getting frantic. Then I saw someone, it seemed to be myself, calmly eating carrots with parsley, indifferent to my search and anxiety. The sight of such calm not helping, just going on eating, made me more and more anxious. My dream went on and on, and I got confused and agitated. I couldn't find the text, the little Shakespeare book I was looking for, and the dream was almost a night-mare.

Without a pause Dr Y gave associations to her dream: obsessional neurosis. I was reading about obsessional neurosis yesterday in a bad paper, feeling I still didn't know or understand it. Hamlet was an obsessional neurotic. About the carrots and the parsley. It was the colours, bright and contradictory, red and green like traffic lights:

253

Stop! Go! It reminds me of trying to work on my paper yesterday (She is writing a paper for a conference). I stopped soon after I began. I felt tired, sleepy, went to get a coffee. Yes, that's it. That's the part of me that interferes, and I'll get no help from it.

Distressed and agitated, Dr Y continued:

> I'm sorry, I know I shouldn't be like this at this stage. I know Hamlet must avenge his father's wrongful death but cannot. Like Hamlet with his obsessional neurosis, I, too, cannot. But is this right? I'd feel better if I could get on with my paper. I'm really sorry for being like this again so near the end of the analysis.

Dr Y was in distress, recognising her regression to an old state of mind, which she at the same time queries. 'Hamlet must avenge his father's wrongful death but cannot. Like Hamlet with his obsessional neurosis, I, too, cannot. But is this right?' she asks in agitated attempts, which she doubts, to find answers not in her own thoughts and feelings, but in Shakespeare's *Hamlet*. I noted the presence of the figure calmly eating red carrots and green parsley. I noted her guilt and apologies, her self-criticisms, and how in the same way she could not work on her conference paper, and still in the state of her dream, Dr Y was struggling on her own in the session, frantic and without resolution. She seemed to have no expectation of getting help from me, or that together we might try something. Foremost, she conveyed loneliness, inner and outer.

After a while I spoke to Dr Y about how she felt alone and without help in her struggle with her dream and her agitation. I said she had lost the analyst she'd come to know over the long period of the analysis – myself, who is ending with her, but who is still here.

A change of atmosphere followed. Dr Y began to cry and for a while could not speak. Then she said: 'What you said made all the difference. You knew who I was.'

I think Dr Y had felt alone with only an obstructive self identified with an inhuman stop–go analyst who is indifferent to her search and anxiety. She had lost a good internal analyst with whom she has a long history. When I communicate to her that I remember who she is, I know she is my patient struggling with the ending of analysis, her inner state changes, and her mind works again. She cries with relief, I think, as she regains contact with her lost good object, and when she can speak, she generously expresses her gratitude: 'What you said made all the difference. You knew who I was.' Dr Y seemed to have life inside her again and she spoke to me in a hopeful way, even with enjoyment, about various things. However, her happier state did not last: I shall return to this in a moment.

Though loss and regaining were foremost, there are other crucial things. One is the figure eating red carrots and green parsley. Melanie Klein notes that envy – 'the worst sin' – (Chaucer), and gratitude – 'the father of the virtues' (Cicero), affect one another differently. Envy *interferes* with gratitude, while gratitude *mitigates* envy. Mitigation is more mysterious than interference. Is the figure of the carrot and parsley eater – present but *not dominant as it once was and now recognised for what it is* – an example of mitigation? Dr Y in her dream 'saw someone, it seemed to be myself, calmly eating carrots with parsley, indifferent to my search and anxiety. The sight of such calm not helping, just going on eating, made me more and more anxious.' And how in her associations she said 'that's the part of me that interferes, and I'll get no help from it.' Something notably different about Dr Y as her analysis moves towards its end is that she is not in the state of melancholic depression in which she began. Earlier, she was often like the figure in her dream: dissociated and depressed in a melancholic way, full of latent bitterness and envy, in identification with an uncaring 'stop–go' object, who the analyst often was for her, a figure connected with undue losses and bitter neglects in her past, and with the ordinary losses that come with life as well.

The carrot and the parsley eater is still in Dr Y's inner world – but her relationship to it is different. It can influence her (e.g., her attempts to work on her conference paper are interfered with and turn into a 'stop–go' as she goes for a coffee), but she is not predominantly identified with it, and she knows its nature. This is a central change that has taken place in the course of her analysis. Could we say that the weakening of the power of this figure is an instance of mitigation? Might Dr Y's gratitude to an analyst 'who knew who she was' have mitigated – that is, *reduced the force and the ascendancy* of – envy and hatred in her personality?

The internal good object is impermanent thrice over: it is vulnerable to damage from internal attack and vulnerable to external circumstances and also to the passage of time. Klein says 'the infant feels he has received from his loved object a unique gift which he wants to *keep*' (Klein 1957: 188, emphasis added). I think Dr Y is struggling to keep her good internal object. She apologises for being anxious, agitated, and unable to work so near the end of her analysis. 'I'm sorry. I know I shouldn't be like this at this stage', she says. She repeats 'I'm really sorry for being like this again so near the end of the analysis.' Consciously, she is guilty for losing her good object; unconsciously, she blames her analyst for this event and for her consequent state of anxiety and agitation. Just as externally, there is, in Klein's words 'the infant's longing for an inexhaustible and ever-present breast' (Klein 1957: 179), so there is a longing for an *everlasting* internal object. Of course, the analyst can neither fulfil desires for an everlasting, inexhaustible object, nor provide the patient with an everlasting internal good object, and nor is it possible for the patient never to lose his good object or to effect an everlasting reparation. All are unrealisables.

Indeed, as we drew towards the end of the session, Dr Y lost her grateful state of mind that – to repeat Klein's words – 'is essential in building up the relation to the good object and underlies also the appreciation of goodness in others and in oneself' (Klein 1957: 187). Her enjoyment of the session ceased, and she seemed more the way she had been at the start of the session: anxious and alone. Dr Y had been unable to keep her internal good object and was suffering an inner loss brought about by the impending loss of the external object (Klein 1935) at this juncture when endings of sessions tended to foreshadow the final ending. I was not sure, though, of the direction of her anxiety. Had she turned away in search of some script, some small volumes of *Hamlet*? Or was she contending with something different: the loss and the pain of mourning the analyst at the end of the session? Was she trying to retreat from these via a regression to her old melancholic state, and yet found she could not – as in her dream she cannot find the text she is looking for, the little Shakespeare volumes of *Hamlet* with its murder of a father, maternal betrayal, and demands for impossible repair? Joan Riviere has described this domain: how the immanent depressive position brings a 'sense of failure, of inability to remedy matters ... so great, the belief in better things is so weak: despair is so near' (Riviere, 1936: 315). 'All one's loved ones *within* are dead and destroyed' (Riviere 1936: 313). Riviere stresses that in this scene in the inner world 'it is *the love for his internal objects*, which lies behind and produces the unbearable guilt and pain' (Riviere 1936: 319).

I think that Dr Y, unable to regress to her former melancholic state and also unable quite to face the ending of the session, was lost somewhere between the condition that Riviere describes where the patient can neither repair nor escape from his damaged, dying, or dead objects, and the different depressive-position problems of the separateness of the self and object, the impermanence of the relation to the object, loneliness, and the pain of mourning the loss of the object. Of course, there is a whole interwoven area here of Dr Y's Oedipus complex, the demands she feels her objects to make of her – you will remember how she apologises: 'I'm sorry. I know I shouldn't be like this at this stage' – her conflicts over reparation, questions of what we have achieved and what hopes have been disappointed, issues of the analyst's failures. But more immediately, there is the end of the session, the painful reality that *time* has entered (Birksted-Breen 2003), that the analyst really is a 'stop–go' analyst.

Throughout *Envy and Gratitude*, Melanie Klein emphasises that emotional life is characterised by losing and regaining the good object. Indeed, impermanence is a central aspect of what she means by her concept of position. Freud called it 'transience' in his wonderful short paper, 'On transience': 'Not long ago I went on a summer walk through a smiling countryside in the company of a taciturn friend and a young but already famous poet' (Freud 1916 [1915]: 305). Freud describes how the poet admired the beauty of the scene but felt no joy in it: 'All that he would otherwise have loved and admired seemed to him to be shorn of its worth by the transience which was its doom' (Freud 1919 [1915]: 305). Dr Y is exposed to the transience of the analysis: the analytic session will end and the analysis will finally stop, with meanings that connect with the long human experience of transience and loss: birth out of the womb in the mother, weaning from the intimacies of feeding from a mother's breast, discoveries that mother is not solely for you – she has other even greater sexual intimacies with father, and perhaps father and mother are parents also of others, and anyway they have more distant tasks, connections and pleasures in the home and out in society. In Dr Y's case, to this natural series of transience must be added early family separations, removals, and losses through death.

In his *Poem of the Deep Song* (*Poema del Cante Jondo*), Federico García Lorca has this refrain: 'Ay, love that went away and never returned!' (Lorca 1921 [1987: 3]).

It is a refrain for the series of human loves that go away and never return. In a few months I will be Dr Y's former analyst, another entry in the series of her life's losses. Freud tells us in his paper how he debated with his companions, arguing that transience does not involve a loss of worth. 'On the contrary,' he said, 'an increase! Transience value is scarcity value in time' (Freud 1916 [1915]: 305). He perceived, however, that he made no impression on them. Freud writes:

> My failure led me to infer that some powerful emotional factor was at work that was disturbing their judgement, and I believed later that I had discovered what it was. What spoilt their enjoyment of beauty must have been a revolt in their minds against mourning … the mind instinctively recoils from anything that is painful.
>
> (Freud 1916 [1915]: 306)

Well, could Freud convince us? Can we keep our memories of enjoyment and gratitude, given the transience of nature and the pain of mourning its loss?

Acknowledgements

A previous edition of this chapter was published in P. Roth and A. Lemma (eds.), *Envy and Gratitude Revisited*, London: IPA, reprinted London: Karnac Books, 2008, pp. 79–91.

20

WHERE IS HERE? WHEN IS NOW?

If I say, like many and diverse colleagues, that I try to work in the *'here and now'* I may conjure up, as well as some contemporary disputes (about which more later), some bits of history about place and time in psychoanalysis. As early as the Project (Freud 1895a) Freud discovered, in relation to problems in his seduction theory, that the *place* with the more determining role in the patient's illness was not external reality but psychic reality with its unconscious phantasies. He developed his psychoanalytic method also through changes he made with regard to *time*. His earlier techniques aimed to bring 'directly into focus the moment at which the symptom was formed' (Freud 1914: 147); the analyst tried to help the patient fill the gaps in his memory – to remember how it happened 'there and then'. Later, with the discovery of transference and the compulsion to repeat, Freud found a different relation of time between 'there and then' and 'here and now' – through the phenomenon of transference the past repeats itself in the present and in a psychoanalysis becomes 'a piece of real life' (Freud 1914: 152) that is 'at every point accessible to our intervention' (Freud 1914: 154). Freud tells us '... we must treat [the patient's] illness, not as an event of the past, but as a present-day force (Freud 1914: 151). All this has implications for analytic technique: the analyst's evenly suspended attention, as I understand it, hovers over, and has a focus on, illuminating psychic reality, while material reality in kept in relative darkness (not darkness, mark you, but relative darkness).

This shifting of analytic focus from external (or practical or material reality as Freud also sometimes called it) to psychic reality was later deepened and extended by Klein's discovery of a whole inner realm of objects, an unconscious world within that is in interplay with external reality. And later still, the Kleinian understanding of the role of projective identification between patient and analyst threw further light on the process of 'transferring' between patient and analyst, showing how it is not only the psychic reality of the patient that is involved but also, though in an importantly different way, the psychic reality of the analyst – for both the transference and the countertransference are, in Freud's phrase, 'a piece of real life'.

This bit of history I give by way of introduction is to remind us that place and time have a distinctive nature in a psychoanalysis: they are 'the here' and 'the now' of psychic reality. In this paper I shall illustrate and try to explore this psychoanalytic 'here' and 'now' with clinical material from the analysis of Mr X: first, with an account of the way his analysis began, and then with a detailed session from 5 years later.

Clinical presentation

Mr X, an anxious, disconnected and young-looking man in his mid-thirties, worked for an international corporation. The youngest of three brothers, he presented himself as 'the little weak one who doesn't know what to do', which seems to have been a life-long role. He said he wanted an analysis because of loneliness and unsettledness; he had few friends and was unsure of his sexual orientation. In the preliminary interview he described one or two homosexual affairs that were intense sexually but which had interfered with his studies and his work; and also some brief relationships with girls who had chosen him rather than his choosing them – except for one, a secretary at work. She fell pregnant, had wanted to have their baby and stay with him, but his parents and brothers told him she was tricking him into a marriage and persuaded him to give her money for an abortion – about all of this Mr X had feelings of guilt and loss. He said his mother was frightening and not interested in him, though his father was a sensitive man and more human.

More immediately, Mr X sought analysis because of a crisis at work: he had become very involved with a male colleague who had then treated him with public contempt, a man who, in Mr X's words 'had messed things up at the firm for him', and then, to his distress, senior management had by-passed him for promotion. He also told me that he had what he called 'a sort of a girl friend' to whom he gave money to buy food for their meals and also for some shopping for herself. She cooked supper for him; they had infrequent sex. Usually he returned to his own flat for the night, sometimes drinking, watching porn on the internet.

Mr X started analysis 'being the new little one who doesn't know what to do', a complex presentation meant to draw me into making a special, gentle pair with him: I would voice his fears and hopes, and tell him what to do. But (I came to realise) the fears, hopes, etc. I was being invited to say were ones he already knew. It was a way of getting us close – and, at the same time, keeping us away from what was new or disturbing. Mr X really was 'a new little one' an anxious new patient, afraid of the impact of analysis and the nature of his analyst, anxious too because of feeling he had little to give in the way of communication to me or for struggling with the forces in himself. However, at the same time, if I listened carefully, I could hear how he was sending himself and me up by acting 'being the little weak one', with an air of not knowing he was doing so and of speaking to an analyst so cut off that she wouldn't notice but would find him little and gentle and pleasing. This whole mixture had its pathos, but it was also irritating, confusing and disabling. Often I didn't know how to think about, or what to select from, the many aspects involved. Did my irritation come from his projection into me of an inner hostile and false maternal figure? Or was I irritated by his acting, which, even as he communicated something, mocked it and spoilt it? Or his debasement of me? Or perhaps all three? Yet I was also aware of his felt need for something, and at the same time, how anxious and inaccessible he was, and how what he said lacked resonance – it was concretely just itself with no under- or over-tones of meaning (see Joseph 1993). Often everything I contemplated saying would seem wrong in some way, and I felt I became like him – I too didn't know what to do. I worried about Mr X getting from me merely 'a sort of analysis', our relations rather like Mr X's relations with his 'sort of a girl friend'.

Often I focused on the overall atmosphere of 'not knowing what to do' – how he wanted something from me and at the same time was hostile and mocked himself and me, and was afraid and didn't know what to do and felt anxious that I too didn't know what to do for him, and so, we would do nothing.

During this opening phase Mr X told no dreams, but one day, unusually, he brought an image. He described how on the way to his session he had noticed a house and its garden outside. It was a tidy garden that had been swept bare, except, that in a corner, there was a plant with two blue, delicate flowers. What seemed to me foremost and new was that Mr X had *noticed* the house and how the garden was, and had been able to bring what he had seen to his session and tell it as a communication. It was a significant movement, I thought, from his usual concrete way of 'acting in' with me, towards awareness and the gaining of an insight with some small degree (Segal, in Quinodoz 2008: 65) of symbolic representation. I spoke to him about how I thought the house and its garden outside expressed his new awareness of how he and I and his sessions were – we are to be like the two blue flowers in a corner, close and delicate with each other, while the session is swept bare of disturbing things – like his hostility, or his fear that I get irritated and restive and might not want to be a delicate blue flower with him.

Mr X's communication of the image of the two blue flowers in a garden outside the house and my interpretations about it are examples of patient and analyst trying to throw light on the 'here and now' of the psychic reality of an analysis. But where is 'here'? In material reality, Mr X is in analysis – he comes for sessions, and, in a corner of my consulting room I sit in my chair and he lies on my couch. However, in psychic reality I think he is in a corner of a garden outside the house of analysis. I also spoke to him about how he tries to get me to join him outside the ordinary frame of analysis and be with him in a special tender way that is perhaps a little blue too – seduced and sexualised together. I think Mr X really understood this. From accounts he gave at this time, this was also the way he tries to manage psychic pressures in his place of work: he pairs closely with someone in the firm, tries to feel they are then in a place apart from the ordinary work-place that is free from the anxieties of rivalry, difference, hostility, competence, etc. Mr X's 'here' can be anywhere, and is, in this sense, unrestricted by the particularities of reality. It is how he is everywhere. Bion has often illuminated the difference between space and time in psychic and in external reality; e.g., he describes (Bion 1957) the vast distances in the mental space and time of the psychotic patient. Indeed, there were times, in the analysis and elsewhere, when Mr X believed he really was in a 'special' place with a special relationship, i.e., he had what Britton (1995) calls a *counter-belief*, a belief of psychic reality that cancels and replaces external reality.

Mr X and I struggled on and slowly he became more able to allow the return of some of the things he had swept out of the sessions. Of particular importance were his fears and doubts about me; his anxious and resentful suspicion that I had no genuine place for him, did not want or accept him; and that I was hostile and devaluing. In the preliminary interview Mr X had described his mother as frightening and with no interest in him; my sense of it was that it might really have been so, and that Mr X had internalised a female figure that was 'a house' that did not let him in but kept him on the outside of her.

If the 'here' where patient and analyst were was changing and becoming a little less bare, what of the 'now'? Mr X had little of the ordinary feeling of the *duration* of his life – he brought no memories, screen or otherwise, from childhood or later – almost all the facts I mentioned at the start of this paper I knew from the preliminary interview. In this first period recollections did not return to him, nor did he experience what Klein calls 'memories in feelings' (Klein 1957: 180). He spoke only of current things in a way, as I remarked above, that had no resonance. And when interpreting myself as a house, a female figure that did not let him in I made no attempt at a construction of the past because, at this stage, Mr X was cut off from his past. Henri Rey (1994) vividly describes patients like Mr X whose illness, in part, is their loss of connectedness: they have broken the thread of life, and as Wollheim (1984) has shown, the thread of a life is at the core of the inner unity of persons and at the centre of personal identity (see Flynn 2008 for a recent discussion).

I shall now leave the first phase of Mr X's analysis and present a session from 5 years later when Mr X had succeeded in obtaining his much longed for senior appointment. On the day before the session I report he had attended for the first time a Senior Managers' meeting in preparation for the new post he would start a few weeks later.

Session

Mr X arrived looking happy. After lying down, he spoke animatedly about the meeting of the day before, telling me about the various people present, the topics discussed and describing his participation. His voluble account, which made me pleased, was so different from his often cautious presentation of himself, that, when he paused, I remarked that today he was able to let me know he was happy: he had joined in and enjoyed being in the Senior Managers' meeting. This remark changed his mood. Angry and with contempt he said, 'It was just childish to be interested in a meeting like that.' And then

263

angrier still, 'You said *they* were the Seniors, not *me.*' 'You said it!', he repeated, now nearly shouting. I remarked on his sudden change from happiness with me to contempt for himself and fury with me. He lay silent. Then, after a while, I said that he had heard me in his mind's ear saying he was not a Senior, but in reality I had not said that. Even as I said this, though, it felt strange to be saying to my patient that I had not actually said, 'They were the Seniors not him', and only after the session, as I discuss below could I begin to understand something about it. In the session itself, in response to my denial, Mr X persisted and repeated, 'You said it.' I responded by suggesting he had been so alarmed by the sudden irruption of his anger and contempt when he called the meeting childish that he had pushed these out of himself and in to me, and then heard me being like a hostile mother – disparaging him. Mr X said nothing.

After a long while, making a noticeable effort, he said he had had a dream the night before.

In his dream he was already working in the section of the firm where he will be doing his new job. He was not dressed properly. He was wearing casual clothes, old jeans and a tee shirt. A secretary came and said: 'Don't you know you shouldn't be dressed like that – you should wear a jacket and tie like Senior Managers do.' She had a jacket, a shirt and a tie ready for him. He took them from her and put them on. Suddenly there was a baby sitting on his shoulder, and then the baby sucked him all over, and made a huge wet mess of his clothes. He realised he couldn't wear them. It was hopeless and he took them off.

As Mr X finished telling his dream he sounded despairing and fell again into a long silence. I reflected on how complicated it all was. His silence now in the session seemed to match his hopeless giving up when the baby messed his clothes in the dream. Yet he had started the session so differently, engaged and happy to talk to me, the very way he had been in the real Senior Manager's meeting of the day before, where, unlike his subsequent dream, he had not needed a secretary to tell him how to present himself properly. As now, I thought, he waits for me to tell him what to do – ask for associations, encourage him to talk, and so on – something of a return to our old 'two blue flowers' place, where I do for him what he knows how to do for himself. Yet, as against that, he had managed to tell me his dream.

And then I wondered, who is the spoiling baby who makes the wet mess in the dream?

As Mr X still lay silent I asked him about the child in the dream. He answered at once that he knew who the child was – it was his brother's child. In external reality, his brother's child is part of all his oldest brother has that Mr X, who has no son and had his one baby aborted, feels painfully and enviously deprived of. In his dream the brother's child who makes a wet mess of him (now in reality 10 or 11 years old) is the baby it was in the past. The dream is set in the future when Mr X will be working in the new Senior section and his dream destroys his pleasurable anticipation that he will do well in his new job. In the session it was Mr X himself who, with angry contempt, spoils his and my pleasure in the Senior Managers' meeting of the day before by saying 'It was just childish to be interested in a meeting like that.' I interpreted that when he'd arrived happy today and told me about yesterday's interesting meeting, he had felt he was my child – not his brother's child, but his parents' child, and that then he was speaking to me, his analyst, as a parent who would be pleased at his success.

After a long pause Mr X said, 'Maybe'.

I went on to speak about how we had seen an opposed side of him who was made angry and envious by yesterday's managers' meeting that went well, and by his pleased regard for me today and the pleasure he thought his achievement gave me; and that that side hated and spoilt these good relations, and miscalled them 'childish'. In his dream, however, he recognises that it is the hostile side who is the baby, the burden he carries on his shoulder.

Mr X replied guardedly, 'It could be so.'

Our time was up and there the session ended.

Discussion of clinical material

I hope it can be seen how over several years Mr X has changed, progressing at his workplace and, in some ways, developing also internally. In the reported session he is not, as he was 5 years before, either in, or aiming to construct, a 'blue-flower' dyad. He has moved – to continue with his telling image of a garden and a house – from pairing in an outside garden, to being in the analytic house, with me and against me, and there some of the things that earlier he had swept out are now beginning to return. His ego has strengthened: he sustains some measure of contact under pressure – e.g., he manages to

265

tell me his dream even after I failed him. That is, Mr X is in a different place. Moreover, events of the session have gained some (though still few) connections with the past and his future: 'now' is no more a schizoid instant, but has regained something of its natural condition, which, as B. J. O'Shaughnessy (1980, vol 2: 312) puts it: 'is internally *... from—towards* ... the life of the self-conscious being [has] ...... one end stretching back to the womb, the other end moving into the unrealised future' (see also Taylor 2005).

When the session starts Mr X is in an Oedipal space, voluble and happy after his successful Managers' meeting of the day before, speaking in a way that gives me pleasure. I am his analyst, who for him at that moment is the 'they' of parents, and he is my patient in the sense of being his parents' child, happy to be doing well and to tell me so. It is when *I* say so out loud that the abrupt changes occur that are the emotional crux of the session. With sudden anger and contempt Mr X says, 'It was just childish to be interested in a meeting like that', and more furious still, 'You said *they* were the Seniors, not *me*.' And repeats, 'You said it!', almost shouting. After his outburst I did something peculiar: I told him I didn't say it, focusing on external reality only and not paying enough attention to and trying to understand his experience – an enactment on my part, an 'acting in', as we say. At that moment I actually became (I am not sure whether from defensiveness in myself or from his projections or both), his internalised Mother who refuses him house room to a central, emotional predicament. Mr X is confusingly conflicted: he wants real human relations and almost simultaneously he interferes with these, gets big and superior to real human relations, which – in a reversal of reality – he calls 'childish'. When I speak of his being with me and enjoying being his parents' child, I rouse his hatred, and furthermore, I rob his hostile side of its bigness, which indeed he had already done himself in his dream of the night before where he had exposed it as a spoiling baby. His destructiveness is thus threatened from within and without, revealed as an infantile burden Mr X carries on his shoulder who makes him feel big through a toxic mix of sexualised destruction – sucking him all over to make a huge wet mess, a big spoiling phallus. All this is to say that in his new and forward-moving Oedipal situation, Mr X's experience is incoherent: enjoyment of success, with feelings of being his parents' son, afflicts him simultaneously with the persecution of exposure and belittlement.

In the session I understood only partially what was happening: I recognised he was in an Oedipal place and that he had instantly to disown and project his spoiling hatred of it into me so that he 'heard' me saying, 'They were the Seniors, not him.' But I did not recognise the terrible incoherence of his experience – how when he succeeds he is also undone. In the session I think Mr X kept some sense of himself as his parents' child and so managed to keep some link to me. He made an effort – you will remember – and told me his dream, though he stayed cautious about what I said to him, saying 'maybe': 'it could be so'. I suspect I was then for him not a totally bad figure, but a disturbing mixture that made him anxious and guarded.

However, I had lost an opportunity to understand and to speak to Mr X about the irruption of his unsettled sexual orientation in the session: how we saw it arise in an Oedipal situation when he identifies with parents and relates with enjoyment to them, and how then a sexualised hatred irrupts in him – in his dream seen as the baby on his shoulder who sucks him all over – that turns him into a big phallus. Conceptualised in terms introduced by Dana Birksted-Breen (1996): Mr X can neither settle into a triangular Oedipal mental space with a penis-as-link nor settle into in a psychic reality of phallic dyads. And indeed, unusually, the next day Mr X returned, worried and depressed, and said he had been thinking a lot about getting so angry with me and also about his dream. He knew it was all very important and he wanted to talk more about it. It was important that he did so, even if it was a little distant and tentative, and I a very uncertain figure for him. His hostility stayed quiescent though I think we both knew it would and, of course, it did, soon erupt again.

If this was 'where' we were, what about 'the now' of the session? It was very much of the present, plus, unlike before, with various connections to the past. In Mr X's dream there is his brother's child (in external reality now a 12 year old) but in the dream seen as the baby he knew in his past who represents his immature hostile side as it was when he was a baby and which still is a baby: in other words it has not developed. And in the session there was my becoming in the transference an early hostile maternal figure who has no place for him. That is, past early difficult relations with parents and brothers are there in the 'now' of the session. And, as well as his past there is now also his future. His dream expresses his foreboding that in the future when he will be actually working in the managerial section in

267

a few weeks' time the baby on his shoulder, the burden he carries of unmitigated envy and destruction, will spoil it.

All this is to say that unlike before, when he existed in a kind of cut-off instant, duration has entered Mr X's psychic reality. There is now something of a connecting thread to his life. To express this in another way: before there was a kind of timelessness, now he lives in time.

Closing comments

In their General Introduction to a selection of Betty Joseph's papers (Joseph 1989), Michael Feldman and Elizabeth Spillius give an excellent account of Joseph's understanding of, and the need in our technique for, psychic immediacy. In my paper, with a Kleinian approach that is influenced by Betty Joseph, I have presented some psychoanalytic work in the 'here and now'. In the contemporary plural scene, analysing in the 'here and now' takes diverse forms in clinical practice, see e.g., the variety of papers in Perelberg (2007) and, as well, misgivings continue to be expressed about this way of working. Analysing in the 'here and now' has been called 'thin'; it has been accused of being an impoverishment of psychoanalysis; anxiety has also been expressed that it will lead to a neglect of the patient's past and his world of unconscious phantasy. This would be specially terrible – if Freud taught us anything it is the force of the past and the power of unconscious phantasy. Of course, analytic work may be thin or impoverished, but such poor work does not come from working in the 'here and now' – on the contrary, it comes from the very opposite. It is due either to some misconception about the 'here' and 'now', for example mistaking the material realities between patient and analyst as being all there is and thus neglecting psychic reality, or it is due to a neglect of what is really present in the 'here and now' of a psychoanalysis where there is always more going on than we could ever know or interpret.

In the clinical situations described above, I think we can see the variation in Mr X's 'here' and his 'now'. He started analysis in an anxious schizoid state, disconnected from memories of his past, merely repeating his past with me in a concrete way that was devoided of phantasy also. He was threatened by unmanageable persecutory anxieties and struggled to protect himself by means of continuous splitting and an appeasing presentation of himself as 'the little weak one who doesn't know what to do', and aimed to restrict and control me into making a gentle dyad with him. On rare occasions, for example when he saw the two blue flowers in a garden outside a house, was Mr X able to find the beginnings of symbolisation by a concrete material equivalent to his psychic situation. Later, as we saw in the detailed session, his phantasy life came more alive: for example, his dream expresses the phantasy of his whole self becoming a big phallus, and mental connection with his past began to be restored, along with anticipations of his future – his dream is about the future. Furthermore, there is an important interplay between external and psychic reality: when Mr X at last obtains his Senior appointment in external reality it affects him internally, which in turn affects also his immediate relations with the analyst. Rather than being thin or impoverished, I submit, the nature of, and the changes in, 'the here and now' of Mr X turn out to be complex and crucial to the analytic process.

Moreover, I think a guideline emerges in regard to technique. The nature of the patient's 'here' and 'now' is a valuable indicator to the analyst for making or not making links with the patient's history, or for speaking or not speaking about phantasy. We have surely to wait until these are there in the patient's psychic reality.

To conclude. This paper is about place and time in psychic reality. I have hoped to show something of the nature of Mr X's problems with place and time, and also as the analysis progressed some of the changes in Mr X's places and in his disconnections and reconnections with time, as he moved from a dyadic towards an Oedipal and family space. For him, as we saw, this was a disturbing, possibly irresolubly difficult and deeply contradictory place. There is a human need for a place – a habitat in material and also in psychic reality, and there is also a natural human need for awareness of duration through memories and anticipations. At the time I leave him in this paper, it was painfully uncertain, I think to patient and analyst, where – in what place, and when – in which kind of time, in psychic and external reality, Mr X would be able to settle, or whether perhaps he would remain unsettled.

Acknowledgements

This chapter was originally presented at a conference at University College, London, in 2008.

269

Part II

REVIEWS

21

MELANIE KLEIN: HER WORLD AND HER WORK

Review of Phyllis Grosskurth (1986)
Melanie Klein, Her World and Her Work.
London: Hodder & Stoughton.
Reprinted, Maresfield Library,
London: H. Karnac Books, 1987

Much hard work was done for this biography, the first written about Melanie Klein. Phyllis Grosskurth consulted many documents and letters (even tracing a lost collection), conducted many interviews (some of people traced down resourcefully), and made herself acquainted with much psychoanalytic theory. She has a narrative gift, and like the experienced biographer that she is, she has organised a mass of material into easy and vivid readability. It is all the more to be regretted, therefore, that what must be the pivot of any biography, the author's relation to his or her subject, has gone awry more often than it has stayed right.

The reader is likely to be made uneasy on the first page:

> Melanie Klein was a woman with a mission. From the moment she read Freud's paper *On Dreams* (1901) in 1914 she was enraptured, converted, and dedicated to psychoanalysis. Captivated by the concept of the unconscious, she followed its seductive lure …

This is language for religion and erotic infatuation and it sets a style the author will use on and off throughout the book in which psychoanalysts, the pursuit of psychoanalysis, and psychoanalytical issues are made sensational, psychologised, or politicised, to the extent that the author at times comes dangerously near to losing sight of whom and of what she is writing about.

One is thankful, however, that Professor Grosskurth has not written in a spirit of piety; but unfortunately she is often possessed – seemingly unawares – by a hostile animus against her subject. It is very obtrusive in Part One where she describes Melanie Klein's early life in Vienna where she was born in 1882. As Phyllis Grosskurth recounts Melanie Klein's relations with her father and mother, her two sisters – one of whom died when Melanie was 4, the later death of her loved and admired brother Emanuel, and the abandonment when she was 18 of her ambition to study medicine and become a psychiatrist for the sake of a mistaken engagement and marriage in which her three children were born, the author judges sufferings and failings harshly and chooses nearly always to place the worst rather than a better construction on events. For example, there is no recognition of the anguish of Emanuel, sick with TB and a rheumatic heart, dying in his early twenties, nor is there authorial sympathy for Melanie Klein, depressed in an unhappy marriage and intellectually stifled in small towns as she struggled through the early years of motherhood. The conjecture that Emanuel was a cocaine and morphine addict is not substantiated. And where is the evidence for saying (the description in the text even indicates the contrary) that Melanie Klein was 'incapable of the task' of caring for her dying mother? And how can the author know that on a specific occasion Melanie Klein 'envied Emily [her oldest sister] for seeming to have the fulfilled emotional life that she herself craved … she still retained the envy of a powerless baby sister'?

From the nature of the author's comments it soon becomes clear that what she is aiming to write is a psychobiography. If this is to be a valid genre, some appraisal is needed of the difference between a psychobiography and a psychoanalysis. Otherwise, as here, too much will become what can only be termed psychospeculation. Even with the privileged access to his internal world which a patient allows to an analyst, unravelling infantile sources of current attitudes is complex and difficult, and a biographer, lacking analytic access, necessarily works from different, more external sources. Phyllis Grosskurth's intrusions into psyches, in my view, hinder her throughout the book from using the findings of psychoanalysis in a more valid writer's way to augment imaginative insight into her subject.

In 1910, because of her husband's work, Melanie Klein moved with him and their children to Budapest. It was there that she came across Freud's book *On Dreams* (Freud 1901) and had the recognition that psychoanalysis was her subject. From intense interest and because of her own need she went to Ferenczi for analysis. Phyllis Grosskurth writes: 'In Klein's case he seems to have been incapable of dealing with her positive transference. It appears that her resistances were so strong that he was unable to penetrate her implacable defences.' How does Grosskurth know? However, when she stops psychologising and writes from a more real and distant stance, she becomes absorbing and informative of Klein and her period, as in the discussion of the poems and prose writings through which Melanie Klein expressed herself until she published psychoanalytic papers. Professor Grosskurth relates Melanie Klein's fictional writings to the literary milieu Klein knew, and here the author can be critical and yet in sympathy with her subject. 'The poetry is derivative, and the prose long-winded; but Klein's translator, Bruni Schling, believes that her writings exhibit considerable creative sensitivity, and the echoes from various poets are a reflection of her wide reading.' Grosskurth traces other interesting literary connexions of the time which made me wish she had also given us more period detail about the Hungarian Psychoanalytic Society. Part One of the biography closes when Melanie Klein has been analysed and encouraged by Ferenczi to start analysing children. She is a member of the Hungarian Psychoanalytic Society and working as psychoanalytical assistant to Anton Von Freund in the Association for Child Research in Budapest. Then in 1919 political upheavals ended in an anti-semitic regime which made it unsafe in Budapest, and Melanie Klein left with her children, parting from her husband, and 2 years later settled in Berlin.

It is a relief to get there. Through the eyes of Alix Strachey in letters to her husband James, Melanie Klein is for the first time seen as a human being – even as the Bloomsbury zest for the ridiculousness of persons is evident, and as well, the extraordinary, original calibre of her mind is recognised. Working as a child analyst and then an analyst of adults, encouraged by Abraham with whom she began analysis in 1924, Klein published her first innovative papers on children. These early papers collided with the approach established in Berlin by Hug-Hellmuth, an approach which also had the support of Anna Freud in Vienna. Phyllis Grosskurth gives a memorable description of the Berlin psychoanalytic scene of the time, even as her psychological speculations continue, directed now not only at Melanie Klein but at the increasing number of analysts who start to throng the book. Over an issue, 'grudgingly Abraham capitulated ...' She wonders if Freud 'was never attracted to Abraham's aloof, self contained manner?' 'There was intense envy and rivalry among these early psychoanalytic pioneers.' 'Jones ... might have been trying to stir up trouble ...'

But when she leaves her gossip's window she gives a serious presentation of psychoanalytic issues. Klein's new play technique had made it possible for prelatency children to express their feelings, anxieties and phantasies to an analyst and was yielding a wealth of material about an internal world of aggression and anxiety, and the symbolic meaning – libidinal and sadistic – of activities at home and at school. One of the most unexpected of Klein's discoveries was the existence of an early cruel superego burdening the weak ego of a small child with anxiety, guilt and depression. In a letter to Freud, Abraham wrote:

> I have assumed the presence of an early depression in infancy as a prototype for later melancholia. In the last few months Mrs Klein has skilfully conducted the psychoanalysis of a three-year-old with good therapeutic results .... The case offers amazing insights into an infantile instinctual life.

Apart from Abraham himself, Karen Horney and one or two others, the Berlin Society met her work with scepticism, as did the Viennese. In 1925 Melanie Klein gladly accepted an invitation to visit London and give a series of papers to the British Society which already had an interest in child analysis, and in the following year she settled permanently in England with her youngest child, Erich. Around the time of her English visit she had a love affair with a married Berlin journalist. Phyllis Grosskurth presents their correspondence – the most personal letters in the book.

In London Melanie Klein found favourable conditions among able and interested colleagues – Jones, Riviere, Strachey, Searle, Gillespie, Bowlby, Sharpe, Winnicott, Payne, and at this stage, Edward Glover. In 1927 'A Symposium on Child Analysis' was held before the British Society. Klein's paper of that name was a reply to Anna Freud's book *Introduction to the Technique of the Analysis of Children* (Freud 1927) and is still today a compelling argument for the view that the same principles – the child forms a transference, his play is the equivalent of an adult's free associations, and the sole function of the analyst is to analyse him – govern child analysis as the analysis of adults. Klein now had an intensely creative period. She wrote a succession of papers which offered a new understanding of criminal tendencies, intellectual inhibition, symbol formation, the creative impulse, and that cornerstone of psychoanalytic theory, the Oedipus complex – its timing, the origins of the superego, female sexual development. She was very grateful to her English colleagues for what they had made possible. On the publication in 1932 of *The Psychoanalysis of Children* (Klein 1932) she wrote to Jones: '… I do not know whether I would have written it if I had stayed in Germany.'

In Vienna Anna Freud was working along different lines on the ego and its defences, and Klein's contentions that object relations, with attendant anxieties, defences and unconscious phantasies begin at birth and lead to the formation of a primitive internal world were not accepted. As part of an exchange of views, Ernest Jones read a paper in Vienna, Riviere went to Vienna to present the Kleinian approach and Waelder came to London to reply on behalf of the Viennese. Though there were background tensions at this time involving Freud, Jones, Anna Freud and Melanie Klein, there was a scientific debate.

Melanie Klein now had two bitter blows. Her eldest son, Hans, died in a mountain accident. His death depressed her deeply. But also her daughter Melitta, a psychoanalyst in the British Society, was increasingly hostile after an analysis with Glover who was also turning against Klein. Melanie Klein's suffering seems to have been an additional personal source for 'A contribution to the psychogenesis of manic depressive states' (Klein 1935) which she published the following year, 1935. The profusion of her previous piecemeal discoveries were welded in this paper into high level formulations with a new concept – the Depressive Position. In this brilliant work Klein began the formulation of a new psychoanalytic theory of development and psychosis.

World events then changed the London psychoanalytic scene. The Nazi invasion of Austria forced the Freuds to leave Vienna and escape to London and so brought the London–Vienna dispute under one roof. What had before been a British Society involved in and proud of Klein's research (with some members who had reservations about it) was now convulsed by a series of Extraordinary Meetings and Controversial Discussions in which Klein was vindictively harassed by Glover as Chairman and also by her daughter Melitta. Professor Grosskurth describes how disputes over clinical and theoretical findings were entangled with personal animosities so extreme as in some cases

277

to be illness. There were deep anxieties on both the Viennese and the London side. The displaced Viennese, who had lost their own Society, were anxious about what they saw as the destruction of psychoanalytic foundations; Klein and her co-workers were anxious about the destruction of scientific developments from these foundations unless freedom of expression and the right of dissent were preserved in the Society. There were wrangles about training and teaching. Grosskurth's narrative grasp of these complex events is impressive as is her grasp of the analytic and training issues, but her sensational language magnifies the personal and political, and tends to reduce everyone involved, and the British Society, to baseness. After all, there was a resolution. Glover resigned and Melitta emigrated to America. Anna Freud chose to exert her main influence not in the British Society but at the Hampstead Clinic. The British Society itself divided into three groups, with a 'Gentlemen's Agreement' – never written down – to give representation to Kleinians, Independents and Anna Freudians in all teaching and on all the main committees of the Society. In an interview with Phyllis Grosskurth, Prof. J. Sandler says:

> Anywhere else in the world the Society would have split. There was something very special about the situation of the Society here which kept it together. And this was a very good thing, because being together made it necessary ... to engage with those who held opposite opinions. It raised the level of British psychoanalysis enormously.

Disagreements continued to arise during Melanie Klein's lifetime, as they still do today, and they were and are contained within the Society.

In 1940 Klein completed her account of the Depressive Position begun in 1935 with a companion paper 'Mourning and its relation to manic depressive states' (Klein 1940). Taken together these two papers describe the second position of development which occurs at 4 to 5 months when the infant begins to change his split relations to part objects to new, more integrated relations to whole objects. Klein's theory is that the infant then begins to experience depressive feelings – anxieties about loss, fears of damage he has done to his object, guilt, mourning and the urge to make reparation. The working through of these feelings from their miniscule beginning to their full elaboration including the negotiation of the Oedipus complex – how it interweaves with the depressive position Melanie Klein described in an important paper in 1945 (Klein 1945) – is the psychic task of the early years of childhood. If successfully accomplished the good object is securely internalised and is the basis of mental stability; if not achieved the inner scene is set for manic depressive states. The earlier position, the Paranoid-Schizoid Position, which had occupied Klein's thinking for many years, she described in 1946 in 'Notes on some schizoid mechanisms' (Klein 1946). This paper posits the existence of a rudimentary ego capable from birth of primitive perceptions, phantasies, and object relations impelled by instincts of love and hate, which result in split and polarised relations to ideal and persecutory objects, externally and internally. It describes the content of gratifying and persecutory phantasies, and the nature of primitive defences against persecutory anxiety, notably projective processes connected with splitting which Klein named 'projective identification'.

These new theories had a widespread impact. Her exploration of schizoid mechanisms which result in states of schizophrenic dissociation and depersonalisation opened a way to the analysis of patients with schizoid disorders. Rosenfeld worked with very ill patients and produced a series of important clinical papers. Segal described the analysis of a schizophrenic; she also, in a seminal paper, connected the development of symbol formation with the depressive position, and, working in another direction, used Melanie Klein's ideas for a new psychoanalytic approach to aesthetics. Bion found in Melanie Klein's work a basis for a new understanding of the primitive processes operating in groups.

In 1952, to mark Melanie Klein's 70th birthday, there were two publications: *Developments in Psychoanalysis* (Klein *et al.* 1952) with a preface by Ernest Jones, contained the papers of the Controversial Discussions of the 1940s, plus some others, the contributors being Klein, Riviere, Isaacs, Heimann (who later left the Klein group) and, as well, there was also a special issue of the *International Journal of Psychoanalysis* dedicated to Melanie Klein, which, with the papers revised and ten new ones added, was later published in book form as *New Directions in Psychoanalysis* (Klein *et al.* 1955), again with a Preface by Ernest Jones and an Introduction by Money-Kyrle. In *New Directions* there is a distinguished list of colleagues and an impressive variety of topics influenced by Klein's work.

Klein's own work continued. At the age of 73 she read a paper to the Geneva Congress, 'A study of envy and gratitude' which became

279

the remarkable book *Envy and Gratitude* (Klein 1957). It formulates hypotheses about the infants' feelings of envy and gratitude towards his original objects, charting the pernicious effect on object relations and character formation if there is a predominance of envy over gratitude at moments of gratification. Bold, original and closely worked out, *Envy and Gratitude* was her final major contribution to psychoanalysis, again one which stimulated clinical and theoretical developments and also aroused much controversy. Until her death in 1960 at the age of 78, Melanie Klein continued writing papers and preparing for publication the manuscript of *Narrative of a Child Analysis* (Klein 1961).

By the end of Prof. Grosskurth's biography the reader has been told of an enormous number of people, incidents, letters, interviews, materials from archives – though nothing from the documents deposited in the Library of Congress on which there is an embargo until the year 2000. There is a useful chronology of Melanie Klein's life, a list of her writings, and an excellent index. Yet, the reader is in two ways unsatisfied. For one, the question of evidence troubles the book throughout. For another, strangely, the reader has not been much enlightened about Melanie Klein as a person or a thinker.

In regard to evidence, the psychologising about Klein and everyone else, the conjectures about low motives (mixed motives and fine motives are rare in this book), the guesses in the latter pages about whose clinical material it is, remain unsubstantiated. Indeed, many adverse authorial judgements seem contradicted by the text itself. Several nasty stories about Klein are unattributed. An unfortunate account of a patient's suicide casts a false slur on Melanie Klein's and also Hanna Segal's competence and concern – the patient killed herself 5 years later than the date given in the book. The author believed Melanie Klein's old housekeeper whose memory was failing. Moreover, there is a special problem about the evidence of analysands: Is it distorted by unresolved transference? Of this matter Prof. Grosskurth has a sophisticated understanding, though she uses it unevenly. While she suggests that unresolved transference and the frailty of old age might account for some of the distortions of fact in Paula Heimann's account of the later bitter relations between herself and Melanie Klein, she accepts the extraordinary account given by Clare Winnicott of her analysis with Melanie Klein which is so at variance with what an analysis is, and so in keeping with what an expression of transference may be, that it surely called for authorial assessment.

What was Melanie Klein like? To make her portrait Phyllis Grosskurth uses two methods. Firstly, she presents a composite formed from the opposed angles from which different people saw Melanie Klein. She writes in her Foreword, 'Few professional women have been subjected to as much distilled malice and rumour accepted as fact as Klein …', and in reporting the perpetrators the book has its full share of malice and rumour. The book also contains accounts by some who were greatly impressed by Klein as an analyst, a thinker, a supervisor, a friend. While the views of others make this disjointed composite which tells of Klein's powerful effect on people but leaves each reader to pick what he wants from it, Phyllis Grosskurth herself is mostly busy with her second method – psychospeculation, and so loses, in my opinion, her chance of creating her own portrait of her subject. In the end, Melanie Klein eludes the book. What were her excellences as a person? Her failings? Her perspective on herself and others? Anxieties, hopes, humour?

The reader may judge something of her from the letters in this volume. One written at the age of 20 to her brother Emanuel shows a most unusual psychological cast of mind, and along with youthful vanity and extremity, an uncommon reflectiveness and plain speaking on difficult matters. Her letters to her Berlin lover express the utterly human feelings of a dignified woman in a passionate affair that will not last. Her later professional letters have courage and dignified directness. Her great care over the smallest detail of a psychoanalytic finding is also evident. And in a letter to Winnicott in which she discusses his obituary of Ernest Jones she gives her own appraisal of Jones – serious, sharply observed, and generous.

Yet, after reading the biography, the nature of the creative forces in Klein's mind are still little known, even though the author describes Klein's findings in detail, traces their sources in Freud, Abraham, and Ferenczi, and discusses debates about them. Prof. Grosskurth staunchly defends Klein on two issues, one, a common misunderstanding, the other, a question of priority. On the charge of ignoring the external world Grosskurth writes:

> Again and again one hears that she ignored environmental factors. Yet for two years Melanie Klein strove to free Erna from her internal tormentors and to bring her into the real world, where she would encounter a loving mother who bore no resemblance to the avenging fury of her phantasies.
>
> (p. 117)

On the question of priority Grosskurth writes:

> ... Klein's pioneering contributions had not been sufficiently acknowledged. From the early twenties she had stressed the developmental processes through relationship to object, so that she may legitimately be described as the parent of object-relations theory.
>
> (p. 372)

Yet for all this attention the biography does not convey that Melanie Klein was *rare*. She worked at the highest level for over 40 years. She started with a new technique for analysing children which yielded a profusion of clinical discoveries. Then, with ideas from Freud and a direction from Abraham, by an imaginative scientific leap she re-aligned psychoanalytical variables – giving equal significance to instincts, object relations and mental phantasy, placing anxiety and the ego's defences against anxiety at the centre of psychic life, and, shedding the last semantic vestiges of hydraulic flow and neurological excitation, she propounded a theory with the new and wholly *psychological* concepts of the Paranoid-Schizoid and Depressive Positions. She concluded her work with a study of two emotions fundamental for development, envy and gratitude. Freud of course was a genius. I think Melanie Klein was a near genius. But how did her mind work? We can see the encounter between a person of extraordinary natural gifts, who instinctively knew her own direction (the youthful ambition Melanie Klein abandoned for marriage was the study of medicine to become a psychiatrist) and the historical moment at which she entered the psychological field: the prior fact that psychoanalysis existed, that Freud with his great work of the twenties – the theory of the life and death instincts, the structural theory of the mind, and his new view of anxiety, was making psychoanalysis ready for a new epoch. We still do not know in what ways Klein thought and worked. How did she write? What did she read? Each day she set aside time for reading and writing. And how did her ideas come?

Acknowledgements

This review was originally published in the *International Review of Psychoanalysis*, 1987, 14: 132–136.

22

HERBERT ROSENFELD

Review of Herbert Rosenfeld, *Impasse and Interpretation*, London: Tavistock Press, 1987

Dr H. A. Rosenfeld died in 1986 after a sudden and short illness at the age of 76. He had completed his work on this book but he did not live to see its publication. It contains the reflections of his last years on the topic at the centre of his professional life – the psychoanalysis of psychosis.

Rosenfeld came to Britain from Nazi Germany in 1935. After retaking his medical examinations he trained as a psychotherapist at the Tavistock Clinic, working meanwhile at the Maudsley and a hospital in Oxfordshire with psychotic patients. In 1942 he began his psychoanalytic training at the Institute and began also an analysis with Melanie Klein. His analysis was, in his own phrase, 'a revelation'. In relation to his work, it confirmed the general view he himself had formed, viz., psychotic patients respond to understanding. Melanie Klein's findings about the ego's relations to its early objects and its defences against primitive anxieties with a psychotic content then suddenly gave Dr Rosenfeld the means with which to try to analyse psychosis.

In 1947 his first famous paper, 'Analysis of a Schizophrenic State with Depersonalization', appeared, the first published account of an adult psychotic treated by psychoanalysis. Further brilliant papers followed, collected in 1965 in a volume called *Psychotic States*, a book widely admired as a pioneering investigation into the nature of, and the psychoanalytic treatment of, the psychoses.

The book under review continues Dr Rosenfeld's interest in the psychoses, but in a different way. Where the clinical evidence for the scientific papers in *Psychotic States* was his own analytic work with very ill patients, *Impasse and Interpretation* rests mainly on supervisory and seminar discussions of the clinical reports of other analysts and therapists whose cases have reached an impasse. The result is a work much looser in its connections and conclusions. Rather than offering compelling scientific evidence, it is more in the nature of an assembling of propositions and opinions on several central problems occurring in work with psychotic and borderline patients.

Those who have tried to work dynamically – including those who use a different terminology – will recognise Dr Rosenfeld's illuminating characterisation of both the patient and the transference – omnipotence, insatiability, confusion between self and analyst or therapist, the taking of others into the self and the putting of the self into others, and the consequent establishment in the treatment of narcissistic, omnipotent object relations, with concrete thinking founded on projective identification.

Throughout the book Dr Rosenfeld emphasises the important clinical fact that omnipotence, however grandiose, is infantile. Beneath or beyond it lies a small lonely infant. He describes the obscurity and confusion from which the patient and his communications suffer, and reiterates that even so there can be intense scrutiny of the analyst and that there is always a transference reference, if we can only find it. Dr Rosenfeld also lays stress on the psychotic patient's continual state of extremity about himself and his therapist. He writes, for instance, 'Psychotic patients tend to exaggerate the extent of their analyst's depression and may delude themselves that the analyst is unfairly treated. Such delusions should be diagnosed early, because to protect the analyst the patient may go so far as to try to kill himself' (Rosenfeld 1987: 241).

The overall plan of *Impasse and Interpretation* is to demonstrate how an impasse may arise in each of three interrelated areas: one, through anti-therapeutic conduct of the therapist; two, through problems connected with the patient's narcissism; and three, from the effect of projective identification in the transference. There are examples of several ways in which a therapist might misunderstand his patient in the pressured obscure climate of the work, of the problems which arise as narcissistic object relations lessen and envy is stimulated, of the hindrance to progress of the patient's state of confusion and of the enormously invasive and controlling power of psychotic projections. Dr Rosenfeld warns us to beware of being ourselves transformed by such projections, and he reminds us that it is our job to do the transforming of the patient's material. And much more.

However, bar one or two exceptions, the format of interposing his own comments on the analyst's or therapist's reports of sessions to show how the impasse can be resolved is not, I think, very successful. More clinical detail is needed to assess both the treatment impasse and its proposed resolution, which otherwise may seem sometimes omnipotently to ignore the very complexities the book is expounding. The problems due to this format are compounded by the nature of psychotic communications which are formed, as Bion has shown, in a particular way of their own. Because of their confused compression and multi-facetedness which split their objects, it is always exceedingly difficult to know what to interpret. Sometimes, the reader may find himself speculating about the clinical material in this book in yet another way from both the luckless therapist in the impasse or Dr Rosenfeld himself. Without very great transference and counter-transference detail, who can know what was most urgent on that day?

Even so, scattered throughout the book are very valuable statements about technique. Let me give just one example. Dr Rosenfeld makes a clinical differentiation between an Oedipal transference and a delusional erotic transference. Where an Oedipal transference calls for interpretation of sexual feelings towards the therapist, this is contra-indicated in the case of a delusional erotic transference – a patient would experience such interpretations as sexual invitations from the therapist with disastrous effect. He advises us to focus instead on the processes of ego-splitting.

Here and there in the book Rosenfeld comments on several topics which held a special interest for him in his last years, including the group of patients who are what he calls 'traumatised', who become 'thin-skinned narcissists', the question of the analyst's neutrality and degree of involvement with his patients, and a new technique of analysing aggression and the negative transference. In this last connection he states that it is important not to break down too quickly our patients' idealisation of ourselves. It is a tricky subject on which I would have welcomed more. On the one hand, it is dangerous for our patients to let idealisation ride, but on the other, out of our fear of its dangers, not least of which is that it taps the analyst's vanity, perhaps we are sometimes afraid of letting idealisation emerge fully.

All during his life, Dr Rosenfeld had a fondness for collating the literature and the book closes with an historical review of the treatment of psychosis by psychoanalysis.

The fundamentals on which this book rests were in part created by Dr Rosenfeld, basing himself on the work of Melanie Klein. To those who have followed Kleinian developments since the 1950s by Rosenfeld, by Bion on psychosis and projective identification and by Segal on pathology of symbol formation, the basic ideas will not be new. But the reader can sense Dr Rosenfeld's long experience with psychosis and his strong grasp of the nature of the patient and the transference. I think many readers will recall with gratitude his fine earlier volume *Psychotic States*, and also what they learnt from him personally in his life-time – including your reviewer, for whom Dr Rosenfeld was a training supervisor and then a seminar leader for many years. They, and others, will find that this late book of his prompts many questions – including the fundamental question: is there a resolution to all these impasses? Or does psychoanalysis sometimes help – or fail to help – these psychotic patients in a quite different way?

Acknowledgements

This review was originally published in the *Journal of Child Psychotherapy*, 1988, 14: 99–101.

23

WILFRED BION

Review of *Wilfred Bion: his Life and Work, 1897–1979* by Gérard Bléandonu, translated by Claire Pajaczkowska, with a foreword by R. D. Hinshelwood. New York: Guildford Press, 1994

In Gérard Bléandonu the life and the work of Wilfred Bion meet – most fortunately – a biographer and an expositor. Bléandonu is a Frenchman and a scholar, who, while cognisant of French traditions, has also had a longstanding regard for Klein (he published *L'École de Melanie Klein* in 1985 (Bléandonu 1985)), and the work of Bion. His aim in the book under review is 'to reveal the meaning of given texts, in relation to the development, the historical context and the internal economy of Bion's oeuvre'.

He begins with biography: Bion's early childhood in India, his schooling in England, a plunge at 19 into the ordeal of the First World War from which he emerged with decorations, years of study – first at Oxford where he read History, captained the swimming team and obtained a rugger blue, then at Poitiers University, in order to study French language and literature, and, finally, after a spell as a teacher, University College, London, where he studied medicine. During his medical studies Bion went to a therapist (name unknown) whom he ironically dubbed 'Mr Feel-it-in-the-past'. On qualifying Bion straightaway launched himself into psychiatry, joining the staff of the Tavistock in 1932, having further therapy from Hadfield. Later Bion approached Rickman, who analysed him between 1937 and 1939. The outbreak of the Second World War terminated this analysis prematurely, and brought patient and analyst together in a pioneering group project in the army. Such are the initial external events in Bion's life for Bléandonu the biographer.

Bléandonu never met Bion. His chief sources for the inner experience and the meaning of these years are the remarkable autobiographical writings of Bion's old age (published posthumously): *The Long Weekend (1897–1919): Part of a Life* (Bion 1982), and *All My Sins Remembered: Another Part of a Life* (Bion 1985) – probably still in draft form – which ends with the Second World War and to which Francesca Bion added letters under the title *The Other Side of Genius: Family Letters*. Later in the book Bléandonu uses Bion's other writings, plus well-researched public sources, to bring to the reader a vivid vision of Bion the man. After all, biography must have a vision of its subject if it is not to remain a mere summation of the facts. Bléandonu is neither voyeuristic nor over-knowing – where he does not know the facts, he has proper authorial hesitation. And he judges his distance from his subject with sensitivity: psychologically aware, while remaining respectful of privacy. Bléandonu admires Bion enormously, especially his creativity, his witty and unusual turn of mind, as well as his courage, both psychological and physical; but he can see also pain, certain failings, and an adverse side of Bion's character. However, the account of the life is subsidiary to the achievements of Bion's work.

Bléandonu divides Bion's work into four 'seasons' of production – most of the book being an exposition in turn of each 'season'. The first is the period of group psychology. As an army psychiatrist Bion tried to introduce leaderless groups for the selection of officers; and, together with Rickman, he set up the Northfield experiment of a therapeutic community. In Bléandonu's view these were 'undeniably a manifestation of creative genius'. Bléandonu describes Bion's disappointment with the army, General J. R. Rees's hostile reaction to him, and the interested responses of notable colleagues, such as Trist, Sutherland, Foulkes, Main, and later Lacan. When the war was over Bion returned to the Tavistock and developed a method of group therapy that had a wide influence, which led Bion to formulate a new theory of group dynamics. Bléandonu himself – he is a community psychiatrist – has been greatly influenced by Bion (he published *Les Communautées thérapeutiques* in 1970 (Bléandonu 1970)) and he gives an excellent account of Bion's ideas of a proto-mental system, of basic assumption groups, and work groups, as might be expected from someone with special experience in the field. He points out that Bion eventually linked these group researches to Klein's discoveries, e.g., basic assumption phenomena were later seen as defences against psychotic anxieties. In 1945 Bion had also resumed his training at the Institute of Psycho-Analysis, and begun an analysis with Klein. Bléandonu remarks that analysis 'awakened in him a deep creativity which was to stay with him until the end of his life'. Bléandonu sees the encounter between Klein and Bion as being 'between a feminine universe and a masculine world', an eccentric vision in this reviewer's eyes, although he has perceptive reflections on both protagonists. And he firmly rebuts the mistaken notion of a division in analytic technique between Bion and other Kleinians.

The second 'season' of work is the period of 'Understanding Psychosis', in which Bion wrote a series of original and brilliant papers. Bléandonu gives a lucid account of all that clusters around the central idea of psychosis as arising from attacks upon links and awareness of links – the pathological use of projective identification, fragmentation of the psychotic ego, a world of bizarre objects made from the expulsion of fragments, hallucination, the incapacitation of verbal thought and an ever-increasing divergence from normal mental functioning. Bléandonu makes the interesting observation that in Bion's view sight is the paramount sense in forming psychosis; he notes Bion's idea that the prime interest of the breast and the penis, and what excites curiosity about them, is their capacity to link objects; and he thinks that Bion found the antithesis of envy, not foremost in gratitude as Klein did, but in creativity. Bléandonu writes an outstanding chapter, 'The intellectual Oedipus' (see Chapter 16), about Bion's new perspective on the Oedipal drama, which brings the vicissitudes of knowledge ('K') rather than sex between the protagonists to the fore.

While President of the British Society, and at the zenith of his creative powers, Bion entered what Bléandonu calls his third 'season' – 'The Epistemological Period'. Following his penetrating insights into disorders of knowing in psychosis, Bion was at this point in search of a theory of knowledge for the ordinary individual: How does he come to know another or himself?; and for the practising psychoanalyst: How does he know the psychic events of a session? Bléandonu's account of Bion's answers to these questions is lucid, well embedded in Bion's strong thinking, and has plenty of his own thought in it too. Bion's theory is that 'knowing' begins with the infant's use of projective identification as a first mode of communication. Development of thought and thinking depends on the internalisation of a mother (the container), who has received, and can herself, in her reverie, think of what her infant transmitted by projective identification (the contained). Equally crucial to the success of this process is the temperament of the infant: it must not be too heavily weighted with death instinct. Such 'learning from experience', Bléandonu thinks, applies to Bion's writings: the reader for Bion is a presence who is to 'remain in a state of uncertainty, or begin to think for himself, while awaiting the author's enlightenment' (Bléandonu 1994: 89), and he sees Bion's texts as 'an intellectual container allowing the reader to introject a state of mind conducive to the search for truth' (Bléandonu 1994: 143). Bléandonu's book will certainly help the reader to gain his own understanding of the formidable terminology Bion developed to express his conceptualisations and clinical findings – such as: alpha-function, beta-elements, contact barrier, beta-screen, dreaming as a continuous process in the mind, a notation for psychoanalytic objects, 'the Grid', psychotic and neurotic transformations, misunderstandings, 'K', the eschewing of 'memory and desire' in the analyst to allow evolution of intuition and the becoming of 'at-one-ment' with 'O'. Bion's overall clinical technique, Bléandonu remarks,

> was rather different from the accepted view of psychoanalysis. Whereas the latter uses conscious material to interpret unconscious-ness, Bion uses the unconscious to interpret a conscious state of mind, linked to the facts known by the analyst. The interpretation of the dream gives the analyst the meaning of the facts and feelings he has experienced.
>
> (Bléandonu 1994: 177)

As Bléandonu charts Bion's life and writings into its fourth and final 'season', when Bion left London for Los Angeles, he describes how it became a time of seminars and lectures. It is Bléandonu's opinion that Bion did not have much more that was new to say in these discussions, nothing that he himself would have taken the trouble to publish – though his followers did: 'A psychoanalyst of renown accumulates a mythic capital … the audience came to see and admire the throned and crowned king' (Bléandonu 1994: 247). The achievement of these last years lay, thinks Bléandonu, in the discovery of new forms of expression. Bion wrote his extraordinary autobiography, which is a work of fine literature, as well as the three-volume *A Memoir of the Future* (Bion 1975, 1977, 1979), of which Bléandonu thinks Bion was very fond. It is a speculation on the future of psychoanalysis in the form of a novel that becomes a play that is also a cryptogram and something of an autobiography. Bion's writings in the fifties and early sixties had been notable for rigour and a daring exactness. As time went on his style grew freer and less definite, and I think that an exuberant evolution of his capacity to be aware of several perspectives, and also of the 'negative capability' he so admired, described by Keats as 'when a man is capable of being in uncertainties, mysteries, doubts, without any irritable reaching after fact and reason', took place and reached its zenith in *A Memoir of the Future*. Bléandonu acknowledges the power of this wild flourishing of perspectives, notations, uncertainties and mysteries to evoke experiences in the reader (and they do indeed to an extent in him) but he sees also a sadder side of the work:

> A sympathetic reader sees an art which reaches the height of freedom because it is no longer bound to proving anything; a critical reader sees the unhappy restlessness of a man who having lost the freshness and energy of his youth, is striving compulsively.
>
> (Bléandonu 1994: 264)

Earlier in his book Bléandonu discusses Bion's importing of terms from other disciplines to introduce new models through their penumbra of 'other' meaning. In this regard, I suspect Bléandonu may be a little too French in the degree of understanding he attributes to Bion of these 'other' fields, especially philosophy: such knowledge, I think, occurs more often in France than in specialist England. However, although Bléandonu recognises that Bion brought arresting insights into psychoanalysis in this way, he also raises the real issue of changes of notation or name that might be merely that, and the related danger of 'conceptual slippage'. About the multivalency of *A Memoir of the Future* he is cautious, even as he admires Bion for keeping until his last days, in Lejeune's phrase (Lejeune 1980), 'the bloom of rebellion'.

One of Bléandonu's chief aims is to reveal the structural unity in Bion's work. He sees this unity – and in this he is surely right – as coming from a lifelong enquiry into the problems and enigmas of knowing: in a group, in an analytic session, as a keeper of analytic records, as a reader of a textbook, as a teacher who disseminates ideas in spoken form (an epistemological problem of interest to Bion in his last years), and of course, in life itself: How to know oneself and significant others? – a question that Bion attempted to answer with his autobiography of *psychic reality*. After all, Freud made the discovery that insight – a special kind of knowing or 'K' – can be curative. I think Bion recognised instinctively that moment in psychoanalysis when its general development, and, as well, Klein's particular contributions, had made it ready for *further work in depth on 'K'*. Bion's scientific achievement lies firstly in what Bléandonu calls an 'original re-theorization of psychoanalysis', Bion's placement of 'K' (trying to know), with 'L' (love), and 'H' (hate), as the three governors of psychic life; and secondly, in his fundamental clinical researches into the nature of 'K' itself. Bléandonu's excellent book offers a portrait of the man, together with an imaginative and scholarly account of Bion's work – work that has in a quiet way in the consulting room caused a revolution in how an analyst may try to know his patient.

Acknowledgements

This review was first published in the *International Journal of Psychoanalysis*, 1995, 76: 857–859.

ANDRÉ GREEN

Review of *The Dead Mother: the Work of André Green*, edited by Gregorio Kohon, London: Routledge, 1999

On the occasion of André Green's 70th birthday, to celebrate Green's distinguished contributions to psychoanalysis, Gregorio Kohon assembled this collection of papers by Michael Parsons, Arnold H. Modell, Christopher Bollas, Jed Sekoff, Thomas H. Ogden, André Lussier, Adam Phillips, Rosine Jozef Perelberg, Martin S. Bergmann, plus one paper by Green himself: 'The intuition of the negative in *Playing and Reality*' (Green 1997).

After a useful introduction in which he summarises both Green's 'The dead mother', from which the book takes its title, and then the papers that follow, Kohon begins the book with a transcript of a long dialogue between Green and himself. In the course of their conversation Green portrays something of both his personal life and his professional journey towards and within psychoanalysis. He reminisces about figures important to him in French psychiatry and psychoanalysis and his early awareness of the plural psychoanalytic scene. He says he saw 'very quickly that each one had his own originality, his own specificity, his own approach, and that one could not talk of "one" psychoanalysis' (Kohon 1999: 22). He recalls his complex relations with Lacan, with whom he eventually quarrelled; their association seems to have left Green with a hatred of Lacan the man, whom he proclaims a cynic and a cruel cheat. Green expresses his regard for Bion, and above all, his deep admiration of Winnicott.

Interspersed with comments on his own ideas, we learn Green's opinions of, among others, Hartmann and Klein, and he and Kohon discuss the differing hypotheses that underlie French and British psychoanalysis. Green gives his perspective on Freud's development, his views on drives, objects and dreams, the ego and the autonomous ego, the centrality of primal phantasies, psychoanalytic institutions and over-publishing in psychoanalysis, and the irrelevance of observation, including infant observation, to psychoanalytic theory – that we learn from the analytic situation is his credo.

The papers that follow are mostly closely linked to 'The dead mother' (Green 1983). Green began this original and insightful paper by remarking on how problems of mourning had become pivotal in analysis and then continued:

> I wish to make it clear that I shall not be discussing here the psychical consequences of the real death of the mother, but rather that of an imago which has been constituted in the child's mind, following maternal depression, brutally transforming a living object, which was a source of vitality for the child, into a distant figure, toneless, practically inanimate .... Thus, the dead mother ... is, so to speak, psychically dead in the eyes of the young child in her care.
>
> (Green 1983: 142)

He described what he named the 'blank mourning' for the dead mother, and marshalled a descriptive and explanatory cluster of ideas – negative hallucination, decathexis of the maternal object, holes in the psyche, blank psychosis, separation and intrusion anxiety, plus the patient's tenacious primary identification with the dead mother, all of which have indications that Green describes for analytic technique.

In response to Green's paper, the authors in this book both develop its ideas and also explore some of the conceptual and clinical issues it raises. For instance, Parsons and Sekoff take negation further; Bollas welds Green's paper to his own technique to illuminate the analysis of a patient; Ogden broadens the issue of aliveness and deadness to cover forms of transference and countertransference; and Lussier extends the notion of inner deadness in 'the dead mother' to apply also to the inner deadness of a father.

Lussier also calls attention to a group of patients who, like Green's, have a dread of nothingness, but who differ in being defensively identified, not with a depressed mother, but with a terrifying mother full of hatred. As Bollas, Sekoff and Modell do, Lussier discusses another of Green's themes: the way in which these patients fail to introject new objects, and instead, in Green's words, 'maintain her [the dead mother] perpetually embalmed' (Kohon 1999: 162). Lussier observes that in this way 'they were proving him [the analyst-father] to be a failure by his inability to bring about any change in them' (Kohon 1999: 160).

In this regard Modell thinks Green's hypothesis that 'a linear causal relationship exists between the experience of the "dead mother" in infancy and childhood and subsequent development' (Kohon 1999: 83) is too narrow. He notes the diversity of individual responses to an emotionally absent mother and suggests:

> It may be useful to distinguish the dead mother syndrome from the dead mother complex. The term dead mother syndrome can be used to denote the intensely malignant clinical syndrome that Green described when there is a primary identification with the emotionally dead mother whereas the term dead mother complex denotes an entire range of an individual's response to a chronically depressed, emotionally absent mother.
>
> (Kohon 1999: 76)

After thus broadening the conceptualisation, Modell goes on to say, 'Both the dead mother syndrome and the dead mother complex are unquestionable responses to the mother's emotional deadness, but primary identification with the mother is only one of the many alternatives' (Kohon 1999: 83). He ends his paper with the statement: 'There is a significant difference between those who remain open to new experience and those who remain prisoners of the past' (Kohon 1999: 85).

How might Modell's significant difference between patients manifest itself in analysis? After analytic work about a dead analysis, might not those patients who are open (even if only a little open) to new experience find that instead of being in a dead analysis they are with an analyst they are deadening – for any number of diverse reasons, like terror of a hostile mother (Lussier); or 'proving him [the analyst-father] to be a failure by his inability to bring about any change in them' (Kohon 1999: 160) (Lussier); or what Sekoff calls the 'solace' they find 'in the certainties of death over the vagaries of life', a death, he adds in which 'no one has ever to die', or what Green himself calls their 'mad passion' to keep the dead mother 'perpetually embalmed'.

Freud spoke of the silent working of the death instinct. During an analysis it could become crucial to differentiate the state of blank mourning in a dead world from the silent destructive deadening of life, and interpret variously, depending on the patient's underlying state of mind, be it terror of the analyst's hatred, terror of his own madness, the patient's hatred of reality, etc. – pace Green, who writes in 'The dead mother': 'I do not believe that the Kleinian technique of the systematic interpretation of destructiveness is of much help here' (Kohon 1999: 155).

This brings me to Green and the plural psychoanalytic scene. In his fine paper Martin Bergmann writes about the history of psychoanalysis. He thinks that a few landmark events have determined the direction of psychoanalysis overall, among them the 1975 debate in London between (on the one side) Leo Rangell and Anna Freud, who argued for classical ego–psychology; and (on the other) Green's 'The analyst, symbolization and the absence in the analytic setting (on changes in analytic practice and analytic experience)' with which, Bergmann says, 'we were transplanted into a different world' (Kohon 1999: 195). And indeed, Green has done more than most in the bewildering plurality of our field. He built his own path through and out of the divergences of French psychoanalysis, taking what he could from Lacan, something of Bion, and most especially from Winnicott, with whom he found a creative affinity. We can see this, for instance, in Green's paper which concludes this book where he explores the link between his ideas on the negative and Winnicott's thinking in *Playing and Reality*.

Any analyst who chooses to grapple with the plural scene has to face its vastness and its variations of terminology, a terminology that is ceaselessly changing. Even in the volume under review, we find Green's interesting new terms from 1984, the 'objectalising function' of the mind, which he defines as 'the power of the human mind to constantly create new objects' (Kohon 1999: 219), and its companion, the 'disobjectalising function', which names 'the process by which an object loses its specific individuality' (Kohon 1999: 220). We also find Ogden's now well-known shifting of the sense of 'countertransference' in papers written over several years. Bollas coins the new term interject to contrast with introject, defining a significant opposition thus:

An interject is an internal object that arrives in the internal world either due to a parental projective identification, interjected into the self, or to a trauma from the real that violates the self, or both. An introject always expresses an aspect of the self's need or desire ... while an interject is an interruption of the self's idiom by the forceful entry of the 'outside'.

(Kohon 1999: 94)

Of course, new terms and shifts of meaning bring with them questions about how they link with already existing ideas. Are they congruent with the old? Or inconsistent? Or overlapping? Do they advance our understanding or even (rarely) take us into a different world?

Furthermore, some approaches speak to us. Others do not. Some raise our hackles. During his conversation with Green, Kohon makes this interesting observation: 'I always think that one writes for somebody, perhaps against somebody, or a mixture of both' (Kohon 1999: 51). Even an outstanding protagonist like Green, who has always professed himself ready for dialogue, runs up against the mass of knowledge, the laborious intricacies of terminology, and the tensions and anxieties inherent in rival approaches.

Green acknowledges Klein's contribution, but feels no affinity with her; on the contrary, his animosity is evident although he and Klein share a belief in the death instinct as a force in mental life and they both believe drives and object relations go together, each shedding light on the other. Green does not use Klein's ideas, even those close to his own, as in the striking instance of the tenacious primary identification with a dead mother, which he does not link with the powerful Kleinian concept of projective identification that would seem to fit it so well.

To call attention to this is not the militantism that Green abhors. There is no imperative upon Green, or any of us, to link our approach to others. However, sometimes, as in this instance, the neglect to do what Roy Schafer calls comparative psychoanalysis, loses us both the validation and the mutual benefit of increased comprehension that comes from the convergence (even if not the identity) of findings in different approaches.

Readers will find this a valuable book – for the lively dialogue between Green and Kohon, its return to Green's major paper 'The dead mother', for the individual authors' impressive responses to it, and for the glimpse of the walls in the present psychoanalytic scene, which Green has both run up against and surmounted.

Acknowledgements

This review was originally published in the *International Journal of Psychoanalysis*, 1999, 82: 619–621.

Bibliography

Abraham, K. (1924) A short study of the development of the libido viewed in the light of mental disorders, in *Selected Papers on Psychoanalysis*. London: Hogarth Press (1927), reprinted by Karnac Books (1979), pp. 418–501.

Anzieu, D. (1989) *The Skin Ego*. New Haven: Yale University Press.

Balint, M. (1959) *Thrills and Regressions*. London: Hogarth.

Barnett Lynn (1988) *Sunday's Child: the Development of Individuality from Birth to Two Years of Age*, Parts I–VIII. Part IX: 2 to 3 years, 1988. Part X: 3 to 6 years, 1989. Concorde Films, 201 Felixstowe Road, Ipswich, Suffolk IP3 9BJ, UK.

Bick, E. (1968) The experience of the skin in early object relations, *International Journal of Psychoanalysis*, 49: 484486. Reprinted in E. B. Spillius (ed.), *Melanie Klein Today*, vol 1. London: Routledge, 1988, pp. 187–191.

Bion, W. R. (1948–51) Experiences in groups, *Human Relations* I–IV, reprinted in *Experiences in Groups and Other Papers*. London: Tavistock, 1961.

Bion, W. R. (1950) The imaginary twin, in *Second Thoughts*. London: Heinemann, 1967, pp. 3–22.

Bion, W. R. (1952) Group dynamics: a re-view. *International Journal of Psychoanalysis*, 33: 235–247. In M. Klein, P. Heimann and R. Money-Kyrle (eds.), *New Directions in Psychoanalysis*, London: Tavistock, 1955, pp. 440–477. Also in *Experiences in Groups and other Papers*, London: Tavistock, 1961, pp. 141–191.

Bion, W. R. (1954) Notes on the theory of schizophrenia. *International Journal of Psychoanalysis*, 35: 13–18. Reprinted in *Second Thoughts*. London: Heinemann, 1967, pp. 23–35.

Bion, W. R. (1955) Language and the schizophrenic, in M. Klein, P. Heimann and R. Money-Kyrle (eds.), *New Directions in Psychoanalysis*, London: Tavistock, 1955, pp. 220–239.

Bion, W. R. (1956) The development of schizophrenic thought. *International Journal of Psychoanalysis*, 37: 344–346. Reprinted in *Second Thoughts*. London: Heinemann, 1967, pp. 3–22.

Bion, W. R. (1957) Differentiation of the psychotic from the non-psychotic personalities. *International Journal of Psychoanalysis*, 38: 266–275. Reprinted in *Second Thoughts*. London: Heinemann, 1967, pp. 43–64.

Bion, W. R. (1958a) On arrogance. *International Journal of Psychoanalysis*, 39: 341–346. Reprinted in *Second Thoughts*. London: Heinemann, 1967, pp. 86–92.

Bion, W. R. (1958b) On hallucination. *International Journal of Psychoanalysis*, 39: 144–146. Reprinted in *Second Thoughts*. London: Heinemann, 1967, pp. 65–85.

Bion, W. R. (1959) Attacks on linking. *International Journal of Psychoanalysis*, 40: 308–315. Reprinted in *Second Thoughts*. London: Heinemann, 1967, pp. 93–109.

Bion, W. R. (1961) *Experiences in Groups and Other Papers*. London: Tavistock.

Bion, W. R. (1962a) *Learning from Experience*. London: Heinemann. Also in *Seven Servants*. New York: Jason Aronson, 1977.

Bion, W. R. (1962b) The psycho-analytic study of thinking. *International Journal of Psychoanalysis*, 43: 306–310. Reprinted as A theory of thinking, in *Second Thoughts*. London: Heinemann, 1967, pp. 110–119.

Bion, W. R. (1963) *Elements of Psycho-Analysis*. London: Heinemann. Also in *Seven Servants*. New York: Jason Aronson, 1977.

Bion, W. R. (1965) *Transformations*. London: Heinemann. Also in *Seven Servants*. New York: Jason Aronson, 1977.

Bion, W. R. (1966) Catastrophic change. *Bulletin of the British Psychoanalytical Society*, 5. Also in *Attention and Interpretation*. London: Tavistock, 1970, Chapter 12.

Bion, W. R. (1967a) *Second Thoughts: Selected Papers on Psychoanalysis*. London: William Heinemann.

Bion, W. R. (1967b) Notes on memory and desire. *Psychoanalytic Forum*, 2: 271–280. Reprinted in E. B. Spillius (ed.), *Melanie Klein Today*: vol. 2, *Mainly Practice*. London: Routledge, 1988, pp. 17–21.

Bion, W. R. (1970a) Lies and the thinker, in *Attention and Interpretation*. London: Tavistock.

Bion, W. R. (1970b) The mystic and the group, in *Attention and Interpretation*. London: Tavistock.

Bion, W. R. (1970c) *Attention and Interpretation*. London: Tavistock.

Bion, W. R. (1975) *A Memoir of the Future, Book One: The Dream*. Rio de Janeiro: Imago Editora; reprinted London: Karnac, 1990.

Bion, W. R. (1977) *A Memoir of the Future, Book Two: The Past Presented*. Rio de Janeiro: Imago Editora; reprinted London: Karnac, 1990.

Bion, W. R. (1979) *A Memoir of the Future, Book Three: The Dawn of Oblivion.* Strath Tay: Clunie Press; reprinted London: Karnac, 1990.

Bion, W. R. (1982) *The Long Week-End 1897–1919: Part of a Life.* Abingdon: Fleetwood Press.

Bion, W. R. (1985) *All My Sins Remembered: Another Part of a Life*; and (ed. F. Bion) *The Other Side of Genius: Family Letters.* Abingdon: Fleetwood Press.

Birksted-Breen, D. (1996) Phallus, penis and mental space. *International Journal of Psychoanalysis*, 77: 649–659.

Birksted-Breen, D. (2003) Time and the *après-coup*. *International Journal of Psychoanalysis*, 84: 1501–1515.

Bléandonu, G. (1970) *Les Communeautées Thérapeutiques.* Paris: Éditions du Scarabée.

Bléandonu, G. (1985) *L'École de Melanie Klein.* Paris: Le Centurion.

Bléandonu, G. (1994) *Wilfred Bion: his Life and Works, 1897–1979*, trans. C. Pajaczkowska. London: Free Association Books.

Blum, H. P. (1983a) The psychoanalytic process and psychoanalytic inference: a clinical study of a lie and a loss. *International Journal of Psychoanalysis*, 64: 7–33.

Blum, H. P. (1983b) The position and value of extratransference interpretation. *Journal of the American Psychoanalytical Association*, 34: 309–328.

Bollas, C. (1987) *The Shadow of the Object: Psychoanalysis of the Unthought Known.* London: Free Association Books.

Brenman, E. (1985) Cruelty and narrow-mindedness. *International Journal of Psychoanalysis*, 66: 273–281. Also in G. F. Spoto (ed.), *Recovery of the Lost Good Object.* London: Routledge, 2006, pp. 48–61.

Brenman Pick, I. (1985) Working through in the counter-transference. *International Journal of Psychoanalysis*, 66: 157–166. A slightly revised version is also published in E. B. Spillius (ed.), *Melanie Klein Today*, vol. 2, *Mainly Practice*, London: Routledge, 1988, pp. 34–47.

Britton, R. (1989) The missing link: parental sexuality in the Oedipus complex, in J. Steiner (ed.), *The Oedipus Complex Today.* London: Karnac Books, pp. 83–102.

Britton, R. (1995) Psychic reality and unconscious belief. *International Journal of Psychoanalysis*, 76: 19–23.

Britton, R. (1998) *Belief and Imagination: Explorations in Psychoanalysis.* London: Routledge.

Britton, R. and Steiner, J. (1994) Interpretation: selected fact or overvalued idea? *International Journal of Psychoanalysis*, 75: 1069–1078.

Bronstein, C. (2002) Borges, immortality and the circular ruins. *International Journal of Psychoanalysis*, 83: 647–660.

Caper, R. (1988) *Immaterial Facts.* Hillsdale, NJ: Jason Aronson.

Caper, R. (1994) What is a clinical fact? *International Journal of Psychoanalysis*, 75: 903–914.

Caper, R. (1998) Review of J. and N. Symington, *The Clinical Thinking of Wilfred Bion*. *International Journal of Psychoanalysis*, 79: 417–420.

Carpy, D. V. (1989) Tolerating the countertransference: a mutative process. *International Journal of Psychoanalysis*, 70: 287–293.

Daitz, E. (1953) The picture theory of meaning. *Mind*, 62: 184–201.

Deutsch, H. (1922) Über die pathologische Lüge (Pseudologia phantastica). *Internationale Zeitung für Psychoanalyse*, 8: 153–167, translated by P. Roazen as On the pathological lie (pseudologia phantastica). *Journal of the American Academy of Psychoanalysis and Dynamic Psychiatry*, 1982, 10: 396–386.

Duncan, D. (1992) Hermeneutics and psychoanalysis. (Unpublished).

Eagle, M. N. (1984) *Recent Developments in Psychoanalysis*. New York: McGraw-Hill.

Eigen, M. (1998) *The Psychoanalytic Mystic*. London: Free Association Books.

Ezriel, H. (1980) *A Psychoanalytic Approach to Group Treatment in Psycho-Analytic Group Dynamics*. New York: International Universities Press.

Feldman, M. (2000) Some views on the manifestation of the death instinct in clinical work. *International Review of Psychoanalysis*, 81: 53–66. Reprinted in B. Joseph (ed.), *Doubt, Conviction and the Analytic Process: Selected Papers of Michael Feldman*. London: Routledge, 2009.

Feldman, M. (2007) The illumination of history. *International Journal of Psychoanalysis*, 88: 609–625. Revised in B. Joseph (ed.), *Doubt, Conviction and the Analytic Process: Selected Papers of Michael Feldman*. London: Routledge, 2009, pp. 72–95.

Feldman, M. (2008) Grievance: the underlying Oedipal configuration. *International Journal of Psychoanalysis*, 89: 743–758. Revised version in B. Joseph (ed.), *Doubt, Conviction and the Analytic Process: Selected Papers of Michael Feldman*. London: Routledge, 2009, pp. 194–215.

Feldman, M. and Spillius, E. B. (1989) General Introduction to *Psychic Equilibrium and Psychic Change: Selected Papers of Betty Joseph*. London: Tavistock/Routledge, 1989, pp. 1–9.

Fenichel, O. (1939) The economics of pseudologia phantastica, in *Collected Papers of Otto Fenichel*, second series. New York: Norton, 1954, pp. 129–140.

Ferro, A. (1992 [1999]) *The Bi-Personal Field: Experiences in Child Analysis*. London: Routledge, 1999.

Flanders, S. (1993) *The Dream Discourse Today*. London: Routledge.

Flynn, D. (2008) Exile: loss of connectedness. *Bulletin of the British Psychoanalytical Society*, 44: 8.

Foucault, M. (1977) What is an author?, in D. F. Bouchard (ed.), *Language, Counter-Memory, Practice*. Ithaca, NY: Cornell UP, 1980.

Freud, A. (1927) *Einführung in Die Technik der Kinderanalyse.* Wien: Internationaler Psychoanalytischer Verlag; trans. L. P. Clark as *Introduction to the Technique of Child Analysis.* Washington: Nervous and Mental Disease Publishing Company, 1928.

Freud, A. (1966) *Normality and Pathology in Childhood.* London: Hogarth Press and Institute of Psycho-Analysis.

Freud, S. (1895a) Project for a scientific psychology. *Standard Edition,* vol. 1.

Freud, S. (1895b) Studies on Hysteria. *Standard Edition,* vol. 2.

Freud, S. (1900) The Interpretation of Dreams. *Standard Edition,* vols. 4 and 5.

Freud, S. (1901) On Dreams. *Standard Edition,* 5: 633–686.

Freud, S. (1911a) Formulations on the two principles of mental functioning. *Standard Edition,* 12: 213–226.

Freud, S. (1911b) Psycho-analytic notes upon an autobiographical account of a case of paranoia. *Standard Edition,* 12: 3–82.

Freud, S. (1913) The disposition to obsessional neurosis. *Standard Edition,* 12: 313–326.

Freud, S. (1914) Remembering, repeating and working-through. *Standard Edition,* 12: 145–156.

Freud, S. (1916 [1915]) On transience. *Standard Edition,* 14: 305–307.

Freud, S. (1917 [1915]) Mourning and melancholia, *Standard Edition,* 14: 239–258.

Freud, S. (1919 [1918]) Lines of advance in psychoanalytic therapy. *Standard Edition,* 17: 159–168.

Freud, S. (1921) Group Psychology and the Analysis of the Ego, *Standard Edition,* vol. 21.

Freud, S. (1923) The Ego and the Id. *Standard Edition,* 19.

Freud, S. (1924a) The economic problem of masochism. *Standard Edition,* 19: 157–170.

Freud, S. (1924b) The loss of reality in neurosis and psychosis. *Standard Edition,* 19: 183–187.

Freud, S. (1930) Civilization and its Discontents. *Standard Edition,* 21: 59–145.

Freud, S. (1933a) Dreams and occultism, Lecture 30 of New Introductory Lectures on Psycho-Analysis. *Standard Edition,* 22: 31–56.

Freud, S. (1933b) New Introductory Lectures on Psycho-Analysis. *Standard Edition,* 22.

Freud, S. (1937) Analysis terminable and interminable. *Standard Edition,* 23: 216–253.

Freud, S. (1940 [1938]) Splitting of the ego in the process of defence. *Standard Edition,* 23: 271–278.

Gabbard, G. O. (2000) On gratitude and gratification. *Journal of the American Psychoanalytic Association,* 48: 697–716.

Gammill, J. (1980) Some reflections on analytic listening and the dream screen, in S. Flanders (ed.), *The Dream Discourse Today.* London: Routledge, 1993, pp. 127–136.

303

Gardner, M. R. (1983) *Self Inquiry*. Hillsdale, NJ: The Analytic Press.

Gardner, S. (1993) *Irrationality and the Philosophy of Psychoanalysis*. Cambridge University Press.

Garza-Guerrero, A. C. (1981) The superego concept: Part 1, historical review; object relations approach. *Psychoanalytic Review*, 68: 321–342.

Gill, M. M. (1983) The point of view of psychoanalysis. *Psychoanalysis and Contemporary Thought*, 6: 523–552.

Gillespie, W. (1940) A contribution to the study of fetishism. *International Journal of Psychoanalysis*, 21: 401–415.

Glasser, M. (1979) Some aspects of the role of aggression, in I. Rosen (ed.), *Sexual Deviation*. Oxford: Oxford University Press.

Green, A. (1975) The analyst, symbolization and absence in the analytic setting (on changes in analytic practice and setting) – in memory of D.W. Winnicott. *International Journal of Psychoanalysis*, 56: 1–22. Also in *On Private Madness*, London: Hogarth, 1986, pp. 30–59.

Green, A. (1983) The dead mother, in *On Private Madness*, London: Hogarth, pp. 142–173.

Green, A. (1993) Pulsion de mort, narcissisme négatif, fonction désobjectalisante, in *Le Travail du Négatif*, Paris: Minuit. Translated by A. Weller as *The Work of the Negative*, 1999, London: Free Association Books.

Green, A. (1997) The intuition of the negative in *Playing And Reality*. *International Journal of Psychoanalysis*, 78: 1071–1084. Also in G. Kohon (ed.), *The Dead Mother: the Work of André Green*, London: Routledge, 1999.

Grinberg, L., Sor, D. and de Bianchedi, E. T. (1975) *Introduction to the Work of Bion*, trans. A. Hahn. Strath Tay: Clunie Press.

Grosskurth, P. (1986) *Melanie Klein, Her World and Her Work*. London: Hodder & Stoughton. Reprinted, Maresfield Library, London: H. Karnac Books, 1987.

Grotstein, J. S. (1981) Wilfred R. Bion: the man, the psychoanalyst, the mystic. A perspective on his life and work, in J. S. Grotstein (ed.), *Do I Dare Disturb the Universe? A Memorial to Wilfred R. Bion*. Beverley Hills: Caesura Press, pp. 1–35.

Hoffer, W. (1954) Defensive process and defensive organization: their place in psycho-analytic technique. *International Journal of Psychoanalysis*, 35: 194–198.

Hoffman, L. (1994) The report of The Kris Study Group of the New York Psychoanalytic Institute on 'superego analysis'. *Journal of Clinical Psychoanalysis*, 3: 161–177.

Hoyer, T. V. (1959) Pseudologia fantastica: a consideration of 'the lie' and a case presentation. *Psychiatric Quarterly*, 33: 203–220.

Joseph, B. (1978) Different types of anxiety and their handling in the analytic situation. *International Journal of Psychoanalysis*, 59: 223–228; reprinted in M. Feldman and E. B. Spillius (eds.), *Psychic Equilibrium and Psychic Change: Selected Papers of Betty Joseph*. London: Tavistock/Routledge, 1989, pp. 106–115.

Joseph, B. (1981) Defence mechanisms and phantasy in the psychoanalytical process, *Bulletin of the European Psychoanalytical* Federation, 17: 11–24. Reprinted in M. Feldman and E. B. Spillius (eds.), *Psychic Equilibrium and Psychic Change: Selected Papers of Betty Joseph*, London: Tavistock/Routledge, 1989, pp. 116–126.

Joseph, B. (1982) Addiction to near-death. *International Journal of Psychoanalysis*, 63: 449–456; reprinted in M. Feldman and E. B. Spillius (eds.), *Psychic Equilibrium and Psychic Change: Selected Papers of Betty Joseph*. London: Routledge, 1989, pp. 127–138.

Joseph, B. (1983) On understanding and not understanding: some technical issues. *International Journal of Psychoanalysis*, 64: 291–298; reprinted in E. B. Spillius and M. Feldman (eds.), *Psychic Equilibrium and Psychic Change: Selected Papers of Betty Joseph*. London and New York: Routledge, 1989, pp. 139–150.

Joseph, B. (1989) *Psychic Equilibrium and Psychic Change*. London: Routledge.

Joseph, B. (1993) *No resonance*, in M. J. Horowitz et al. (eds.), *Psychic Structure and Psychic Change. Essays in Honour of Robert S. Wallerstein*. Madison: International Universities Press.

Karpman, B. (1949) From the autobiography of a liar. *Psychiatric Quarterly*, 23: 277–307.

Kennedy, R. (2007) Restoring history to psychoanalysis, in *The Many Voices of Psychoanalysis*, London: Routledge, pp. 109–123.

Kernberg, O. F. (1992) Psychopathic, paranoid and depressive transferences. *International Journal of Psychoanalysis*, 73: 13–28.

Khan, M. (1974) *The Privacy of the Self*. London: Hogarth Press.

Klein, G. S. (1976) *Psychoanalytic Theory*. New York: International Universities Press.

Klein, M. (1925a) The importance of words in early analysis. *Writings*, vol. 3, p. 314.

Klein, M. (1925b) A contribution to the psychogenesis of tics. *Writings*, vol. 1, pp. 106–127.

Klein, M. (1927) Symposium on child analysis. *Writings*, vol. 1, pp. 139–169.

Klein, M. (1928) Early stages of the Oedipus conflict. *International Journal of Psychoanalysis*, 9: 167–180. Also in *Writings*, vol. 1, pp. 186–198.

Klein, M. (1932) The Psychoanalysis of Children. *Writings*, vol. 2.

Klein, M. (1935) A contribution to the psychogenesis of manic–depressive states. *Writings*, vol. 1, pp. 236–289.

Klein, M. (1937) Love, Guilt and Reparation. In *The Writings of Melanie Klein*, vol. 1, pp. 306–343. London: Hogarth Press, 1975.

Klein, M. (1940) Mourning and its relation to manic-depressive states. *Writings*, vol. 1, pp. 344–369.

Klein, M. (1945) The Oedipus complex in the light of early anxieties. *Writings*, vol. 1, pp. 370–419.

Klein, M. (1946) Notes on some schizoid mechanisms. *International Journal of Psychoanalysis*, 27: 99–110. A slightly revised version appears in Klein M., Heimann P., Isaacs S. and Riviere J. (1952) *Developments in Psychoanalysis*. London: Hogarth Press, 1952, pp. 292–320. Also in *Writings*, vol. 3, 1975, pp. 10–24.

Klein, M. (1948) On the theory of anxiety and guilt. In *The Writings of Melanie Klein*, vol. 3, pp. 25–42. London: Hogarth.

Klein, M. (1952a) Some theoretical conclusions regarding the emotional life of the infant. *Writings*, vol. 3, pp. 61–93.

Klein, M. (1952b) The origins of transference. *International Journal of Psychoanalysis*, 33: 433–438. Also in *Writings*, vol. 3, pp. 48–56.

Klein, M. (1955) On identification, in M. Klein, P. Heimann and R. Money-Kyrle (eds.), *New Directions in Psychoanalysis*. London: Tavistock, pp. 309–345. Also in *Writings*, vol. 3, pp. 141–175.

Klein, M. (1957) *Envy and Gratitude*. London: Tavistock. Also in *Writings*, vol. 3, pp. 176–235.

Klein, M. (1958) On the development of mental functioning. *Writings*, vol. 3, pp. 236–246.

Klein, M. (1961) *Narrative of a Child Analysis*. London: Tavistock. in *Writings*, vol. 4.

Klein, M. (1975, 1980) *The Writings of Melanie Klein*, vol. 1, *Love, Guilt and Reparation*, vol. 2, *The Psychoanalysis of Children*, vol. 3, *Envy and Gratitude and Other Works*, vol. 4, *The Narrative of a Child Analysis*. London: Hogarth Press and the Institute of Psychoanalysis.

Klein, M., Heimann, P., Isaacs, S. and Riviere, J. (1952) *Developments in Psychoanalysis*. London: Hogarth Press.

Klein, M., Heimann, P. and Money-Kyrle, R. (eds.) (1955) *New Directions in Psychoanalysis*. London: Tavistock.

Kohon, G. (ed.) (1999) *The Dead Mother: the Work of André Green*, edited by Gregorio Kohon. London: Routledge.

Kohut, H. (1971) *The Analysis of the Self*. New York: International Universities Press.

Kuhn, T. S. (1962) *The Structure of Scientific Revolutions*. Chicago: University of Chicago Press.

Langs, R. (1976) *The Therapeutic Interaction*. New York: Jason Aronson.

Langs, R. (1980) Truth therapy/lie therapy. *International Journal of Psychoanalysis*, 8: 3–34.

Laplanche, J. and Pontalis, J.-B. (1967) *Vocabulaire de la Psychanalyse*. Paris: Presses Universitaires de France. Published in English as *The Language of Psychoanalysis*, trans. D. Nicholson-Smith. London: Hogarth Press, 1973.

Lejeune, P. (1980) *Je est un autre*. Paris: Seuil.

Lewin, B. D. (1946) Sleep, the mouth, and the dream screen. *Psychoanalytic Quarterly*, 15: 419–434.

Lewin, B. D. (1955) Dream psychology and the analytic situation. *Psychoanalytic Quarterly*, 25: 169–199.

Lichtenberg, J. D. and Slap, J. W. (1971) On the defensive organization. *International Journal of Psychoanalysis*, 52: 451–457.

Locke, J. (1690) Of identity and diversity, Chapter II.xxvii of *An Essay Concerning Human Understanding*, in P. Nidditch, (ed.), *The Works of John Locke*. Oxford: Oxford University Press, 1975.

Lorca, F. G. (1921) *Poema de Cante Jondo*, trans. by C. Baur as *Poem of the Deep Song*. San Francisco: City Lights Books, 1987.

McGinn, C. (1991) *The Problem of Consciousness*. Oxford: Blackwell.

Mahler, M. (1961) On sadness and grief in infancy and childhood: loss and restoration of the symbiotic love object. *Psycho-Analytic Study of the Child*, 16: 332–351.

Malcolm, R. R. (1999) The constitution and operation of the superego, in P. Roth (ed.), *On Bearing Unbearable States of Mind*. London: Routledge, pp. 53–70.

Matte-Blanco, I. (1975) *The Unconscious as Infinite Sets*. London: Duckworth.

Meltzer, D. (1978) *The Kleinian Development*. Strath Tay: Clunie Press.

Midgley, M. (1994) *The Ethical Primate: Humans, Freedom and Morality*. London: Routledge.

Money-Kyrle, R. (1944) Towards a common aim: a psychoanalytic contribution to ethics, in D. Meltzer and E. O'Shaughnessy (eds.), *The Collected Papers of Roger Money-Kyrle*. Strath Tay: Clunie Press, 1978, pp. 176–197.

Money-Kyrle, R. (1956) Normal counter-transference and some of its deviations. *International Journal of Psychoanalysis*, 37: 360–366.

Money-Kyrle, R. E. (1958) On the process of psycho-analytical inference. *International Journal of Psychoanalysis*, 39: 129–133. Reprinted in D. Meltzer and E. O'Shaughnessy (eds.), *The Collected Papers of Roger Money-Kyrle*. Strath Tay: Clunie Press, 1978, pp. 343–352.

Money-Kyrle, R. E. (1961) *Man's Picture of His World*. London: Duckworth.

Money-Kyrle, R. (1965) Success and failure in mental maturation, in D. Meltzer and E. O'Shaughnessy (eds.), *The Collected Papers of Roger Money-Kyrle*. Strath Tay: Clunie Press, 1978, pp. 397–406.

Money-Kyrle, R. (1968) Cognitive development. *International Journal of Psychoanalysis*, 49: 691–698; reprinted in D. Meltzer and E. O'Shaughnessy (eds.), *The Collected Papers of Roger Money-Kyrle*. Strath Tay: Clunie Press, 1978, 416–433.

Nagel, T. (1986) *The View from Nowhere*. Oxford: Oxford University Press.

Ogden, T. (1982) *Projective Identification and Psychotherapeutic Technique*. New York: Aronson.

O'Shaughnessy, B. J. (1980) *The Will*. Cambridge: Cambridge University Press.

O'Shaughnessy, B. J. (1991) The anatomy of consciousness, in E. Villanueva (ed.), *Consciousness: Philosophical Issues, 1*. Atascedero, California: Ridgeview Publishing Company.

O'Shaughnessy, E. (1952) I can if I choose. *Analysis*, 12: 125–132.

O'Shaughnessy, E. (1964) The absent object. *Journal of Child Psychotherapy*, 1: 39–43.

O'Shaughnessy, E. (1980) Interminably a patient. *International Journal of Psychoanalytic Psychotherapy*, 8: 573–579.

O'Shaughnessy, E. (1981a) A clinical study of a defensive organization. *International Journal of Psychoanalysis*, 62: 359–369. Reprinted in E. B. Spillius (ed.), *Melanie Klein Today*, vol. 1. London: Routledge, 1988, pp. 293–310.

O'Shaughnessy, E. (1981b) A commemorative essay on W. R. Bion's theory of thinking. *Journal of Child Psychotherapy*, 7: 181–192. Reprinted as: W. R. Bion's theory of thinking and new techniques in child analysis, in E. B. Spillius (ed.), *Melanie Klein Today*, vol. 2. London: Routledge, 1988, pp. 177–190.

O'Shaughnessy, E. (1983) Words and working through. *International Journal of Psychoanalysis*, 64: 281–289. Reprinted in E. B. Spillius (ed.), *Melanie Klein Today*, vol. 2. London: Routledge, 1988, pp. 138–151.

O'Shaughnessy, E. (1986) A 3½-year-old boy's melancholic identification with an original object. *International Journal of Psychoanalysis*, 67: 173–179.

O'Shaughnessy, E. (1987) Melanie Klein. Her world and her work. *International Review of Psychoanalysis*, 14: 132–136.

O'Shaughnessy, E. (1988) The invisible Oedipus complex, in E. B. Spillius (ed.), *Melanie Klein Today*, vol. 2. London: Routledge, 1988, pp. 191–205. Reprinted in J. Steiner (ed.), *The Oedipus Complex Today*. London: Karnac Books, 1989: 129–150.

O'Shaughnessy, E. (1989) Seeing with meaning and emotion. *Journal of Child Psychotherapy*, 15: 27–31.

O'Shaughnessy, E. (1990) Can a liar be psychoanalysed? *International Journal of Psychoanalysis*, 71: 187–282.

O'Shaughnessy, E. (1992a) Enclaves and excursions. *International Journal of Psychoanalysis*, 73: 603–614.

O'Shaughnessy, E. (1992b) Psychosis: not thinking in a bizarre world, in R. Anderson (ed.), *Clinical Lectures on Klein and Bion*. London: Tavistock/Routledge, pp. 89–101.

O'Shaughnessy, E. (1994) What is a clinical fact? *International Journal of Psychoanalysis*, 75: 939–947.

O'Shaughnessy, E. (1995) Wilfred Bion: his life and work, 1897–1979. *International Journal of Psychoanalysis*, 76: 857–859.

O'Shaughnessy, E. (1999) Relating to the superego. *International Journal of Psychoanalysis*, 80(5): 861–870.

O'Shaughnessy, E. (2004a) Dreaming and not dreaming, in M. Lansky (ed.), *The Dream after a Century*. New York: International Universities Press.

O'Shaughnessy, E. (2004b) On being Frankenstein, in E. Hargreaves and A. Varchevker (eds.), *In Pursuit of Psychic Change*. London: Routledge.

O'Shaughnessy, E. (2005a) A projective identification with Frankenstein. *Bulletin of the British Psychoanalytical Society*, pp. 2–10.

O'Shaughnessy, E. (2005b) Whose Bion? *International Journal of Psychoanalysis*, 86: 1523–1528.

O'Shaughnessy, E. (2007) Mental connectedness. *Bulletin of the British Psychoanalytic Society*, pp. 3–8.

O'Shaughnessy, E. (2008a) *Intrusions*. Paper given at conference in 2000 on Herbert Rosenfeld, in J. Steiner (ed.), *Rosenfeld in Retrospect*, London: Karnac Books.

O'Shaughnessy, E. (2008b) *Gratitude*, in P. Roth and A. Lemma (eds.), *Envy and Gratitude Revisited*, London: IPA, reprinted London: Karnac Books.

O'Shaughnessy, E. (2008c) Where is here? When is now? Paper given at UCL conference in 2008.

O'Shaughnessy, E. and Arundale, J. (2004) Edna O'Shaughnessy in conversation with Jean Arundale. *British Journal of Psychotherapy*, 20: 527–539.

Perelberg, R. J. (ed.) (2007) *Time and Memory*. London: Karnac Books.

Poincaré, H. (1905) *Science and Hypothesis*. London: Walter Scott Publishing Co. Reprinted as *Science and Method*. New York: Dover Publications, 1952.

Pontalis, J.-B. (1974) Dream as object. *International Review of Psychoanalysis*, 1: 125–134.

Quinodoz, J.-M. (1999) Dreams that turn over a page. *International Journal of Psychoanalysis*, 80: 225–238.

Quinodoz, J-M. (2008) *Listening to Hanna Segal: Her Contribution to Psychoanalysis*. London: Routledge.

Rey, H. (1994) The schizoid mode of being and the space-time continuum, in J. Magagna (ed.), *Universals of Psychoanalysis in the Treatment of Psychotic and Borderline States*. London: Free Association Books.

Riviere, J. (1936) A contribution to the analysis of the negative therapeutic reaction. *International Journal of Psychoanalysis*, 17: 304–320. Reprinted in A. Hughes (ed.), *The Inner World and Joan Riviere*, London: Karnac Books (1991), pp. 134–153.

Rosenfeld, H. (1947) Analysis of a schizophrenic state with depersonalisation. *International Journal of Psychoanalysis*, 28: 130–139; in *Psychotic States*, London: Hogarth (1965), pp. 13–33.

Rosenfeld, H. (1952) Notes on the psychoanalysis of the superego conflict in an acute schizophrenic patient. *International Journal of Psychoanalysis*, 33: 111–131, and in *Psychotic States: a Psychoanalytical Approach*. London: Hogarth, pp. 52–103.

Rosenfeld, H. (1954) Considerations regarding the psycho-analytic approach to acute and chronic schizophrenia, Chapter 6 of *Psychotic States*. London: Hogarth, pp. 117–127.

Rosenfeld, H. (1962) The superego and the ego-ideal. *International Journal of Psychoanalysis*, 43: 258–263.

Rosenfeld, H. (1964) An investigation into the need of neurotic and psychotic patients to act out during analysis, in *Psychotic States*. London: Hogarth, 1965, pp. 200–216.

Rosenfeld, H. (1965) *Psychotic States: a Psychoanalytical Approach*. London: Hogarth.

Rosenfeld, H. (1971) A clinical approach to the psychoanalytical theory of the life and death instincts: an investigation into the aggressive aspects of narcissism. *International Journal of Psychoanalysis*, 52: 169–178. Also in E. B. Spillius (ed.), *Melanie Klein Today* vol. 1, *Mainly Theory*. London: Routledge: 1988, pp. 239–255.

Rosenfeld, H. (1987) *Impasse and Interpretation*. London: Tavistock.

Sabbadini, A. (1989) Boundaries of timelessness. *International Journal of Psychoanalysis*, 70: 305–313.

Sandler, J. (1976) Countertransference and role responsiveness. *International Journal of Psychoanalysis*, 57: 43–48.

Schafer, R. (1959) Generative empathy in the treatment situation. *Psychoanalytic Quarterly*, 28: 342–373.

Schafer, R. (1960) The loving and beloved superego in Freud's structural theory. *Psychoanalytic Study of the Child*, 15: 163–188.

Schafer, R. (1976) *A New Language for Psychoanalysis*. New Haven: Yale University Press.

Schafer, R. (1983) *The Analytic Attitude*. London: Hogarth Press.

Schafer, R. (1997) *Tradition and change in psychoanalysis*. Madison, CT: International Universities Press.

Searle, J. R. (1992) *The Rediscovery of the Mind*. Cambridge, MA: MIT Press.

Segal, H. (1956) Depression in the schizophrenic. *International Journal of Psychoanalysis*, 37: 339–343. Reprinted in *The Work of Hanna Segal*. New York: Jason Aronson, 1981, pp. 121–129.

Segal, H. (1957) Notes on symbol formation. *International Journal of Psychoanalysis*, 38: 391–397. Reprinted in *The Work of Hanna Segal*,

New York: Jason Aronson (1981) pp. 40–65, and in E. B. Spillius (ed.), *Melanie Klein Today* (1988), pp. 160–177.

Segal, H. (1972) A delusional system as a defence against the re-emergence of a catastrophic situation. *International Journal of Psychoanalysis*, 53: 393–401.

Segal, H. (1979) *Klein*. London: Fontana.

Segal, H. (1980) The function of dreams, in S. Flanders (ed.), *The Dream Discourse Today*. London: Routledge, 1993, pp. 100–107.

Segal, H. (1987) What is therapeutic and counter-therapeutic in psycho-analysis? (Unpublished).

Segal, H. (1991) *Dream, Phantasy and Art*, London: Routledge.

Shelley, M. (1818) *Frankenstein, or The Modern Prometheus*, ed. M. Joseph. Oxford: Oxford University Press, 1969.

Sherick, I. (1983) Adoption and disturbed narcissism: a case illustration of a latency boy. *Journal of the American Psychoanalytic Association*, 31: 487–513.

Smith, S. (1972) The golden phantasy: a regressive reaction to separation anxiety. *International Journal of Psychoanalysis*, 58: 311–324.

Sodré, I. (1999) Death by daydreaming: *Madame Bovary*, in D. Bell (ed.), *Psychoanalysis and Culture: a Kleinian Perspective*. London: Duckworth, pp. 213–234.

Sodré, I. (2005) 'As I was walking down the stair, I saw a concept which wasn't there …': or, *après-coup*: A missing concept? *International Journal of Psychoanalysis*, 86: 7–10.

Sohn, L. (1985) Narcissistic organization, projective identification, and the formation of the identificate. *International Journal of Psychoanalysis*, 66: 201–213. Also in E. B. Spillius (ed.), *Melanie Klein Today*, vol. 1, *Mainly Theory*, London: Routledge (1988), pp. 271–292.

Spence, D. (1982) Narrative truth and theoretical truth. *Psychoanalytic Quarterly*, 51: 43–69.

Spence, D. (1994) What is a clinical fact? *International Journal of Psychoanalysis*, 75: 915–926.

Spillius, E. B. (1983) Some developments from the work of Melanie Klein. *International Journal of Psychoanalysis*, 64: 321–332.

Spillius, E. B. (ed.) (1988) *Melanie Klein Today*, vol. 1 *Mainly Theory*; vol. 2 *Mainly Practice*. London: Routledge.

Spillius, E. B. (1989) On Kleinian language. *Free Associations*, 18: 90–110.

Spillius, E. B. (1994) Developments in Kleinian thought: overview and personal view. *Psychoanalytic Inquiry*, 14: 324–364.

Spillius, E. B. (1999) Introduction. In: Ferro (1992 [1999]).

Steiner, J. (1989) The psychoanalytic contribution of Herbert Rosenfeld. *International Journal of Psychoanalysis*, 70: 611–617.

Steiner, J. (1993) *Psychic Retreats: Pathological Organizations in Psychotic, Neurotic and Borderline Patients*. London: Routledge.

Steiner, J. (1996) The aim of psychoanalysis in theory and practice. *International Journal of Psychoanalysis*, 77: 1073–1085.

Steiner, R. (1992) Some historical and critical notes on the relationship between hermeneutics and psychoanalysis. (Unpublished).

Stewart, H. (1973) The experiencing of the dream and the transference, in S. Flanders (ed.), *The Dream Discourse Today*. London: Routledge, 1993, pp. 122–126.

Stewart, H. (1990) Interpretation and other agents for psychic change. *International Journal of Psychoanalysis*, 17: 61–70.

Stolar, D. and Fromm, E. (1974) Activity and passivity of the ego in relation to the superego. *International Review of Psychoanalysis*, 1: 297–311.

Strachey, J. (1934) The nature of the therapeutic action of psychoanalysis. *International Journal of Psychoanalysis*, 15: 127–159; reprinted in *International Journal of Psychoanalysis*, 1969, 50: 275–292.

Strenger, C. (1991) *Between Hermeneutics and Science: an Essay on the Epistemology of Psychoanalysis*. Madison: International Universities Press.

Symington, J. and Symington, N. (1996) *The Clinical Thinking of Wilfred Bion*. London: Routledge.

Taylor, D. (2005) Interpretation and anticipation. Paper for 'Bion To-day' Conference at University College, London.

Tustin, F. (1972) *Autism and Child Psychosis*. London: Hogarth.

Tustin, F. (1986) *Autistic Barriers in Neurotic Patients*. London: Karnac.

Wallerstein, R. S. (1988) One psychoanalysis or many? *International Journal of Psychoanalysis*, 69: 5–21. Reprinted in R. S. Wallerstein (ed.), *The Common Ground of Psychoanalysis*. Northvale, NJ: Aronson, 1992.

Winnicott, D. W. (1945) Primitive emotional development. *International Journal of Psychoanalysis*, 26: 137–143. Reprinted in *Through Paediatrics to Psychoanalysis*, London: Hogarth Press (1975), pp. 145–156.

Wollheim, R. (1980) On persons and their lives, in A. O. Rorty (ed.), *Explaining Emotions*. Berkeley and Los Angeles: University of California Press.

Wollheim, R. (1984) *The Thread of Life*. Cambridge: Cambridge University Press.

Index